A FEAST
OF DAYS

A FEAST OF DAYS

A Saint and a Diary Extract
for Every Day of the Year

Paul Jennings

With Decorations by
Sue Scullard

MACDONALD & CO
LONDON & SYDNEY

First published in Great Britain in 1982 by
Macdonald & Co (Publishers) Ltd
London & Sydney

Maxwell House
74 Worship Street, London EC2A 2EN

ISBN 0 356 07901 5

Filmset, printed and bound in Great Britain by
Hazell Watson & Viney Ltd, Aylesbury, Bucks

CONTENTS

ACKNOWLEDGEMENTS

The author and publishers wish to thank the following for permission to quote extracts from the works listed below:

Blackie and Son Limited: *The Suffolk Scene* by Julian Tennyson
Cambridge University Press: *I Too Am Here* by A. Simpson and M. H. Simpson
Jonathan Cape Ltd: *A Young Victorian in India* edited by Ethel Waley Cohen; *Carrington: Letters and Extracts from her Diaries* edited by David Garnett (thanks also to the David Garnett Estate and to the Sophie Partridge Trust); *The Letters of T. E. Lawrence* edited by David Garnett (thanks also to the Letters of T. E. Lawrence Trust); *The Cecil King Diary 1970–1974* by Cecil King; *Kilvert's Diary* edited by William Plomer (thanks also to Mrs. Sheila Hooper)
Chatto and Windus Ltd: *Ancestral Voices* by James Lees Milne; Author's Literary Estate and Chatto and Windus Ltd: *Diaries and Letters of Marie Belloc Lowndes*, ed. Susan Lowndes.
Constable Publishers: *Nurse at the Russian Front* by Florence Farmborough; *The Wandering Scholars* by Helen Waddell
J. M. Dent & Sons Ltd: *Schubert: A Documentary Biography* by Otto Deutsch
Hart-Davis, Granada Publishing Ltd: *My American Journey* by James Agate (taken from *A James Agate Anthology* edited by Alan Dent)
Miss Norah Hartley: letter by L. P. Hartley in *Diaries and Letters of Marie Belloc Lowndes*
Author's Literary Estate and The Hogarth Press Ltd: *The Diary of Virginia Woolf: Vol. II. 1920–24* edited by Anne Olivier Bell
Mary Lutyens: *Lady Lytton's Court Diary* edited by Mary Lutyens
Macmillan, London and Basingstoke: *Mozart Letters* by Eric Blom; *Arthur Young and His Times* by G. E. Mingay
Macmillan, New York: *Journal of Henri Frederic Amiel* translated by Van Wyck Brooks
John Murray (Publishers) Ltd: *Creevey's Diaries* edited by John Gore; *Elizabeth Barrett to Miss Mitford* edited by Betty Miller
Reprinted by permission of Oxford University Press: *The Letters of Thomas Moore* edited by Wilfred S. Dowden (2 vols.); *The Journals and Papers of Gerard Manley Hopkins* (2nd ed. 1959), edited by Humphry House, completed by Graham Storey, © The Society of Jesus 1959; *Journals of Dorothy Wordsworth* edited by Mary Moorman, © The Trustees of Dove Cottage 1971; Wilfred Owen: *Collected Letters* edited by Harold Owen and John Bell, © Oxford University Press 1967; *The Letters of Sydney Smith* edited by Nowell C. Smith (2 vols. 1953)
Reprinted by permission of A. D. Peters & Co. Ltd: *Diary of a Provincial Lady* by E. M. Delafield; *Letters to a Sister* by Rose Macaulay
Reprinted by permission of Penguin Books Ltd: *A Dictionary of Saints*

PREFACE

Before I started on this book I had a vague idea that it would catch, in its arbitrary, happened-on-the-same-day net, the infinite capacity of human behaviour to surprise; and at the same time there would be some rudimentary impression of whatever it was that formed Europe, the hammering out of basic Christian beliefs (however eroded nowadays) and their incorporation into everything from legal systems to folk memory, followed by the diary or letter entries, basically 18th and 19th century not only for obvious copyright reasons but because this was when saints were getting a bit thin on the ground. From constant to unpredictable, from tradition to change, from faith to doubt . . .

Of course it didn't quite come out like that. One glance at the saints will show you there's nothing constant about *them*. There are good solid, deeply admired figures like St Anselm (*see April 21*) or St Francis of Assisi (longest entry in the book, *see October 4*); but there are people like St Keverne (*see November 18*) throwing stones after someone who had pinched his chalice (and *that* was a saint too) or the St Ruadhan who had the dispute with King Dermot (*see April 15*) whose conclusion I owe to Baring-Gould, who was my chief source for the saints, together of course with Bishop Butler, Attwater, and the other proper, real hagiographers.

I know saints come in all kinds of character, and periods; there is the canonization this very year, for instance, of the Franciscan Fr Kolbe who offered himself in place of an Auschwitz prisoner condemned to be starved to death—and was accepted. But I don't think (*pace* St Augustine) that many, if any, in the church would say today that moral heroism is confined to members of it. Since Catholicism doesn't look just yet like being literally Catholic, *kath' holou*, for the whole world, maybe it wouldn't be a bad idea if the UN or some such body set up a secular canonization tribunal of some kind, if they could manage for once to keep politics out of it and agree what kind of love it is that makes saints.

ix

The rest of the book, inevitably, reflects that whole world, dotty and often very unsaintly; and it certainly does not lack surprise. People in introductions are always thanking their wives for their forbearance etc., but mine didn't just forbear, she helped in the research (well, it is 730 pieces). It was she who discovered the accident-prone William Coe (January 23 and 29, February 16, March 27, April 8, May 26, June 4, June 23, July 31, October 18, November 18, December 7).

Thomas Blaikie, the "Scotch Gardener" who worked for the Duc d'Orléans and other French grandees and, among other things, laid out the Parc Monceau in Paris, really did spell the way he is printed here, and Joseph Farington, in his fascinating diaries, did always use a capital H for 'he'.

In short, there has been no cheating. Since very few of the diary/letter entries actually refer to the time of year, flowers, weather, etc., it would have been theoretically easy enough to change the date of some interesting item to fit a date still blank. A little thought will show that the further the work progressed the stronger the temptation became to do this, as is clear, for instance, in February (a dismal month). Although you would not think so from what I eventually found for it, at first it remained obstinately empty. But a kind of mad determination to stick to the rules seized me, and in fact I only cheated once, and have said so when I did (September 11).

One soon learns whose diaries contain short pithy bits that can be lifted out to stand on their own. How we came to love Beatrix Potter, and of course good old standards like Horace Walpole and Dr Johnson. But there are plenty of unfamiliar names here too, I hope; plenty of, what was that word again, ah yes, *surprise*.

The sort of surprise one does *not* want in a work of this kind is inaccuracy. Every effort has been made to guard against this, but if I have offended, *mea* (I trust, not *maxima*) *culpa*.

JANUARY

January 1

ST ODILO, 5th Abbot of Cluny (962–1049) supported an institution called the Truce of God, whereby military operations were regularly suspended at certain periods (as it might be the present one).

1676: The wind being fair all night hath brought us to the middle of Candia this morning, whereabouts we expect to see our adversaries the Tripolines every hour.

A NEW YEAR'S GIFT TO OUR CAPTAIN
ACROSTICON

W—hen Phoebus did this morning first appear
I—nriching with his beams our hemisphere,
L—eaving the darksome night behind him, and
L—onging to be at his meridian;
I—magine then the old year's out of date,
A—new one unto Jove let's dedicate—
M—an should not be like an old almanack.
H—eavens guide you, Sir, that Paul's words may be
O—ld things are done away, all things are new; [true]
U—nto the rich endowments of your mind
L—ift up your noble courage: Fortune's kind
D—irections bid you forwards; your *Assistance*
I—s begged by Mars for th' Trypolines' resistance.
N—'er man more fit bold acts to undertake,
G—od with his blessings make you fortunate.

Rev Henry Teonge (Chaplain on HMS Assistance*) (1621–1690)*

January 2

ST SERAPHIM OF SAROV; born at Kursk in 1759. He lived alone in the forest for sixteen years, and returned to his monastery for a few months after being beaten up by robbers. He then left again to spend much of his time in prayer on a high outcrop of rock. Attwater says that whatever elements of legend grew up around him "he summed up in himself the Russian ideal of the holy monk and elder (*starets*); and the more-than-natural facial transfiguration recorded in the conversation with Motovilov—a spiritual irradiation manifesting itself outwardly in a blinding light—is a phenomenon recorded of other outstanding holy men in both East and West."

1803: [To Mrs Beach].... After all, my dear Madam, are you doing right in keeping William any longer from the University? Are you not listening rather to your affection than your reason? One of the great objects of education is to accustom a young man *gradually* to become his own master.... To accustom men to great risks, you must expose them, when boys, to lesser risks. If you attempt to avoid all risks, you do an injury infinitely greater than any you shun....

Sydney Smith (1771–1845)

January 3

ST GENEVIEVE (Genoveva), patron saint of Paris. Born at Nanterre in 422. As a child she met St Germanus of Auxerre, on his way to Britain to fight the heresy of the British monk Pelagius (who denied original sin and said people could be saved through their own efforts, though grace *helped;* a real British compromise). She told him she had already decided to consecrate her virginity to God. She was attacked by a Paris mob for persuading them not to run away from the Huns, but when the Huns turned off to Orléans this was attributed to her. Some priests whom she asked to start building a church in honour of St Denis declined because they said they could not get any lime for the mortar. She told them to cross the city bridge and report what they heard. They heard one swineherd say to another, "whilst I was following one of my pigs the other day, it led me into the forest to a large limekiln" (Roman building arts almost forgotten in Dark Ages).

1903: Am writing an essay on the life-history of insects and have abandoned the idea of writing on "How Cats Spend their Time."

W. N. P. Barbellion (1889–1917)

January 4

St Pharaildis (in Flemish Veerle or Verelde) seems to have come from a family of saints, being the daughter of Theodoric of Lorraine and his wife St Amalberga. A brother on her mother's side was St Emenbert Bishop of Cambrai, and her sisters were St Rainelda and St Gudula. And she was brought up by an aunt; St Gertrude. She appears in art as patroness of Ghent, with a goose in her arms, *gans* being Flemish for goose and *Gantum* the Latin for Ghent. She is also shown with loaves, because of a legend that a woman's request for bread for her child was refused by her sister, who said she had none, whereupon the woman said, "may St Pharaildis change the bread into stones if there be any here." Whereupon some loaves the sister had by her were petrified.

1871: At 8 p.m. I went out on the terrace. There was a keen clear frost and the moon was bright in a cloudless sky. Some men were beating the holly bushes along the old bridle lane at the top of Parson's Ground. They probably had a clap net and were beating for blackbirds, &c. "Look out," cried one man. I could hear their voices quite distinctly across the fields in the silence of the frost. Children's voices seemed to be calling everywhere. I heard them from the village and across the common. A number of children must have been out. Perhaps they were sliding in the moonlight.
Francis Kilvert (1840–1879)

January 5

St Simeon Stylites, was, as nearly everyone knows, the one who lived on a pillar, for the last 36 of his 69 years (390–459) at Telanissus (Dair Sem'an, Turkey). Among the people who crowded to see him and hear his preaching was his own mother, but she was not allowed even into the enclosure at the bottom of the pillar. After three days' anguished, and presumably shouted conversation, she died. They took her body to a point where he could see it. He wept.

1849: Mr Pugin, the architect, one day entered one of his rooms just as his child had broken its arm, through a fall from a high chair. The child was being raised by a clerk, at the moment when Mr P. entered, accompanied by the historical painter and convert Mr H. The father went off in a swoon, and Mr H. threw himself down before a crucifix. So, there was the clerk, with one hand holding the child, with the other throwing cold water on the swooning father. On another occasion, a friend who had been travelling all night, had placed his loaded pistols on a table in one of the rooms. One of Mr Pugin's sons entered the room, and not knowing the pistols were loaded, took one and fired it at the window. The ball went through one of the panes, leaving a small round hole. When Mr P. came in, he saw the hole, and made enquiries about it. On learning how it had been caused, he began kicking the child; and after doing so, he fainted. When he recovered he said to his clerk, "You should have said a *Te Deum.*" The man gravely answered, "We went into the chapel and said one." These facts demonstrate how superstition unmans a man. They were told me by an artist, my friend —, who knows the certainty of them. Mr P. was afterwards in an asylum for a time.

John Epps (1805–1869)

January 6

THE MAGI. According to Baring-Gould, the names of GASPAR, MELCHIOR and BALTHASAR "are not found in any writers before the twelfth century". Even so, they are said to have been baptised by St Thomas and preached in Persia. Perhaps the nicest tradition is that they were Shem, Ham and Japhet, who had fallen asleep in a cave, woke only at the Nativity of Christ, came to adore Him, returned to their cave and died: not so much kings, as representatives of all branches of the human race.

1752: [To his son] In Roman Catholic countries, inform yourself of all the forms and ceremonies of that tawdry* church. . . . attend their most remarkable cere-

---

* Gay and showy; *tawdry* had not quite its present signification in Chesterfield's time

monies; have their terms of art explained to you, their *tierce, sexte, nones, matines, vêpres, complies; their bréviaires, rosaires, heures, chaplets, agnus*, etc., things that many people talk of from habit, though few know the true meaning of any of them.

Lord Chesterfield (1694–1773)

January 7

ST CEDD, or Ceadda, is not to be confused with his brother, St Chad. Trained in the Iona usage, at Lindisfarne, he lived in Bradwell (Essex) and Tilabury (Tilbury), teaching the East Saxons "to observe the discipline of regular life, as far as those rude people were then capable." But he returned to the north quite frequently, and founded the Abbey of Lastingham (Yorkshire). King Oswy up there had a wife, Queen Eanfleda, who followed the Roman rite, with its different date for Easter, so he and his earls and thanes were troubled at their Easter feasting by the sight of her and her servants still fasting at the end of a wearisome Lent, since for her it was still only Palm Sunday. St Cedd was present at the Synod of Whitby which decided that all should follow the Roman use.

1908: It is officially announced that the "Times" is to be turned into a Limited Liability Company under the chairmanship of Walter and that the director manager is to be Pearson. This means that the old "Times" is indeed dead. . . . I cannot help, however, regretting the old Thunderer now he is gone.

Wilfrid Scawen Blunt (1840–1922)

January 8

ST SEVERINUS, (d. 482) was a pioneer of Christianity from Vienna and along the Danube during the chaotic German and Hun invasions. During one of the frequent famines he reproached a rich woman, Procla, for hoarding grain, and told her she might as well throw it into the Danube for all the good it would do her. Abashed, she gave it to the poor "and a little while afterwards, to the astonishment of all, vessels came down the Danube laden with every kind of merchandise. They had been frozen up for many days near Passau, but the prayers of God's servant had opened the ice-gates, and let them down the stream before the usual time."

1841: ... For my Husband he is as usual—never healthy, never absolutely ill—protesting against "things in general" with the old emphasis—with an increased vehemence just at present, being in the agonies of getting under way with another book. He has had it in his head for a good while to write a life of Cromwell and has been sitting for months back in a mess of great dingy folios, the very look of which is like to give me lock-jaw. .... (*See also Jan. 10*)

Jane Welsh Carlyle (1801–1866)

January 9

Sᴛ Fɪʟᴀɴ (7th century) was the son of a saintly mother, Kentigerna, and a not so saintly father, Feriach, who ordered him to be thrown into the lake near his castle when shown him at birth, for he was "somewhat unshapely". Through the prayers of his mother and the ministry of the angels, however, he floated ashore. He was educated by St Mungo (also, rather confusingly, known as Kentigern). As he wrote in his cell at night he held up his left hand, and it shone so brilliantly that he was able to write in its light with his right.

1924: At this very moment, or fifteen minutes ago, to be precise, I bought the ten years lease of 52 Tavistock Sqre London W.C.1 ... music, talk, friendship, city views, books, publishing, something central & inexplicable, all this is now within my reach, as it hasn't been since August 1913, when we left Cliffords Inn, for a series of catastrophes which very nearly ended my life, & would, I'm vain enough to think, have ruined Leonard's. So I ought to be grateful to Richmond & Hogarth, & indeed, whether its my invincible optimism or not, I am grateful. Nothing could have suited better all through those years when I was creeping about,

7

like a rat struck on the head, & the aeroplanes were over
London at night, & the streets dark, & no penny buns in the
window. Moreover, nowhere else could we have started the
Hogarth Press, whose very awkward beginning had rise in
this very room, on this very green carpet. Here that strange
offspring grew & throve; it ousted us from the dining room,
which is now a dusty coffin; & crept all over the house.

Virginia Woolf (1882–1941)

January 10

S⊤ Peter Orseolo (928–987). There have been many St Peters
besides the first one: St Peter Orseolo was certainly the only
one who had also been a Doge of Venice; but he ended his life
as a hermit in the Pyrenees, and was canonized forty years after
his death.

1843: ... Dear I will tell you a secret but see that you
keep it to yourself—Carlyle is no more writing about
Oliver Cromwell than you and I are! I have known this for a
good while—you will wonder that I should not have known
it all along—the fact is his papers were a good time more
resembling hierogliphics than finished manuscript. I could
not be at the trouble of making them out—then when I
came to find, on days when I chanced to look, pages about
the *present fashion of men's coats*—about the rage for novel-
ties—puffing every thing or anything except *"Cromwell
Oliver"*—I had no misgivings—I know he has such a way of
tacking on extraneous discussings to his subject—but when
I found at last a long biography of that *Abbot Samson!* then
indeed—I asked what on earth *has* all this to do with
Cromwell—and learned that Cromwell was not begun—that
probably half a dozen other volumes will be published
before that.

Jane Welsh Carlyle (c. 1801–1866)

January 11

S T THEODOSIUS. If he was born at Marissa, in Cappadocia in 423, he was 106 when he died in 529. Known as the Coenobiarch, which means Arch-monk, he began in solitude in the cave where the Magi were said to have rested on their way to Bethlehem. Then, having attracted other monks in spite of his desire for solitude, he wandered about Palestine with a censer containing unlit charcoal and ince se. At Gultilla, by the Dead Sea, it began to give forth fragrant smoke. He founded a monastery there "like a city of saints in the midst of the desert." It had four churches; one for Greek-speakers, one for Arab, and one for Armenian, and one for recovering lunatics.

1927: [To Mrs Thomas Hardy] The knowing you & having the freedom of Max Gate has been a delightful privilege of mine for nearly four years. I cannot tell you how grateful I am to you both: and how much I look forward to finding you there when I come back. Eighty-six is nothing of an age, so long as its bearer is not content with it; in fact it is still fourteen years short of a decent score in cricket. . . .

T. E. Lawrence (1888–1935)

January 12

S T BENEDICT BISCOP (628 (?)–690) (often abbreviated to St Benet Biscop). A Northumbrian noble who was abbot and founder of a monastery at Wearmouth. Its builder, too, for from one of his numerous journeys to Europe (he went to Rome six times) he brought back masons, masters of the stone arch which delighted the Saxons. He also brought books, indeed chant and the whole Benedictine tradition of culture. Having been succeeded as abbot, in the democratic Benedictine way, by Easter-win (his nephew, twenty-two years younger) he returned to find him, and a lot of other monks, dead in an epidemic. At nearby Jarrow, which he had also founded, the only survivors were the abbot and a boy. The latter grew up to become the Venerable Bede, the father of English history.

9

1967: An unseen scullerymaid was cleaning knives; and as she cleaned, she sang: "I love Robin," she sang, "and Robin he loves me." Down in her dark hole beneath the doorsteps the scullion scrapes and sings: and over her head, young ladies trip and tattle at their ease.

A. J. Munby (1828–1910)

January 13

Sᴛ Hɪʟᴀʀʏ ᴏꜰ Pᴏɪᴛɪᴇʀs, or Pictavium (d. 368) was a very tough character, known as *malleus Arianorum*, the hammer of the Arians (whose heresy was that Christ wasn't consubstantial with the Father, just an exceptionally good man. Lot of them about). The Emperor Constantius favoured the Arians, so he was banished to Phrygia. He tried to appear at an Arian council in 360 (*four* different creeds had been published the preceding year). He was refused, although later he did "defeat" an Arian bishop, Auxentius, in a public disputation at Milan.

1833: They who grow cotton are merciful taskmasters in comparison with those who manufacture it. Robert Hildyard (whom you know) told me the other day that Marshall, the Member for Leeds, showed him one of his manufactories, and upon his remarking the extreme delicacy of the children, replied they were consumptive, that a great proportion of them never reached the age of twenty, and that this was owing to the *flew* with which the air was always filled. He spoke of this with as little compunction as a General would calculate the probable consumption of lives in a campaign ... I know not how a cotton-mill can be otherwise than an abomination to God and man.

Robert Southey (1774–1843)

January 14

Sᴛ Kᴇɴᴛɪɢᴇʀɴ (d. 601) is the patron saint of Glasgow. The apostle of Strathclyde, the region between the Clyde in southern Scotland and the Mersey in northern England, then as

Celtic as Wales, he did actually spend some time in Wales, founding the famous monastery of St Asaph. He lived in a good time for legends. E.g., king's wife gave lover a ring, king saw it on his hand when he was asleep during rest out hunting, with difficulty restrained himself from killing lover, simply threw ring into Clyde, then asked queen where it was, she very troubled confided to St K. who, remembering his own mother's illegitimacy, prayed for her. The ring turned up in the belly of a salmon, all forgiven. But he did have historic meeting with St Columba and his monks from Iona.

1827: "Often, my own productions seem wholly strange to me. To-day, I [Goethe] read a passage in French, and thought as I read: 'This man speaks cleverly enough—you would not have said it otherwise': when I look at it closely, I find it is a passage translated from my own writings!"
Johann Peter Eckermann (1792–1854) Conversations with Goethe.

January 15

TWO GOOD saints today. ST PAUL (d. 341) was known in Egypt as the "father of hermits". When he died, aged over 100, two lions came and dug his grave.

ST MAURUS (d. 584) was one of the first Benedictine saints. From Monte Cassino he crossed the Alps, carrying the weights for the bread and the measures for the wine according to that famous moderate Rule of St Benedict, and set up the monastery of Glanfeuil which, says Baring-Gould, "among the vineyards of Anjou, merits the grateful glance of every traveller who is not insensible to the advantages which flowed from that first Benedictine colony over the whole of France."

1806: . . . As for news, Fenwick is coming to town on Monday (if no kind angel intervenes) to surrender himself to prison. He hopes to get the rules of the Fleet. On the same day, or nearly the same day, Fell, my other friend and quondam drinker, will go to Newgate, and his wife and four children, I suppose, to the parish. Plenty of reflection and motives of gratitude to the wise Dispenser of all things in *us,* whose prudent conduct has hitherto insured us a warm fire and snug roof over our heads . . . maybe I may, at last, hit upon some mode of collecting some of the vast superfluities of this money-voiding town. Much is to be got, and I do not want much. All I ask is time and leisure; and I am cruelly cut off for them.

Charles Lamb (1775–1834)

January 16

S⊤ FURSEY (d. about 653) is credited with the first "vision" of hell, which some credit as a primary source for the *Divina Commedia*—although that was to be written, one might remember, almost as long after St Fursey as St Fursey was after Christ. His relics are at Peronne; he left a war-ravaged East Anglia to found a monastery at Lagny.

1803: Intensely cold. Wm had a fancy for some gingerbread I put on Molly's Cloak and my Spenser, and we walked toward Matthew Newton's. I went into the house. The blind Man and his Wife and Sister were sitting by the fire, all dressed very clean in their Sunday's Clothes, the sister reading. They took their little stock of gingerbread out of the cubboard and I bought 6 pennyworth. They were so grateful when I paid them for it I could not find it in my heart to tell them we were going to make Gingerbread ourselves.

Dorothy Wordsworth (1771–1855)

January 17

S⊤ ANTHONY THE GREAT (251–356), is called the father of monasticism. It is true he was himself a solitary hermit for many years—indeed he is *the* type of the young man wrestling for perfection; everyone knows the famous story of the Temptations. But he was not a fanatic; in fact his rudimentary organization of the many hermits in the desert and his counselling worked against fanaticism. Among other things he was credited with curing erysipelas, hence its name of "St Anthony's Fire".

1803: Marchi told me today that during the latter part of Sir Joshua Reynolds life, He used as a vehicle in painting the Macgilp only (mastic varnish and drying oil) which He sometimes would lay on a part of his picture without mixing any colour with it, but making it serve as a tint. This did not answer, for in a few months it was sure to become yellow or brown & obliged to be taken off.

Joseph Farington (1747–1821)

January 18

ST DEICOLUS lived "at the beginning of the 7th century", a time when saints wandered about a lot. He left his native Ireland with St Columbanus, went to East Anglia, became a hermit in Burgundy. Once he hung his coat on a sunbeam. Asked in his youth why he was always smiling he replied, "because no one can take my God away from me".

1790: In point of cleanliness, I think the merit of the two nations is divided; the French are cleaner in their persons, and the English in their houses. . . . A *bidet* in France is as universally in every apartment as a basin to wash your hands . . . on the other hand, their houses are temples of abomination; and the practice of spitting about a room, which is amongst the highest as well as the lowest ranks, is detestable. I have seen a gentleman spit so near the clothes of a duchess that I have stared at his unconcern.

Arthur Young (1741–1820)

January 19

ST WULSTAN (c. 1012–1095) is the great saint of Worcester. After the Norman Conquest the Normans tried to get rid of him because he was "ignorant" (i.e., did not speak French), but relented when the bishop's staff which he cheerfully yielded could not be got out of the stone where he left it standing except by him. He was very strongly for the celibacy of priests and very against the slave trade (in Bristol even then; the English used to sell them to the Irish).

1729: Yesterday I was at the rehearsal of the new opera composed by Handel: I like it extremely but the taste of the town is so depraved, that nothing will be approved of but the burlesque. The Beggar's Opera entirely triumphs over the Italian one.

Mrs Pendarves to Mrs Ann Granville

January 20

ST SEBASTIAN was *not* killed by arrows. The legend is that Sebastian, a tribune in Diocletian's army, saved some Christian prisoners by converting the governor, was indeed pierced with arrows, but recovered after being left for dead. Seeing the Emperor pass in a procession later, St Sebastian once more called on him to renounce his pagan gods; and was then beaten to death. All that is known for sure is that he *was* a martyr.

1825: I have discovered a new means of exercise, that is, by running up and down stairs a dozen times at a stretch, and then walking along the passage, which measures exactly 30 feet in length; there are 14 stairs, so that pacing backwards and forwards will give 168 stairs in 12 descents and ascents, and walking 24 times along the passage at 10 yards each time will give 240 yards. This, repeated alternately for an hour, will afford as strong an exercise as can be required, indeed much stronger than horse exercise or common walking. . . .

John Skinner (1772–1839)

January 21

S T AGNES certainly existed, although the legends of her miraculous survival in the brothel to which she was sent, and on the fire, are doubtful. But she was certainly very young ("twelve or thirteen" says Attwater), did resist a pagan marriage, and was executed by stabbing of the throat.

1875: I went round the premises late at night to see if the outhouses were locked up. All was still and the white pig lying in the moonlight at the door of his house, fast asleep, with the moon shining on his white face and round cheek.

Francis Kilvert (1840–1879)

January 22

S S VINCENT and ANASTASIUS, it says for today in the old Catholic Missal. St Anastasius (d. 628) longed to be a martyr. He was flogged, had an enormous beam laid across his legs, was hung up by one arm with weights attached, flogged again, and finally strangled. He was pleasantly surprised, according to the Acts concerning him, that this final treatment was not more drawn out. 300 years earlier Vincent had died, at Valencia, under Diocletian, from tortures, said to have included a red-hot gridiron.

1768: I have no acquaintance, at present, among the gentlemen of the navy: but have written to a friend, who was a sea-chaplain during the late war, desiring him to look into his minutes, with respect to birds that settled on their rigging during their voyage up or down the channel. What Hasselquist says on that subject is remarkable: there were little short-winged birds frequently coming on board his ship all the way from our channel quite up to the Levant, especially before squally weather. What you suggest, with regard to Spain, is highly probable. The winters of Andalusia are so mild, that, in all likelihood, the soft-billed birds that leave us at that season may find insects

15

sufficient to support them there. Some young man, possessed of fortune, health, and leisure, should make an autumnal voyage into that kingdom; and should spend a year there, investigating the natural history of that vast country.

Gilbert White (1720–1793)

January 23

S⊤ JOHN THE ALMSGIVER, was Patriarch of Alexandria (d. 616). A lot of charming stories are told about him. Once he took a Bishop called Troilus round a quarter where he had built simple domed huts for his beloved poor, and shamed him into giving them money. Then the bishop took ill, and when John went to see him it was clear he was ill with rage at not having kept the money to buy a certain silver drinking cup. So he said "I only borrowed the money" and as soon as Troilus saw it back in his hand his illness vanished. "Come and dine with me, if you are now well," said St John. After dinner the bishop fell asleep and dreamed he saw a house of unearthly beauty on which it said THE ETERNAL MANSION AND PLACE OF REPOSE OF TROILUS, THE BISHOP, but there came One with attendants who were ordered to change this to THE ETERNAL MANSION AND PLACE OF REPOSE OF JOHN, ARCHBISHOP OF ALEXANDRIA, PURCHASED FOR THIRTY POUNDS.

1715: I sett up my foot on the ladder as it lay in my stable at Milden town . . . & as I was setting my foot down my heel stuck on the end of one of the broad staves of the ladder. I could not recover myselfe, but fell down with my head and shoulders first to the ground, but God be praised got noe harm. (*See also Jan. 29*)

William Coe of Mildenhall (1680–1729)

January 24

S T TIMOTHY, Bishop of Ephesus, was the most famous of St
Paul's converts. Indeed the two Letters to him are part of the
New Testament. He was stoned and beaten to death in his own
city; according to tradition, after exhorting to decency the
orgiasts at the annual pagan feast of the Catagogii.

1842: [To Bernard Barton] A letter has been sent from
the Secretary of the Ipswich Mechanics' Institution
asking me to Lecture—any subject but Party Politics or
Controversial Divinity. On my politely declining, another,
a fuller, and a more pressing letter was sent urging me to
comply with their demand: I answered to the same effect,
but with accelerated dignity. I am now awaiting the third
request in confidence: if you see no symptoms of its being
mooted, perhaps you will kindly propose it. I have prepared
an answer. . . .
This is a day like May: I and the children have been
scrambling up and down the sides of a pit till our legs ache.
Edward Fitzgerald (1809–1883)

January 25

S T POPPO (978–1048) ought to be remembered for various
charitable actions, not the least of which must surely have
been that of dissuading the Emperor Henry II from the sport of
smearing a naked man with honey, putting him among bears,
and watching him elude their attempts to lick it off.

1787: Rode to Ringland this morning and married one
Robert Astick and Elizabeth Howlett by licence, Mr
Carter being from home, and the Man being in Custody,
the Woman being with Child by him. The Man was a long
time before he could be prevailed on to marry her when in
the Churchyard; and at the Altar behaved very unbecoming.
It is a cruel thing that any Person should be compelled by
law to marry.
James Woodforde (1740–1803)

17

January 26

MOST SAINTS either come from glamorous-sounding places like Assisi or—Antioch, or (like Mother Theresa or Father Damien) go to very unglamorous centres of poverty and disease to work. But *ordinary* places? There are going to be in this book two saints from Barking, Essex, 8 miles from Liverpool Street. At Barking Creek is the outfall of the north London sewer. Well this is the feast-day of ST THEORITGITHA (7th century), a sister in the great convent there.

1916: I send a letter out of sheer loving kindness, seeing there is no fact, complaint, desire, fear, regret or fancy to be addressed unto you, but only the fact of my sonship, and my greetings to the most gentlest of mothers. . . . We are now—at last—on our Musketry Course. Many are falling sick about me, by reason of January, and the dead season. . . . I may be going for the 5th Manchester Regiment. Did you know that no officers can be sent to the Firing Line without 5 months waiting in England.

Wilfred Owen (1893–1918)

January 27

ST JOHN CHRYSOSTOM ("golden-mouthed") (c. 345–407) is one of the four great Eastern Doctors of the Church (with St Gregory of Nazianzen, St Athanasius and St Basil). After years as a desert ascetic he became archbishop of Constantinople. He became famous for his preaching, which was not only against idle monks and a licentious court, but for the virtues of Christianity, expressed concretely, not in learned abstractions. The Arians, who at this time had no church, used to sing hymns expounding their doctrines outside public buildings, and he answered with nightly processional hymn-singing—the first example of hymns in the church.

1884: A gentleman had a favourite cat who he taught to sit at the dinner-table where it behaved very well. He was in the habit of putting any scraps he left on to the cat's

18

plate. One day puss did not take his place punctually, but presently appeared with two mice, one of which it placed on its master's plate, the other on its own.

Beatrix Potter (1866–1943)

January 28

IN THE old Missal, many of the greater feast-days were commemorated with an Octave, eight days later. But ST AGNES (*see 21st January*) is a special case. Today is simply called The Second Feast of St Agnes, and commemorates the fact that eight days after her martyrdom her parents went to pray at her tomb and had a vision of her in a blaze of light surrounded by other virgin saints.

1805: The rooms are not half so agreeable as they were some years ago, when the late London hours were not thought of; and how prejudicial must they be to the health of all, is very visible in the young as well as the old. Formerly youth was seldom ill; now, from thin clothing and late hours, you hardly see a young lady in good health, or not complaining about rheumatism, as much as us old ones! Sixteen thousand strangers at Bath in the season 1805!

Mrs Philip Libbe Powys (1739–1817)

January 29

ST FRANCIS DE SALES (1567–1622) was educated at Annecy, seat of the Catholic bishops of Geneva after the Calvinist takeover. He endured some kind of mysterious crisis of faith in adolescence, and emerged as a tireless and above all good-tempered preacher. "You can catch more flies with a spoonful of honey than with a hundred barrels of vinegar," he said, and "what is good makes no noise; what is noisy does no good." One Calvinist minister in Geneva said, "if we honoured any man as a saint, I know no one since the days of the apostles more worthy of it than this man." He is the patron saint of journalists.

19

1715: I fell from the top of our Kitchen stairs to the Bottom, my Heels slipt up & I slidd down on my back & Praised be God I got noe hurt. (*See also Feb. 16*)

William Coe of Mildenhall (1680–1729)

January 30

ST ADELELM (d. about 1100) was a noble of Lyons; first a soldier, then a monk. When ordained priest he refused to officiate, after hearing that the bishop who ordained him had obtained the office corruptly, until a successor was appointed. On his way to see that successor, on a dark stormy night, St Adelelm gave a companion a candle to show the way and it was not blown out. It is from this legend that the static electricity round ships' mastheads is known as St Elmo's Fire. He died as Abbot of Burgos in Spain.

1687: I heard the famous eunuch Cifaccio, sing in the new Popish chapel this afternoon; it was indeed very rare, and with great skill. He came over from Rome, esteemed one of the best voices in Italy. Much crowding— little devotion.

John Evelyn (1620–1706)

January 31

ST JOHN BOSCO, 1815–1888, was recognized as a pioneer in the work of caring for and training boys, begun in Turin, long before his eventual canonization in 1934. He was a gentle man who did it all by kindness and example. The work of the order which he founded spread all over the world. He is commemorated within two days of the saint he admired so much—St Francis de Sales (*see January 29*)—after whom he named his order—the Salesians.

1836: . . . It occurs to me I have not noticed as I ought Wordsworth's answer to the charge brought by Wilson against Wordsworth that he never quotes other poems than his own. In fact, I can testify to the falsehood of the statement; but Wordsworth in addition remarked: "You know how I love and quote, not even Shakespeare and Milton, but Cowper, Burns, etc. As to the modern poets—Byron, Scott, etc.—I do not quote them because I do not love them. Byron has great power and genius, but there is something so repugnant to my moral sense that I abhor them."

Henry Crabb Robinson (1775–1867)

FEBRUARY

February 1

RATHER LESS is known for certain of this ST BRIDGET (d. about 525) than of the St Bridget who founded the Bridgettine order of nuns and was Swedish. This one, by contrast, belongs to the Irish legendary period. As she had to travel a lot, the bishop ordained her coachman a priest; once he turned to preach to her and a companion, all becoming so engrossed that no one noticed a horse had slipped its yoke and the coach was running "all on one side".

1877: [To C. E. Norton] I only want to have Crabbe read more than he is. Women and young People never will like him, I think: but I believe every thinking man will like him more as he grows older. . . . Campbell observed his "shrewd Vigilance" awake under all his *"politesse"*, and John Murray said that Crabbe said uncommon things in so common a way that they escaped recognition. It appears, I think, that he not only said, but wrote, such things: even to such Readers as Mr Stephen [Leslie Stephen, father of Virginia Woolf] who can see very little Humour, and no Epigram, in him. I will engage to find plenty of both.
Edward Fitzgerald (1809–1883)

February 2

THERE IS an old joke about the three things that even God doesn't know: what a Dominican is thinking, what a Jesuit is doing, and how many orders of nuns there are in the church. Well, one of the best-known of them, that of the Sisters of Notre Dame (of Bordeaux) was founded by today's ST JOAN DE LESTON-NAC (1556–1640). Not, however, canonized till 1949.

1774: We have no news public or private; but there is an ostrich-egg laid in America, where the Bostonians have canted three hundred chests of tea into the ocean. Lord Chatham talked of conquering America in Germany; I believe England will be conquered some day or other in New England or Bengal. I think I have heard of such a form in law, as such an one of the parish of St Martin's-in-the-Fields in Asia: St Martin's parish literally reaches now to the other end of the globe, and we may be undone a twelve-month before we hear a word of the matter—which is not convenient, and a little drawback on being masters of dominions a thousand times bigger than ourselves. . . .

Horace Walpole (1717–1797)

February 3

Sᴛ Bʟᴀsɪᴜs, Blase, Blayse, Blays, Blaise (or sometimes in England, Blazey) was martyred under Diocletian in 316. He once saved the life of a child being choked by a bone, and until the post-Vatican II disappearance of such things there used to be a ceremony on this day in which people's throats were touched with two blessed candles with a prayer for deliverance from throat disease. Today is also the feast of St Werburga, the patroness of Chester.

1830: Dined with Goethe. We talked of Mozart. "I saw him," said Goethe, "when he was seven and gave a concert while travelling our way. I myself was about fourteen, and remember perfectly the little man with his frisure and sword." I stared; it seemed to me almost wonderful that Goethe was old enough to have seen Mozart when a child.

Johann Peter Eckermann, Conversations with Goethe, 1827
(1792–1854)

February 4

Sᴛ Gɪʟʙᴇʀᴛ ᴏꜰ Sᴇᴍᴘʀɪɴɢʜᴀᴍ (in Lincolnshire), about 1085 to 1189, but certainly a very old man, deserves remembering if only for his reply when the bishop wanted to make him archdeacon. "I know of no shorter road to perdition," he said when refusing. A man of austere and ascetic habits, he founded the only specifically English religious order, the Gilbertines, in which, curiously, the men were Augustinian canons and the women followed the Rule of St Benedict. All its houses, of which there were over twenty, were suppressed by Henry VIII.

1793: [To her father, Dr Burney] How exactly do I sympathize in all you say and feel, my dear sir, upon these truly calamitous times! I hear daily more and more affecting accounts of the saint-like end of the martyred Louis. When the King left the Temple to go to the place of sacrifice, the cries of his wretched family were heard, loud and shrill, through the courts without! Good heaven! what distress and horror equalled ever what they must then experience?

When he arrived at the scaffold, his confessor, as if with the courage of inspiration, called out to him aloud, after his last benediction: "Fils de Saint Louis, montez au ciel!" The King ascended with firmness, and meant to harangue his guilty subjects; but the wretch Santerre said he was not there to speak, and the drums drowned the words, except to those nearest the terrible spot. To those he audibly was heard to say: "Citoyens, je meurs innocent! Je pardonne à mes assassins; et je souhaite que ma mort soit utile à mon peuple."

Fanny Burney (1752–1840)

February 5

ST AGATHA (another of those mentioned by name in the Mass) was tortured to death in the 3rd century, under the Emperor Decius, and there is a persistent legend that this included the cutting off of her breasts. Twenty-six Martyrs of Japan, whose feast is also today, were canonized in 1862. In the persecution, starting in 1597, of the church started by St Francis Xavier, which flourished, and was then wiped out, many of them were crucified, burnt near slow fires and then drenched with water, hacked to pieces or lowered into sulphur pits.

1870: . . . Paris shines from afar with the lustre of the New Jerusalem. When I first arrived there, still haunted by the memory of Florence, I was oppressed and irritated by its pretentious splendor and its pedantic neatness and symmetry: but gradually its immense merits began to impress me and I have now quite succumbed to it as the perfect model of a mighty capital. . . .

Henry James (1843–1916)

February 6

S<small>T</small> V<small>EDAST</small> (d. about 540) was a fairly important figure in the development of what used to be known as Christendom Clovis, King of the Franks, who after victories over the Visigoths settled in Paris, was converted to Christianity partly by his Christian wife , Clotilda, and partly by the saint. He has also been known as Vaast, Vaat Wast, Wat (hence presumably Wat Tyler, of the Peasants' Revolt), Gaston; and in England, Vastes, Fastes, Fastres, Faster, Faister and Fauster, not to mention Foster. His church in Foster Lane in the City was known, before the Great Fire (1666) as St Foster's.

1842: . . . I think Handel never gets out of his wig: that is, not out of his age: his Hallelujah chorus is a chorus not of angels, but of well-fed earthly choristers. . . . There is a little bit of Auber's, at the end of the Bayadère when the God resumes his divinity and retires into the sky, which has more of pure light and mystical solemnity than anything I know of Handel's: but then this is only a scrap: and Auber could not breathe in that atmosphere long: whereas old Handel's coursers, with necks with thunder clothed and long resounding pace, never tire. Beethoven thought more deeply also: but I don't know whether he could sustain himself so well. . . .

Edward Fitzgerald (1809–1883)

February 7

S<small>T</small> P<small>ARTHENIUS</small>, Bishop of Lampsacus, was authorized by Constantine, the first Christian Emperor (c. 288–337) to overthrow heathen idols and temples. He found a man possessed by a demon, which at first refused to be cast out, saying, "I know thee; thou wilt cast me out and bid me enter a swine." The saint said no, he would offer it a man to dwell in. Then the demon came out, and the Bishop said "I am the man. Enter if thou canst." The demon fled.

1833: MY DEAR LORD ASHLEY, There is one thing, connected with these accursed factories which I have long intended to expose, and that is the way in which Sunday Schools have been subservient to the merciless love of gain. The manufacturers know that a cry would be raised against them if their little white slaves received no instruction; and so they have converted Sunday into a school-day, with what effect may be seen in the evidences.

This is quite a distinct question from that of the good or evil to be expected from Sunday Schools, as originally intended, and existing in most places. Upon the latter subject I have something to say when opportunities will allow me.

Robert Southey (1774–1843)

February 8

ST CUTHMAN (9th century) was one of those strong saints. A shepherd originating from Devon, he was reduced to great poverty when he could not work and look after his aged mother. He therefore pushed her, on a handcart, taking casual work on the way, till he fetched up at Steyning in Sussex, where, single-handed, he built a church. By this time, the local people had given him two oxen. When these were stolen he went to the two young men who had done this, yoked them to his cart, and made them take the building materials to the church.

1645: There was little more to be seene in the rest of the civil world, after Italy, France, Flanders, and the Low Countrys but plaine and prodigious barbarisme.

John Evelyn (1620–1706)

February 9

Sᴛ Tᴇɪʟᴏ (d. about 651) is co-titular, with St Peter, St Dubricius (his teacher), and the perhaps mythical (according to Attwater) St Oudoceus, of Llandaff Cathedral, which is as good as to say Cardiff Cathedral, since it is two miles from the city centre. St Teilo was its original builder, Llandaff being his point of rest after a journey eastward from his native Tenby. He is said to have founded twelve other churches.

1878: My dear Sallie,—Please tell Jessie I meant it all for nonsense, so I hope she won't give me a pincushion, for I've got three already. I've forgotten what I said in my letter to her, and *she* knows it all by heart; so you can see this is what happened—the letter has gone out of *my* mind into *her* mind: it is just like a person going into a new house. I wonder if it found Jessie's mind warm and comfortable, and if it liked it as well as its old house? I *think*, when it first got in and looked round and said "Oh, dear, oh dear! I shall *never* be comfortable in this new mind! I wish I was back in the old one! Why, there's a great awkward sofa, big enough to hold a dozen people! And it's got the word 'KINDNESS' marked on it. Why, I shan't be able to have it all to myself. Now, in my old home there was just *one* chair—a nice soft arm-chair that would just hold me; and it had the word 'SELFISHNESS' marked on the back; so other people couldn't come bothering in, because there were no chairs for them. And what a stupid little stool that is by the fire, marked 'HUMILITY'!"

C. L. Dodgson (Lewis Carroll) (1832–1898)

February 10

Sᴛ Bᴇɴᴇᴅɪᴄᴛ had a twin sister called Scholastica (for their birth date I have so far seen everything from 540 to 548). She directed, in a valley near Monte Cassino, the nuns who followed her brother's famous Rule. The well known story about her is that she came to see him and St Benedict at first refused, since such things were against the Rule; but her tears, followed by a

29

violent storm appearing from nowhere out of clear air, persuaded him otherwise, and they passed the night "speaking of heavenly things". Three days later she died, while St Benedict in his cell had a vision of her soul ascending as a dove.

1770: The last Vases were not, some of them, what they were intended to be, & it will very often happen so in Pebble Vases, but I have often observ'd that what we have esteem'd a *great fault*, has been admir' by some as a peculiar beauty wch makes me easier about such mishaps. . . .

Josiah Wedgwood (1730–1795)

February 11

S^T Caedmon (d. about 680) was a monk at Whitby Abbey (ruled by a woman, St Hilda, as often happened in Celtic Christianity). When the harp came down the table towards him he would refuse it and leave, having no training in music or poetry. But God appeared to him in a dream and ordered him to sing; and, unlike most of us who dream marvellous dreams, he remembered it in the morning. He became famous as a bard, and translated Genesis, Exodus, a lot more Old Testament, the Life and Passion of Jesus and the Acts of the Apostles into Anglo-Saxon, in that metaphor-rich style where the sea is "the path of sails" or "the whale's road" or "the swan's pathway", and fog is "the helmet of the air". He had over thirty metaphors for Noah's Ark. As a French critic remarked "these poets instinctively put their own feelings into Jewish history, and pictured a Judaea washed by the sullen and icy waters of the North Sea".

1866: . . . Miss Durant was interesting to me, because she is a refined type of that character which is so noble in low life: a strong and handsome woman, dignified and self-reliant; and moreover, ladylike, highbred, blazing, as it were, with talent, and sleek with cultivation; just the person to impress some men with awe and admiration. Yet, in a drawingroom creature, such selfasserting strength looks somewhat masculine and out of place: whereas the form it takes in working women is simply heroic. I hold, for

30

instance, that Kitty, queen of milkmaids, with her calm
lofty endurance and her grand silent ways, is a nobler being
than Miss Durant. . . .

A. J. Munby (1828–1910)

February 12

THE FOURTH LATERAN COUNCIL (1215) forbade the establishment
of new orders of friars, and the Council of Lyons in 1274
condemned all but the four main orders of mendicants to gradual
extinction. The Servite Order ("Servants of Mary"), however,
was approved by Pope Alexander IV in 1233. Today is the feast
of its Seven Founders, led by St Buonfiglio Menaldo (d. 1261).
They were all well-born citizens of that rich and sumptuous
place, Florence. The order flourished particularly in France,
Germany and Poland.

1870: The slate slabs of the urinals even are frosted in
graceful sprays. [Dec. 31 1870. I have noticed it here
also at the seminary: it comes up when they have been
washed.]

Gerard Manley Hopkins (1844–1889)

February 13

THE NAME Gregory instantly suggests St Gregory the Great,
Pope Gregory I, who sent St Augustine to Britain, gave his
name to the serene chant now so casually abandoned and
altogether overshadows today's saint, who is GREGORY II
(669–731). Yet the latter was a key figure in the great conflict
with the Iconoclasts or image-breakers. Although Byzantine
Emperors (such as Leo the Isaurian, with whom our St Gregory
was often in conflict) and the generally spiritualized, contemplative, "un-physical" Eastern church are mainly associated with
this movement, it was in fact the Byzantine Empress Irene who
got the Council of Nicaea (787) called, which restored images.

1695: You would never believe how vulgar and ill-
mannered the French have become in the last twelve or

31

thirteen years. You won't find two young people of quality who know how to be polite in word or deed. There are two reasons for this: the piety prevailing at Court, and the excesses prevailing amongst the men. For one thing, it is no longer seemly for men and women to be seen speaking together; for another, men no longer wish to please anyone but each other, and the more debauched and impertinent they are, the more they are admired.

Elizabeth Charlotte (Liselotte), Princess Palatine and Duchess of Orleans (1652–1722)

February 14

THE ONE saint's day that everybody knows; and I don't mean Ss Vitalis, Fechula and Zeno, St Eleucodius of Ravenna (d. 112), St Viventine of Teramo (d. 273), St Maro of Syria (d. 390), St Auxentius of Bithynia (about 470), St Antonine, Abbot of Sorrento (about 830), or St Bruno and Eighteen Companions (martyred in Prussia, 1008). ST VALENTINE was a Roman martyr of the third century; and the practice of sending love-cards (anonymous or otherwise) on this day has nothing whatever to do with him, but possibly something to do with an old belief that this was the date when birds started mating.

1477: Address: Unto my ryght welbelovyd Voluntyn, John Paston, Squyer, be this bill delyvered, &c.

Ryght reverent and wurschypfull and my ryght welebeloved Voluntyne, I recommande me unto yowe full hertely, desyring to here of yowr welefare, whech I beseche Almyghty God long for to preserve unto hys plesure and yowr hertys desyre. And yf it please yowe to here of my welefare, I am not in good heele of body ner of herte, nor schall be tyll I here from yowe;

For ther wottys[1] no creature what peyn that I endure,
And for to be deede, I dare it not dysecure.[2]. . . .

But yf that ye loffe me, as I tryste verely that ye do, ye will not leffe me therfor; for if that ye hade not halfe the lyvelode[3] that ye hafe, for to do the grettyst labure that any

[1] knows
[2] reveal
[3] property

32

woman on lyve myght, I wold not forsake yowe.

And yf ye commande me to kepe me true whereever I go, I wyse I will do all my myght yowe to love and never no mo.

And yf my freendys say that I do amys, thei schal not me let so for to do.

Myn herte me byddys ever more to love yowe
Truly over all erthely thing.

And yf thei be nev er so wroth, I tryst it schall be bettur in tyme commyng.

No more to yowe at this tyme, but the Holy Trinite hafe yowe in kepying. And I besech yowe that this bill be nor seyn of non erthely creature safe only your selfe, &c. And thys lettur was indyte[4] at Topcroft wyth full hevy herte, &c.

Be your own M.B.

Margery Brews (d. 1495) to John Paston III

February 15

WHEN THE Irish ST BERACH was baptized by his uncle, St Froech, the latter, when Berach's mother wanted him back, said, "no, let me have the bringing up of this little one; God will provide for his sustenance." So St Froech took him, and when the baby cried for the breast of his mother, his uncle gave him the lobe of his ear to suck, and thence flowed a copious supply of honey.

1874: What always astonishes me is the kind of impetuous enthusiasm with which women side against the accused. A prisoner is in their eyes a culprit. Far from distrusting their own passion they glory in it; they have an antipathy to impartiality, to calm, to the spirit of justice. . . . They know only love and hatred and do not conceive even the fringe of justice. These gentle creatures are truly ferocious the moment they cease to be partial. Beware then of the women with the knitting needles, the women who pour petroleum on the flames, those that light the pyres. Having a horror of reason, they are the prey of every extravagance

<hr>

[4] written

and they can go to every extreme. The moment the feminine element dominates, over-excitement and orgies are imminent; religions, art, poetry, customs, states are impaired and fall into decadence.

Frédéric Amiel (1821–1881)

February 16

IN 309, five Egyptian Christians on their way back from trying to help some friends sentenced to slave labour (unheard of nowadays, of course) in Cilicia, were stopped at the gates of Caesarea, and asked what their native city was. "Jerusalem," they said, and they did not mean it geographically. What were their names? Either because they said so, or because these were the names on which they called, they are recorded as ELIAS, JEREMIAH, ISAIAH, SAMUEL and DANIEL. They were tortured to death.

1722: I was at the Ds of Grafton's funerall at Euston Church & as I was going over the vault (where all that family are deposited) to read the Lord Arlington's inscription on white marble against the wall, the Corner of a seat Catched my Clothes & put me suddenly back & if I had not Catched hold of the seat I had fallen backwards down the vault (a great steep) wch must inevitably have done me a great mischief, but blessed be God I saved my selfe as above said. (*See also May 26*)

William Coe of Mildenhall (1680–1729)

February 17

ST FINAN (d. 661) succeeded St Aidan as abbot of Lindisfarne. His conversion of Sigebert, king of the East Saxons, and Peda (son of the bloody-minded Penda), king of the Midland Angles, is a reminder that the Christianization of the whole of Britain was a kind of spiritual pincer movement, operating from the north as well as from the mission established at Canterbury by St Augustine in 597.

1830: I feel very unwell, and think it is the bile which hangs about me. I strive to amuse myself by reading novels, and have finished that of the "Black Dwarf" by Sir Walter Scott. I must be reduced to a sad state when I feel obliged to such nonsense for a pastime.

John Skinner (1772–1839)

February 18

S⊤ ANGILBERT ("some French martyrologies") (d. 814) married, after he was ordained priest, Bertha, daughter of Charlemagne, "by the king's consent." He vowed that he would embrace the monastic life if he recovered from an illness. But when he did recover he was summoned to resist Danish pirates who had come up the Somme, and (says Baring-Gould) "buckling on his harness, he fell like a thunderbolt on the pirates and utterly defeated and exterminated them." *Then* he embraced the monastic life, and so did his wife.

1918: (Scarborough) And we got excited. What excited us, who shall say? We jumped about, we bumped about, we sang praises, we cursed Manchester; we looked in at half open doors and blessed the people inside. We saw Shakespere in a lantern, and the whole of Italy in a Balcony. A tall chimney became a Greek Column; and in the inscriptions on the walls we read romances and philosophies.

It was a strange way of getting drunk. I wonder if the people in the officers' bar suspected that evening, how much more cheaply a man can get fuddled on fresh air and old winding passages?

Wilfred Owen (1893–1918)

February 19

S⊤ BELINA (d. 1153) was canonized in 1203 and is one of a host of saints who died in defence of their virginity (*see, for instance, St Maria Goretti, July 6*). The local lord of the manor, called Lord of Pradines and d'Arcy, wanted her (she was a peasant girl, engaged to a peasant) as his mistress and killed her when she resisted. This was at Landreville, in the diocese of Troyes.

1885: British army retreating. Papa met Mr Gladstone walking in Bond Street this afternoon. Mr Gladstone half stopped, and so did his shadow, the detective, but papa wouldn't take his hat off, and went on. I'd have stopped and given him a piece of my mind.

Beatrix Potter (1866–1943)

February 20

AVILA IS of course famous for one of the great mystics of the west, St Teresa (and this may be the place to tell of the splendid lady I met at a party who said, when some Jehovah's Witnesses got their foot in her door, "it's no good talking to me, I'm a *mystic.*" On this they retired down her front path, and she heard one say to the other in the accents of Kansas, "What's a mystic?" "I dunno," said his friend, "they're sure not in the Bible.") But February 20 has been the feast there of a much more curious and legendary saint; ST PAULA THE BEARDED. She was very beautiful but wished to discourage a young man who clearly had evil intentions. She prayed and after her prayer a beard and moustache immediately grew on her.

1858: Had to go to Huntingdon. In returning, met in a railway carriage with a most intelligent man from Leeds, a member of the Society of Friends. He thinks, with many, that much railway-travelling is injurious to the brain. Certainly it throws the whole action of the body on the junction of the neck with the head.

John Epps (1805–1869)

February 21

S<small>T</small> Z<small>ACHARIAS OF</small> J<small>ERUSALEM</small> (d. 631) was a figure in one of the countless battles that have centred round that city. In 614 it was taken by the Persians under Chosroes, many Christians being massacred; Zacharias and others managed to escape to Alexandria, where they were helped by St John the Almsgiver (*see January 23*). In 628 peace was restored with the Emperor Heraclius by Siroes, son of Chosroes (and his assassinator, as a matter of fact), and the next year Zacharias returned and was able to identify the relics of the True Cross.

1930: Lady B. calls in the afternoon—not, as might have been expected, to see if I am in bed with pneumonia, but to ask if I will help at a Bazaar early in May. Further enquiry reveals that it is in aid of the Party Funds. I say What Party? (Am well aware of Lady B.'s political views, but resent having it taken for granted that mine are the same—which they are not.). . . .

She asks after Robert, and I think seriously of replying that he is out receiving the Oath of Allegiance from all the vassals on the estate, but decide that this would be undignified.

E. M. *Delafield*, Diary of a Provincial Lady

February 22

S<small>T</small> M<small>AXIMIAN OF</small> R<small>AVENNA</small> (d. 556), when he was just a deacon at Pola, ploughed up an enormous treasure. He put a lot of the money, and his pair of goatskin boots, in the belly of his ox and presented the rest to the Emperor Justinian. When the latter asked if he had any more treasure trove he equivocated with "only what is in my boots and belly", a contemporary phrase for "a trifling amount.". . . . Later, as Archbishop of Ravenna, he used the money to build and adorn churches; so if we owe any of those marvellous mosaics to him it was equivocation in a good cause.

1770: In June last I procured a litter of four or five young hedge-hogs, which appeared to be about five or six days old; they, I find, like puppies are born blind and could not see when they came to my hands. No doubt their spines are soft and flexible at the time of their birth, or else the poor dam would have but a bad time of it in the critical moment of parturition. . . .

Gilbert White (1720–1793)

February 23

ST Peter Damian (1007–1072) was one of those life-long ascetics who remain totally uncorrupted when called to high office—in his case office as Bishop of Ostia and papal emissary on such delicate missions as dissuading Henry IV of Germany from divorcing his wife Bertha.

1889: If the first movement of this [Mendelssohn, E Flat] quartet was not "a model of construction", it would perhaps be a genuine piece of music instead of the mere dummy that it is. Surely the musical critics ought to leave to their inferiors, the literary reviewers, the folly of supposing that "forms" are anything more than the shells of works of art. Though Bach's natural shell was the fugue, and Beethoven's the sonata, can anybody but an academy professor be infatuated enough to suppose that musical composition consists in the imitation of these shells: a sort of exercise that is as trivial as it is tedious? The fugue form is as dead as the sonata form; and the sonata form is as dead as Beethoven himself. Their deadliness kills Mendelssohn's St Paul and the "regular" movements in his symphonies and chamber music. Fortunately, the people are sound on this question. They are not indifferent to the merits of the first and second subjects in a formal sonata; but to the twaddling "passages" connecting them to the superfluous repeat, the idiotic "working out" and the tiresome recapitulation they are either deaf or wish they were.

George Bernard Shaw (1856–1950)

38

February 24

VERY LITTLE is known for certain about ST MATTHIAS. He is said to have died by crucifixion; a Gospel is said to have been put out falsely under his name. But one thing is certain. He was the man elected by the other eleven Apostles to make up their Twelve again after the defection of Judas.

1777: [To Dr Johnson]... Be assured, my dear Sir, that my affection and reverence for you are exalted and steady. I do not believe that a more perfect attachment ever existed in the history of mankind. And it is a noble attachment; for the attractions are Genius, Learning, and Piety. Your difficulty of breathing alarms me, and brings into my imagination an event, which although in the natural course of things, I must expect at some period, I cannot view with composure. . . .

James Boswell (1740–1795)

February 25

IN THE tiny church of St Martin in Canterbury, said to be the oldest parish church in England that has been in continuous use (since the 6th century), there is a tradition that ST ETHELBERT, King of the East Saxons, was baptized from the ancient font. He had married a Christian, Bertha, granddaughter of Clovis (whose conversion was a key one in the Christianization of the Atlantic west); and he was still a pagan when, obviously with Bertha's urging, he allowed St Augustine to begin his historic mission.

1944: . . . The bombing debates were interesting. . . . I wonder what it is about any plea for greater humanity or civilised care in war that makes so many people see red. I have heard the most passionate references to "those old bishops" in shops; one woman said it was lovely to think of the way we "gave Berlin a doing" on Tuesday night; and she'd like to "throw old Chichester on top of the bonfire." It is nonsense of Lord Latham to say "there is no gloating or exultation" among the English. . . .

Rose Macaulay (1881–1958)

February 26

S⊤ PORPHYRIUS (d. 420) was made Bishop of Gaza when the people there still worshipped a god called Marnas (to whom it is said human sacrifices were offered). In spite of an Elijah-type miracle bringing rain, and no doubt *because* of the support of the Christian Emperor who sent military help, he had his house set on fire and had to escape over the roof with his deacons.

1804: . . . I have as yet found no place to preach in; it is more difficult than I had imagined. Two or three random sermons I have discharged, and thought I perceived that the greater part of the congregation thought me mad. The clerk was as pale as death in helping me off with my gown, for fear I should bite him. . . .

Sydney Smith (1771–1845)

February 27

S⊤ GELASIUS (d. 269) was Second Clown of the theatre at Helio-polis, in Phoenicia. He had an act mimicking Christian baptism, with another clown pouring water over him. He saw "a dazzling light" in the font and declared himself a Christian; upon which the audience dragged him outside and stoned him to death.

1942: Invitation from Churchill to be Lord High Commissioner to the General Assembly of the Church of Scotland. I saw there was a letter from his office but I didn't open it; took it up to Muriel in bed with the other post. Next time I went up she told me there was something to refuse "from that cur".

Sir John Reith (1889–1971)

February 28

BARING-GOULD states firmly that "ST OSWALD", (d. 992), "is the only saint commemorated on February 29," and indeed the pre-Vatican II Missal also says that the man who founded the Benedictine monastery at Worcester (which became the cathedral) and also founded the famous Abbey of Ramsey, in Huntingdonshire, and must surely have been the only man to become Archbishop of York without resigning the See of Worcester, died after washing the feet of twelve poor men on the 3rd Sunday of Lent, which *was* February 29 that year. His feast, however (in the Catholic Diocese of Birmingham at any rate), is given as February 28, for obvious reasons.

1922: Life here [Vienna] is just as expensive as England and the food is horrible. Everything has an overcoat of batter. The meat often wears two waistcoats and two mackintoshes to conceal its identity. The very cakes wear masks. The butter is ashy pale and tasteless. I had chicken last night that tasted of fried mongoose and then one's lunch costs 4/-, each bed and breakfast 5/- each, and the room had stained glass windows, and was practically a dentist's consulting room. The Pension Franz is *much* better.

Carrington (1893–1932) to Gerald Brenan

41

MARCH

March 1

ST DAVID (d. 544), the patron saint of Wales, established a dozen monasteries in Wales, and took an eloquent and successful part against Pelagianism (our own native British heresy. Pelagius, a Briton, in the days when that meant "Celt", taught that there is no original sin, and grace is not necessary to avoid sin, it can be done by free will, although grace is, well, a help). He consented to become Archbishop if the see could be moved to quiet Mynyw from busy Caerleon, which it was. Later it was named St David's after him, and became a shrine so important that two pilgrimages to it were counted the equal of one to Rome itself.

1776: Certainly the very best thing that can happen to a very young man, is to fall desperately in love with a woman of fashion, who is clever, and who likes him enough to teach him to endeavour to please her, and yet keep him at his proper distance.

Lady Pembroke to Rev. W. Coxe (her son's tutor)

March 2

ST CHAD (d. 672) was the brother of St Cedd (*see January 7*). He became bishop of York soon after the famous Synod of Whitby (664) had proclaimed the victory of the Roman rite and method of fixing Easter over the Celtic, and his acceptance of this at "Celtic" hands caused the next archbishop of Canterbury, Theodore, to question his legality—a question he accepted with such instant readiness to retire that he was confirmed in the office. Later he was made bishop of Lichfield. He was well known for his unwillingness to visit his people on horseback, preferring to go on foot "like the Apostles".

1884: Our moving from Alipur to this house was effected by the bearer on Saturday, while I was at office. It is wonderful that, even in Calcutta, if you go into the street and engage 50 coolies whom you have never seen before and give no names or addresses, and if you load

44

them with property and send them from one house to another, they arrive all right without there being any risk of their absconding on the way.

H. M. Kisch (1850–1942)

March 3

S<small>T</small> W<small>INWALOE</small> was born about 455. His father, Fragan, was governor of Leon, or Lyonesse. When he was about fifteen he was "given to a holy man, possibly St Budock, and lived there with his brothers Gwethenoc and Jacut, on the islet of Islevert, serving God." Landewednack on the southernmost tip of Britain, the Lizard peninsula, is named after him. A Celtic sea-saint.

1828: I drove to Mells to attend a clerical meeting, and arrived a little after two. We sat down fourteen to dinner, which was an uncomfortable one owing to there being only one waiter. After some rather desultory conversation one of the party, of the name of Bumstead, asked me what was the etymon of his name. I did not perceive it at the time, but have every reason to believe, on account of what afterwards occurred, that it was done purposely to put me on the subject of Etymology for the amusement of the company. The expense of the dinner was eight shillings, my horse and ostler one-and-sixpence.

John Skinner (1772–1839)

March 4

S<small>T</small> C<small>ASIMIR</small> (1458–1484) was the second son of King Casimir III of Poland. Like his part-contemporary Henry VI of England, he was deeply religious. At *fifteen* he was put at the head of an army in an attempt to make him King of Hungary (at the request, they said, of Hungarian nobles). He was pleased, and his father was angry, when this did not succeed. He was not allowed to return to Cracow, but stayed in the castle of Dobzki. He took a vow of celibacy, which doctors advised him to break for his health's sake, although, as his disease was tuberculosis, they would have been, as usual, wrong. He was famous for his devotion to the Passion of Christ and for his charity to the poor. He is the patron saint of Poland.

1875: Old William Halliday told me he had heard from the old people of Allington and especially from the Taverners, when he was young, strange tales of ancient times and how the world was once full of "witches, weasels (wizards) and wolves". Old William also told the story of how old Squire Sadler Gale of Bulwich House at Allington made himself wings and flew off the garden wall. "Watch I vlee!" he cried to the people. Then he dashed down into the horsepond.

Francis Kilvert (1840–1879)

March 5

IT IS a pity to steal the thunder of St Jerome (*September 30*); but the story of the lion and today's saint, GERASIMUS (d. 475), which perhaps got transferred because of the similarity of names, is so charmingly told by Baring-Gould that I cannot resist quoting it verbatim.

"One day as the old abbot was walking on the banks of the Jordan, he saw a lion limping and roaring with pain. The lion, instead of attempting to escape, held up its paw, which was much swollen, and Gerasimus taking it on his lap, examined it, and saw that a sharp splinter had entered the flesh. He withdrew the piece of reed, and bathed the paw. The lion afterwards gratefully followed him to his cell, and never after left him, but was fed by the abbot. There was an ass belonging to the monastery which brought water from the Jordan, and Gerasimus sent the ass out to pasture under the guardianship of the lion. One day the lion had gone away from his charge, and an Arabian camel driver passing by, stole the ass. In the evening the lion returned depressed in spirits to the monastery, without the ass. Gerasimus naturally concluded that the lion had eaten the animal, and he cried out, 'Sirrah, where is the ass?' The lion stood still, and looked back over his shoulder. 'You have eaten him!' said the abbot; 'Let us praise God. Well, what the ass did, you shall do now.' And thenceforth the lion carried the water for the brethren.

"Now one day a certain soldier came to the monastery, and seeing the lion toiling under the water bottles, he pitied the lordly beast, and gave the abbot some money to buy an ass on the next opportunity, and release the lion from its office of water-carrier. Some days after this, as the lion was near Jordan, there came by the man who had stolen the ass, with three camels, and the stolen beast itself. The lion set up its mane and roared, and made towards the man, whereupon the driver took to his heels. Then the lion caught the end of the ass's halter, and drew it along with the camels to the door of the monastery. And thus the abbot learned that he was wrong in accusing his dumb friend of having devoured his charge.

"For five years the lion was the constant companion of the old abbot, going in and out among the monks; and at the expiration of that time Gerasimus died. Now the lion was out when he departed to his rest; but when the lion returned home, he went about searching for the old man. Then the abbot Sabbatinus, a disciple of the dead saint, seeing the uneasiness of the lion, said to him 'Jordan (for by that name the lion was called), our old friend has gone away and left us orphans, and has migrated to the Lord; but here is food, take and eat.' But the lion would not, and paced to and fro seeking the dead man, and every now and then throwing up his head, and roaring. Then Sabbatinus and some of the other brethren came and rubbed his neck, and said, 'The old man is departed to the Lord, and has left us.' But this did not appease the lion; and the more they caressed him, and spake to him, the more agitated he became, and the louder he roared, 'showing with mouth and eyes how great was his distress, because he saw not the old man.' Then the abbot Sabbatinus said to him, 'Come along with me, as you will not believe me, and I will show you where our old friend is laid.' And he led the lion to the place where Gerasimus was buried; and the abbot Sabbatinus, standing at the tomb, said, 'See, here is where he is buried.' And then he knelt, and wept upon the grave. So when the lion saw this, he went and stretched himself on the grave, with his head on the sand, and moaned, and remained there, and would not leave the place, but was found there dead a few days later."

1814: I am sorry to hear there has been a rise in tea. I do not mean to pay Twining till later in the day, when we may order a fresh supply.

Jane Austen (1775–1817)

March 6

SS PERPETUA and FELICITAS were early martyrs, at Carthage, under the Emperor Severus, in 203. Felicitas was heavily pregnant (and a slave); Perpetua was still suckling her child. Both were condemned to face wild beasts at a public show for the soldiers. Perpetua, who had several remarkable visions, had to face the entreaties of her father, a pagan, that she should renounce Christianity, when he appeared at the hearing with her child, now weaned. Felicitas was asked, crying out during the birth of her child in prison, how she would face the worse pains in the arena. "It is I who am suffering these pains now," she replied, "but then there will be another who suffers with me." They were both exposed to the attacks of a wild cow. They were not killed, however; and the people crying out that it was enough, they were taken to the gate to be killed by the sword. Both saints are mentioned in the Canon of the Mass.

1846: [To Frederic Tennyson] ... the dirt, both of earth and atmosphere, in London, is a real bore. But enough of that. It is sufficient that it is more pleasant to me to sit in a clean room, with a clear air outside, and hedges just coming into leaf, rather than in the Tavistock or an upper floor of Charlotte Street. And how much better one's books read in country stillness, than amid the noise of wheels, crowds etc. or after hearing them eternally discussed by no less active tongues! ....
Edward Fitzgerald (1809–1883)

March 7

ST THOMAS AQUINAS (1225, 6 or 7 to 1274) was the Angelic Doctor, the supreme codifier of the *philosophia perennis*, the "eternal philosophy" of Christianity. He was the supreme thinker, as Dante was the supreme poet, of the century when the Christianity of hermits and monasteries and barbarian kings was coalescing into the High Gothic civilization. His stupendous work, the *Summa Theologica*, began with the study of existence, being, and God, passed on to consider man, and only then dealt with specifically Christian revelation. He sought (always in the same formal manner, stating a point, raising possible objections, then answering them) to show how Christianity was consonant with reason, though reason could never reach it alone. Taught by the famous Albertus Magnus at Cologne and Paris (he later succeeded—and excelled him), St Thomas had extraordinary powers of concentration and absorption (and could dictate on knotty problems to three or four scribes simultaneously). St Thomas also wrote hymns, and the office for the new feast of Corpus Christi, including the magnificent hymn *Lauda Sion*. After an ecstasy he abandoned the *Summa*. *Mihi ut palea videtur,* "it all seems like straw to me", said the greatest mind of his age about his life's work, after his glimpse of Heaven. Falling ill on a journey, he died in a Benedictine monastery, surrounded by monks of the order who had taught him as a boy. And in view of later rivalries it is good to remember that he had a profound friendship also with his great opposite number in the Franciscan Order, St Bonaventure.

1778: I must tell you that I was absolutely horrified and that tears came into my eyes when I read in your last letter that [you have to go about so shabbily dressed]. My very dearest Papa! That is certainly not my fault—you know it is not! We economise in every possible way here; food and lodging, wood and light have cost us nothing, and what more can we want! As for dress, you surely know that in places where you are not known, it is out of the question to be badly dressed, for appearances must be kept up. . . . I mean to work with all my strength so that I may soon have the happiness of helping you out of your present distressing circumstances. . . .

Wolfgang Amadeus Mozart (1756–1791)

March 8

S^T FELIX (d. 654) a native of Burgundy, established his bishopric at Dunwich in Suffolk. A less widely held theory is that it may have been at Domnoc, a site now visible at low tide

49

from the Edwardian resort of Felixstowe named after him. There is nothing very much except a cliff-top caravan site at Dunwich now, and a few ruins. Most of it has been swallowed up by the sea. Six of its large number of churches still remained in 1631. The last one fell over the cliff in 1919.

1797: Harrison, the architect, remarked to Marchant that the Cathedral of St Paul's will sustain great injury from the *doors* being so constantly kept shut, which is done to oblige people to pay for admittance.—He said that from want of a due circulation of air, that which is inclosed is generally so damp that it must corrode the walls of the building.—The doors and windows of St Peter's at Rome are opened every day.

Joseph Farington (1747–1821)

March 9

Sᴛ Dᴏᴍɪɴɪᴄ Sᴀᴠɪᴏ (1842–1857) was a pupil of St John Bosco (*see January 31*), the founder of the Salesians. While there is uncertainty about the age of, for example, St Agnes (*see January 21*), he is certainly among the youngest to have been canonized in modern times (1954).

1930: Barbara goes to Evening Service, and I go to look in on her mother, whom I find in shawls, sitting in an armchair reading—rather ostentatiously—enormous *Life of Lord Beaconsfield*. I ask how she is, and she shakes her head and enquires if I should ever guess that her pet name amongst her friends used to be Butterfly? (This kind of question always so difficult, as either affirmative or negative reply apt to sound unsympathetic. Feel it would hardly do to suggest that Chrysalis, in view of the shawls, would now be more appropriate.) However, says Mrs Blenkinsop with a sad smile, it is never her way to dwell upon herself and her own troubles. She just sits there, day after day, always ready to sympathise in the little joys and troubles of others and I would hardly believe how unfailingly these are brought to her. People say, she adds deprecatingly, that just her Smile does them good. She does not know, she says, what they mean. (Neither do I.)

E. M. Delafield, Diary of a Provincial Lady

March 10

THE FORTY MARTYRS OF SEBASTE were victims of Agricola, the governor of Cappadocia and Armenia under the Emperor Licinius, who had broken with his brother-in-law Constantine (first Christian Emperor) and proscribed Christianity. These Martyrs were soldiers who, after torture, were stripped and left on a frozen pond swept during the night by icy winds from the Caucasus, within sight of fires and warm baths if they should recant. One did, and his place was taken by a guard.

1932: Shaw's plays are the price we pay for Shaw's prefaces.

James Agate (1887–1947)

March 11

ST CONSTANTINE (d. about 576) son of Padarn, king of Cornwall, entered a monastery in Ireland without saying who he was. This was discovered by chance, and he was instructed and ordained. He then worked with St Columba and St Kentigern, preaching in Galloway and eventually becoming abbot, almost certainly in Glasgow.

1806: Dear Rickman I send you the papers about a salt-water soap, for which the inventor is desirous of getting a parliamentary reward, like Dr Jenner. . . . The patent, you see, he has got. A contract he is about with the Navy Board. Meantime, the projector is hungry . . . is there any chance of success in application to Parliament for a reward? . . . I vouch nothing for the soap myself; for I always wash in *fresh water*, and find it answers tolerably well for all purposes of cleanliness. . . .

Charles Lamb (1775–1834)

March 12

ST GREGORY THE GREAT (540–604) personified the Papal title of *Pontifex* ("bridge-builder") more than any other holder of that office. It is always a bit of a shock to recall that, a member of a noble family, he held the office of *praetor* in Rome during the first invasion of the Lombards—an office which had existed long before it became elective in 366 *Before Christ*. Somehow he typifies Rome as the physical historical bridge between past and present. Having spent six years as legate at Constantinople he had an understanding of the Eastern Church, and when he became Pope he established the real foundations of the relationship of the medieval papacy with the still-confused agglomerations that were to become France and Spain and other European nations—perhaps most notably England. It was he, of course, who had wanted to come here personally after seeing the fair-haired slaves and making his famous comment *non Angli, sed Angeli*, "not Angles, but Angels." In the event he was elected Pope soon afterwards and sent St Augustine.

A Benedictine monk, he became the great pre-medieval establisher and founder-figure. It was under him that the liturgy achieved a definitive form. "Gregorian Chant has always been considered the supreme model of sacred music," said a Vatican *Motu Proprio* in 1903.

St Gregory is one of the four great Latin Doctors, the others being St Ambrose, St Augustine and St Jerome.

1768: Gray has added to his poems three ancient Odes from Norway and Wales . . . our human feelings, which he masters at will in his former pieces, are here not affected. Who can care through what horrors a Runic savage arrived at all the joys and glories they could conceive, the supreme felicity of boozing ale out of the skull of an enemy in Odin's hall?

Horace Walpole (1717–1797)

52

March 13

Sᴛ Gᴇʀᴀʟᴅ (d. 732). After the famous Synod of Whitby of 664, where the final decision for the Roman rite against the Irish one was made, St Colman, a leader on the Irish side, resigned his bishopric. He retired eventually to the island of Inishbofin, with both Irish and English monks. The latter complaining that they had to do all the harvest work, a separate monastery was set up for them in Mayo, and of this St Gerald was the first abbot.

1817: [To Fanny Knight] Single Women have a dreadful propensity for being poor—which is one very strong argument in favour of Matrimony. . . .

Jane Austen (1775–1817)

March 14

Sᴛ Mᴀᴛɪʟᴅᴀ (d. 968) was dynastically married to Henry, King of Germany, probably without having her wishes too much consulted, since he was divorced and already had a son called Thankmar. Her life with Henry was happy, however. After his death her son Otho, who was elected Emperor, sent her away from court "because she had lavished the money of the empire on charities." Eventually St Matilda retired to what must have been a good-sized convent, for she gathered about her "three thousand sisters", (says Baring-Gould, although Butler says it was the monastery at Polden, one of several she founded, which had three thousand *monks*).

1907: Have been reading through the Chemistry Course in the Harmsworth Self-Educator and learning all the latest facts and ideas about radium. I would rather have a clear comprehension of the atom as a solar system than a private income of £100 a year. If only I had eyes to go on reading without a stop!

W. N. P. Barbellion (1889–1917)

March 15

USUALLY THOSE in the Society of St Vincent de Paul are practical and unobtrusive practitioners of charity. The Society is named after the saint whose feast is on July 19. ST LOUISE DE MARILLAC (1591–1660) was St Vincent's great assistant in the work for the poor, the sick and the imprisoned which he organized. She was the foundress of the Sisters of Charity, who already had more than forty houses at the time of her death.

1803: Oberne, the Bishop of Meath, preach'd an excellent sermon at this season at Bath against card-parties, and concerts on Sunday evenings. His wife, Mrs Oberne, went the day after to pay a morning visit to an old lady, who told her she was very angry with her husband, as she had just received twenty-eight cards of refusals to her next Sunday's party. "Oh, how glad I am," says Mrs Oberne, "to hear this."

Mrs Philip Libbe Powys (1739–1817)

March 16

SS ABRAHAM and MARY (6th century). He became a hermit in the wilderness in Mesopotamia, after a marriage had been arranged for him by wealthy parents. Mary was his niece, orphaned at seven. A cell was built for her near his, and he brought her up until a young man fell in love with her, took her away, and then abandoned her. She became a prostitute at Assos, in the Troad. Eventually Abraham, disguised as a soldier, went to the brothel, upon which she burst into tears and he took her back. She lived five years after his death at seventy "and God wrought miracles of healing by her hands, to comfort the penitent soul, and assure her that her tears had blotted out her transgression."

1815: .... In a few days we heard that Bonaparte, whom we had concluded to be, of course, either stopped landing or taken prisoner, or forced to save himself by flight, was, on the contrary, pursuing his route unimpeded to Lyons. The project upon Paris became at length obvious yet its success was little feared, though the horrors of a civil war seemed inevitable. M d'Arblay began to wish me away; he even pressed me to depart for England to rejoin Alexander and my family: but I knew them to be in security, whilst my first earthly tie was exposed to every species of danger, and I besought him not to force me away. (*See also March 17*)

Fanny Burney (1752–1840)

March 17

Sᴛ Jᴏsᴇᴘʜ ᴏf Aʀɪᴍᴀᴛʜᴀᴇᴀ. Described as "rich" by St Matthew, "a counsellor" by St Mark, a "secret disciple" by St John. St Luke says "there was a man named Joseph, a counsellor; and he was a good man, and a just: (the same had not consented to the counsel and deed of them;) he was of Arimathaea, a city of the Jews: who also himself waited for the kingdom of God. This man went unto Pilate, and begged the body of Jesus. And he took it down, and wrapped it in linen, and laid it in a sepulchre that was hewn in stone, wherein never before man was laid."

He was the patron saint of Glastonbury, to which he was a legendary visitor.

In Ireland; the feast of St Patrick (d. about 465).

1815: .... but on the 17th, hope again revived. I received these words from my best friend, written on a scrap of paper torn from a parcel, and brought to me by his groom from the palace of the Tuileries, where their writer had passed the night mounting guard: "*Nous avons de meilleures nouvelles. Je ne puis entrer dans aucun detail; mais sois tranquille, et aime bien qui t'aime uniquement.* God bless you." This news hung upon the departure of Marshal Ney to meet Bonaparte and stop his progress, with the memorable words uttered publicly to the King, that he would bring him to Paris in an iron cage.* (*See also March 18*)

Fanny Burney (1752–1840)

* On the contrary he joined forces with Napoleon, and commanded at Quatre Bras.

March 18

ST CYRIL OF JERUSALEM (about 315–389) occupied the see of that
city, with intervening periods of banishment because of
emperors favourable to Arianism. When Julian the Apostate was
emperor one of his plans was to rebuild the Temple of Jerusalem,
not out of any regard for the Jews but to spite the Christians. Not
surprisingly St Cyril prophesied the failure of this enterprise,
which was attended by earthquakes and thunderstorms. St Cyril
wrote several "mystagogic" instructions for catechumens before
and after their reception into the Church. In view of the
embarrassment still expressed by some at Communion taken in
the hand today it is interesting to see that in one of these he
wrote "putting your left hand under your right, form a throne of
your right hand to receive the king; hold it hollow, receiving on
it the Body of Christ. Answer, Amen . . ."

*1815: . . . . the next day, the 18th of March, all hope
disappeared. From north, from south, from east, from
west, alarm took the field, danger flashed its lightnings: yet
in Paris there was no rising, no disturbance, no confusion—
all was taciturn suspense, dark dismay, or sullen passive-
ness.*

Fanny Burney (1752–1840)

March 19

ST JOSEPH. The humblest and often least regarded figure in the
whole mysterious scheme of the Incarnation. Of the four
Evangelists, St Mark and St John begin with Jesus already a
man, and being announced by St John the Baptist: St Luke tells
the marvellous story of the Annunciation ("how shall this be,
seeing I know not a man?") and the Magnificat; it is St Matthew
who begins with the genealogy of St Joseph from David, and
tells of his two dreams. ". . . before they came together, she was
found with child of the Holy Ghost. Then Joseph her husband,
being a just man, and not willing to make her a publick example,
was minded to put her away privily. But while he thought on
these things, behold, the angel of the Lord appeared unto him

in a dream, saying, Joseph, thou son of David, fear not to take unto thee Mary thy wife: for that which is conceived in her is of the Holy Ghost . . ."

And after the Magi had departed, "the angel of the Lord appeareth to Joseph in a dream, saying, Arise, and take the young child and his mother, and flee into Egypt, and be thou there until I bring thee word. . . ."

Joseph. A carpenter.

1789: Most part of the Day fine but Air very cold. I took a little Rharbarb this Evening going to bed being rather dull and melancholy.

James Woodforde (1740–1803)

March 20

S⊤ Cuthbert (d. 687) became abbot of Lindisfarne, then lived a tough solitary life as a hermit, on the small island of Farne, and was then begged to become bishop of Hexham, but returned to Farne to die. The great saint, with Bede, of Northumbria. At one end of the mighty Durham Cathedral is Bede's tomb. At the other is St Cuthbert's shrine (though not his bones, which were removed, no one is sure where to, by monks keeping them from marauding Danes).

1827: My sermons were little or nothing; their excellence is in your own desire to excel, and in your disposition to be pleased. Politics, domestic and foreign, are very discouraging; Jesuits abroad—Turks in Greece— No-Poperists in England! A. panting to burn B.; B. fuming to roast C.; C. miserable that he cannot reduce D. to ashes; and D. consigning to eternal perdition the three first letters of the alphabet.

Sydney Smith (1771–1845)

57

March 21

WHEN ST BENEDICT (480–543), that quiet light steadily burning in a howling and confused darkness and miraculously diffusing its own *pax*, came to build his famous monastery at Monte Cassino people were still worshipping Apollo there. The Rule he wrote not only made monastic life available to "ordinary" men, it also provided a rule-book for democracy (e.g. abbot elected for a limited period, then he is just Dom So-and-so again, unless he is re-elected). Benjamin Franklin visited an exiled English Benedictine community in Paris and may have got some of its ideas into the American Constitution.

The Benedictine vows are not, as some popularly suppose, poverty, chastity and obedience, but "obedience, *stabilitas* and *conversio morum*." Stability, staying in one place; and change of morals. St Augustine who converted England, St Boniface who converted Germany, were Benedictines. From time to time there were returns, such as that made by the Cistercians, to an "original" toughness. He *was* tough. But for 1500 years the Black Monks have shown the world that if you want Stability, theirs is a good motto to follow. *Ora et labora*; pray and work.

1956: Of course as regards right living, all good religions sincerely held incline to this, according to the character of the holder; it would be difficult in Christianity to say that more right living is achieved by one kind than another. But it is certain that, for right living, each individual had better try to find the kind of beliefs that suit his own mind; if he tries to hold those unsuited to him he will make little of them. ... Luckily there is something for everyone.

Rose Macaulay (1881–1958)

March 22

BLESSED NICOLAS VON DER FLUE (1417–1487), having been a soldier in various internal campaigns in Switzerland, married, became the father of ten children, and governor of Obwald, then "with the consent of his family" became a hermit at his native place of Melchthal.

1776: On Friday, March 22, having set out early from Henley, where we had lain the preceding night, we arrived at Birmingham about nine o'clock, and, after breakfast, went to call on his old schoolfellow Mr Hector. A very stupid maid, who opened the door, told us that "her master was gone out; he was gone to the country; she could not tell us when he would return". In short, she gave us a miserable reception; and Johnson observed, "She would have behaved no better to people who wanted him in the way of his profession." He said to her, "My name is Johnson; tell him I called. Will you remember the name?" She answered with rustic simplicity in the Warwickshire pronunciation, "I don't understand you, Sir."—"Blockhead," said he, "I'll write." I never heard the word *blockhead* applied to a woman before, though I do not see why it should not, when there is evident occasion for it. He, however, made another attempt to make her understand him, and roared loud in her ear, "*Johnson*", and then she catched the sound.

James Boswell (1740–1795)

March 23

S⊤ ETHELWALD (d. about 723) inherited the island of Farne after St Cuthbert (*see March 20*). Bede says that one of his miracles was to create, by his prayers, a calm patch of sea in the middle of a storm, thus saving the lives of two monks who had come over from Lindisfarne to visit him.

1770: You know I have always some favourite, some successor of Patapan. The present is a tanned black spaniel, called Rosette. She saved my life last Saturday night, so I am sure you will love her too. I was undressing for bed. She barked and was so restless that there was no quieting her. I fancied there was somebody under the bed, but there was not. As she looked at the chimney, which roared much, I thought it was the wind, yet wondered, as she had heard it so often. At last, not being able to quiet her, I looked to see what she barked at, and perceived sparks of fire falling from the chimney, and on searching farther perceived it in flames. It had not gone far, and we easily extinguished it. I wish I had as much power over the nation's chimney. Adieu!

Horace Walpole (1717–1797) to Sir Horace Mann.

March 24

ST GABRIEL, ARCHANGEL. There are only three angel feast days, the others being St Michael (*September 29*) and on the first free day after that, which turned out to be October 2, the Guardian Angels. Angels are messengers of the Lord. This last is of course what the word *angelos* means in Greek. Gabriel was the supreme messenger, as far as the human race is concerned, announcing to Daniel when Christ would be born, to Zachary the birth of John the Baptist, and to Mary the news which is celebrated in tomorrow's feast.

1902: Took my niece Mary Milbanke, it being Lent, to a medieval morality play, *Everyman*, being just now revived, a terribly dreary business, which more than half reconciled me to having been born in the nineteenth century. . . . There is a brutality in the view of all pleasure being sinful, which is only tolerable when mixed with a large dose of scepticism, as in Boccaccio. These north of Europe plays with their serious intention are like having a bucket of cold and very dirty water poured over one for a joke.

Wilfrid Scawen Blunt (1840–1922)

March 25

THE ANNUNCIATION. In countless paintings, the bright folded wings of the imagined kneeling flaming spirit; in a secret room, or on a terrace from which one sees Umbrian hills with feathery trees, or opulent Venetian hangings; or under cloistered arches. Somewhere, a silent Woman hearing those words uttered for the first time. *Hail, full of grace! The Lord is with thee, blessed art thou amongst women.* . . .

1804: The evening was passed not in conversation but in listening to a succession of opinions, & explanations delivered by Coleridge. . . . I particularly noticed that His illustrations generally disappointed me, & rather weakened than enforced what He had before said. He read some lines written by Wordsworth upon "The Maid of Loch Lomond," a pretty girl they found residing there; and also some lines upon Westminster Bridge & the scenery from it. His Dialect particularly when reading, is what I shd. call *broad* Devonshire, for a gentleman. . . . His mother is 80 years of age, from which I judge Him to be 35.

Joseph Farington (1747–1821)

March 26

S͏ᴛ Lᴜᴅɢᴇʀ (about 744–809), apostle of the Frisians and Saxons. He came to England to study under the famous Alcuin at York (the same Alcuin who instructed Charlemagne). He visited Rome and Monte Cassino, and founded the monastery which gave the city of Munster its name.

1870: So this is the place that I have heard old Hannah Whitney talk of so often, the place where the old miller sleeping in the mill trough used to see the fairies dancing of nights upon the mill floor.

Francis Kilvert (1840–1879)

March 27

S͏ᴛ Rᴜᴘᴇʀᴛ (d. about 700), a Frankish noble, was bishop of Worms, ". . . but that people being for the most part idolaters, could not bear the lustre of such a sanctity. They beat him with rods, loaded him with all manner of outrages, and expelled him the city." However Theodon, Duke of Bavaria, gave him hospitality and, with his people, was converted by him. He ended his life as the bishop of, and great church-builder in, the old Roman town of Juvavia; now better known to us as Salzburg.

1700: My wife narrowly escaped Choaking haveing a pinn in her mouth wch by drawing her breath sliped into her throat, but by God's great mercy it came vp again. (*See also May 26*)

William Coe of Mildenhall (1680–1729)

March 28

S^t J_{OHN} _{OF} C_{APISTRANO} (1385–1456) was governor of Perugia and married before he received dispensation to become a Franciscan friar. The Turks had taken Constantinople in 1453 and Europe faced the danger of another Islamic invasion when he preached a crusade. Unfortunately there were Hussites in Moravia, and Jews in Silesia, to whom he would certainly not have appeared as a saint.

1885: There are signs that the domestic animals are revolting. From Holborn comes news that one Mr Ashton, returning home, discovered his black tom had two visitors in the passage, whom Mr Ashton proceeded to eject, but all three set on him, and after a violent struggle Mr Ashton was driven precipitously out at the front door, and fell into the arms of two policemen who took him to the hospital.

Beatrix Potter (1866–1943)

March 29

S^t J_{ONAS} (d. 327) had molten lead poured into his nostrils and eyes, was hung up by one foot, had fingers, toes and tongue cut off and was finally pressed to death. St Barachisius (d. 327) was killed by piercing with many spikes, before he too, was put into the press. "Under their most exquisite tortures," says the eye-witness account, "they thought they had bought heaven too cheap."

1824: O imagination! thou greatest treasure of man, thou inexhaustible wellspring from which artists as well as savants drink! O remain with us still, by however few thou art acknowledged and revered, to preserve us from that so-called enlightenment. . . .

Franz Schubert (1797–1828)

March 30

St John Climacus (about 525–606) was abbot of the monastery of Mount Sinai. He had "a weakness for talking excessively, and condemned himself to rigorous silence for a twelvemonth." St Gregory the Great sent him beds and money for his hospital. Once when he was entertaining 600 pilgrims, he saw a very old and dignified man ministering to the guests, and afterwards vanishing, "a curious instance of the very widely diffused belief in the Wandering Jew" (although St John in this case thought it was Moses).

His surname comes from his "Climax, or Ladder of Perfection, containing in 30 chapters rules for attaining the thirty steps of religious perfection."

1883: A certain Mr Montgomery, father of Marchioness of Queensberry went into a bird shop and enquired: "Cucker cucker can thutter thutter this be-ird talk?", whereupon the enraged shopman answered, "if he could not talk better than you, I'd wring his neck."

Beatrix Potter (1866–1943)

March 31

St Renovatus (d. about 633) was abbot of Merida in Spain. There was a gluttonous monk in his monastery whom whipping could not cure, so the abbot then said he could either leave, or help himself to food and wine. He took a tremendous picnic which he consumed in a pleasant spot. This went on "for some days;" then, going out "with a fat capon and some wine," he heard the schoolboys reciting the antiphon they were learning: *"considera judicium terribile Domini,"* consider the terrible judgment of the Lord. With a fever already on him after his gluttony he was stricken with remorse, confessed his sins, and died a few days later.

1860: [I] felt a boyish delight in meeting so many light blue rosettes in the Strand, and in hearing that Cambridge had won by two boats' lengths. This is not merely fellow feeling & *esprit de corps*: it is the pathetic joy with which one clings to anything that recalls a younger and lovelier life, now gone for ever.

A. J. Munby (1828–1910)

APRIL

April 1

ST GILBERT OF CAITHNESS (d. about 1211). When the people of Caithness killed their bishop, King Alexander III "took a horrible revenge, mutilating all males in the diocese to the fourth and fifth generation." Later St Gilbert was appointed to this see.

1821: The mind and feeling which produced the "Selborne" is such an one as I have always envied. The single page alone of the life of Mr White leaves a more lasting impression on my mind than that of Charles the fifth or any other renowned hero—it only shows what a real love for nature will do—surely the serene & blameless life of Mr White, so different from the folly and quackery of the world, must have fitted him for such a clear and intimate view of nature. It proves the truth of Sir Joshua Reynolds' idea that the virtuous man alone has true taste.

John Constable (1776–1837)

April 2

ST JOSEPH THE HYMNOGRAPHER (d. 883) is venerated by the Greeks, but not, evidently, by Dr Neale, author of *Hymns of the Eastern Church*, who wrote "of the innumerable compositions of this most laborious writer it would be impossible to find one which, to Western taste, gives the least sanction to the position which he holds in the East. The insufferable tediousness consequent on the necessity of filling eight odes into the praises of a saint, of whom nothing, beyond the fact of his existence, is known, and doing this sixty or seventy times, the verbiage, the bombast, the trappings with which scriptural simplicity is *elevated* to the taste of the corrupt court, are each and all scarcely to be paralleled. He is by far the most prolific of hymn-writers."

1781: It has been said that the eyes of fishes are immoveable: but these apparently turn them forward or backward in their sockets as their occasions require. They take little notice of a lighted candle, though applied close to their heads, but flounce and seem much frightened by a

66

sudden stroke of the hand against the support whereon the bowl is hung; especially when they are motionless, and are perhaps asleep. As fishes have no eyelids, it is not easy to discern when they are sleeping or not, because their eyes are always open.

Gilbert White (1720–1793)

April 3

Sᴛ Fʀᴀɴᴄɪs ᴏꜰ Pᴀᴏʟᴀ (1416–1508) was the founder of the Minims, an ultra-strict branch of the Franciscans with much emphasis on humility and fasting, observing a "perpetual Lent." He acquired a European reputation for wisdom and sanctity, and when Louis XI (who among other things annexed Provence to France) was dying he asked for St Francis. . . . the king thought the saint's "refusal" to work a miracle for him was due to his not having offered enough gold. In the end the saint seems to have worked the perhaps greater miracle of composing the king's mind before his death. Louis died in the saint's arms.

1798: Went to Mrs Lutwyche's party (always at home on Tuesdays). We thought there were numbers of people, but Mrs Lutwyche express'd herself quite hurt that Mr Powys and I should be there the first time when she had hardly any company, "only seven tables, and that is so very few, you know, Ma'am." I really am very ignorant, for I did not know it, and thought it a squeeze; but how unfashionable I am in disliking these immense parties I kept secret.

Mrs Philip Lybbe Powys (1739–1817)

April 4

Sᴛ Isɪᴅᴏʀᴇ (about 570–636) is a Doctor of the Church. There is a legend that as a boy he ran away from school, feeling that it was all too hard, and stopped by a spring where the water had worn a hole in the rock. This had the same effect on him as Bow Bells had on Dick Whittington, only in a perhaps higher sphere, since he lived to become bishop of Seville.

1838: We have had Alfred Tennyson here; very droll, and very wayward: and much sitting up of nights with pipes in our mouths: at which good hour we would get Alfred to give us some of his magic music, which he does between growling and smoking; and so to bed. All this has not cured my Influenza as you may imagine: but these hours shall be remembered long after the Influenza is forgotten.

Edward Fitzgerald (1809–1883)

April 5

ST JULIANA (1191–1258) was abbess of the convent of Cornillon, outside Liège. In 1208 she had a vision in which she saw that the cycle of feasts in the church year, beginning with Advent, following the life of Jesus to His Ascension, and ending with Pentecost (Descent of the Spirit into the world through the church) and Trinity Sunday, lacked a final one that would commemorate the continued presence of Christ in the sacrament of Communion. The feast of Corpus Christi was at first kept only in the local diocese of Liège, and the first office for it was one composed by a young monk called John of Cornillon. When the feast spread throughout the Christian world it was replaced by that written by St Thomas Aquinas (*see March 7*).

1913: . . . As for Turkey, down with the Turks! But I am afraid there is, not life, but stickiness in them yet. Their disappearance would mean a chance for the Arabs, who were at any rate once not incapable of good government. One must debit them with algebra though. . . . .

T. E. Lawrence (1888–1935)

April 6

NOTKER BALBULUS ("the Stammerer"), who died in 912, is not a saint, merely beatified (i.e. he is Blessed Notker). He was a monk at the famous Swiss monastery of St Gall, where one of the two texts containing authentic Gregorian chants and hymns which Charlemagne requested from Rome was kept, since various "impurities" had crept in—presumably in places like St Gall itself, since its chronicler, the dean Eckhardt, wrote in the 13th century quoting an earlier author, "they received the sweet melodies incorrupt, but the levity of their minds, which made them intrude some of their own tunes into the Gregorian song, and their natural barbarity, made them lose them in their integrity. And indeed Alpine bodies with their own thundering voices are not adapted to sweet modulations of tone. The barbarous hugeness of those tippling throats, when endeavouring to utter a soft song full of inflections and dipthongs, makes a great roar, as though carts were tumbling down steps headlong."

Notker is credited with perfecting the *sequence*, the verse-like piece in the Mass before the singing of the Gospel, which was originally intended to replace the (perhaps Byzantine-inspired) long phrases of some of the alleluias.

c. 1891: Eggs for breakfast simply shocking; sent them back to Borset with my compliments, and he needn't call any more for orders. Couldn't find umbrella, and though it was pouring with rain, had to go without it. Sarah said Mr Gowing must have took it by mistake last night, as there was a stick in the 'all that didn't belong to nobody. In the evening, hearing someone talking in a loud voice to the servant in the downstairs hall, I went out to see who it was, and was surprised to find it was Borset, the butterman, who was both drunk and offensive. Borset, on seeing me, said he would be hanged if he would ever serve City clerks any more—the game wasn't worth the candle. I restrained my feelings, and quietly remarked that I thought it was *possible* for a City clerk to be a *gentleman*.

George and Weedon Grossmith, The Diary of a Nobody

April 7

ST Nilus of Sora (about 1433–1508) was canonized by the Russian Orthodox Church in 1903. Having spent some time on the famous Mount Athos in Greece, he established a monastery by the river Sora where many Greek mystical works were translated. He was, says Attwater, "essentially a man of freedom and moderation" but severe and uncompromising about monks possessing property of any kind, and thought that even their churches should be bare and unadorned, so as not to distract.

1765: Now, for my disaster; you will laugh at it, though it was woful to me. I was to dine at Northumberland-house, and went a little after four: there I found the Countess, Lady Betty Mackenzie, Lady Strafford; my Lady Finlater, who was never out of Scotland before; a tall lad of fifteen, her son; Lord Drogheda, and Mr Worseley. At five, arrived Mr Mitchell, who said the Lords had begun to read the Poor-bill, which would take at least two hours, and perhaps would debate it afterwards. We concluded dinner would be called for, it not being very precedented for ladies to wait for gentlemen:—no such thing. Six o'clock came—seven o'clock came,—our coaches came,—well! we sent them away, and excuses were we were engaged. Still the Countess's heart did not relent, nor uttered a syllable of apology. We wore out the wind and the weather, the Opera and the Play, Mrs Cornelys's and Almack's, and every topic that would do in a formal circle. We hinted, represented—in vain. The clock struck eight: my Lady, at last, said she would go and order dinner; but it was a good half-hour before it appeared. We then sat down to a table for fourteen covers: but instead of substantials, there was nothing but profusion of plates striped red, green, and yellow, gilt plate, blacks and uniforms! My Lady Finlater, who had never seen these embroidered dinners, nor dined after three, was famished. The first course stayed as long as possible, in hopes of the Lords: so did the second. The dessert at last arrived, and the middle dish was actually set on when Lord Finlater and Mr Mackay arrived!—would you believe it?—the dessert was remanded, and the whole first course brought back again!—Stay, I have not done:—just as this second first course had done its duty, Lord Northumberland, Lord Strafford and Mackenzie came in, and the whole began a third time! The second course and the dessert! I thought we should have dropped from our chairs with fatigue and fumes! When the clock struck eleven, we were asked to return to the drawing-room, and drink tea and coffee, but I said I was engaged to supper, and came home to bed . . .

Horace Walpole (1717–1797)

April 8

S T WALTER became abbot of St Martin, Pontoise, in 1060. He was clearly a better abbot than the one in charge of the monastery he joined as a young man, at Rebais, in the diocese of Meaux. Finding a peasant locked up and left to starve for some offence against the monastery, St Walter helped him escape, upon which they "beat him unmercifully." Like many of the best abbots he did not want to be one.

1710: .... in the coach the footboard fell down just att the River Bridge at Barton Mills & frightened the horses, who runn away over the white bridge & through the little bridge water (the man all this time hanging upon the pole) but the water stopped their speed so that the man recovered himself (tho' almost stifled in the water) & gott hold of the reines & stopped them so soon as they came out of ye water & by God's great mercy there was noe mischief done. . . .
(see also May 26)

William Coe of Mildenhall (1680–1729)

April 9

B ISHOP BUTLER says "St DOTTO founded and governed a great monastery in the sixth century," in the Orkneys. "In the same island stood other monasteries and churches dedicated to God under the patronage of St Brendan. Though all the isles of Orkney are recommended for the healthfulness of the air, and longevity of the inhabitants, this of St Dotto is remarkable above the rest on these accounts. Our saint lived near one hundred years."

1801: [Lawrence] requested me to urge him to exertion saying that at times He is incapable of any, at other times is full of it. He alluded to the state of his affairs.—I told him there was only one way which was to look his situation fairly in the face and to acquire a habit of regular application, which He might obtain by each day taking up that picture which required finishing that He felt most inclined to work upon.—He said He was sure his picture of

71

[Kemble, the actor as] Hamlet had not taken him more than 10 days to paint it, supposing each day to be from 9 o'clock till 5.

Joseph Farington (1747–1821)

April 10

Sт BADEMUS, an abbot, had been in prison for four months, each day receiving a certain number of lashes. Another Christian prisoner, called Nersan, was promised freedom and restitution if he would perform the execution of St Bademus with the sword. The poor man made a nervous and botched job of it (the date was 376), and got the worst of both worlds, for later he was tortured and executed apparently for some other offence than that of being a Christian; though no doubt St Bademus interceded for and perhaps saved him.

1712: It was *Petronius* his Merit that he died in the same Gaiety of Temper in which he lived; but as his Life was altogether loose and dissolute, the Indifference which he showed at the Close of it, is to be looked upon as a Piece of natural Carelessness and Levity, rather than Fortitude. The Resolution of *Socrates* proceeded from a well-spent Life, and Prospect of a happy Eternity. If the ingenious Author above-mentioned was so pleased with Gayety of Humour in a dying Man, he might have found a much nobler Instance of it in our Countryman *Sir Thomas More. . . .*

Joseph Addison (1672–1719)

April 11

Sт GUTHLAC (d. 714) renounced a military career to become a hermit on what was then the island of Crowland (just northeast of what is now Peterborough) in the wild, undrained fens. Later a great wooden abbey arose on the site of St Guthlac's hermitage, and "the French abbot of Crowland sent French monks to open a school under the new French donjon, in the little Roman town of Grantebrigge, whereby—so does all earnest work grow and spread in this world, infinitely and for ever,—St Guthlac, by his canoe voyage into Crowland Island, became the spiritual father of the University of Cambridge."

1830: The wedding was much of the same cast as the Camerton weddings in general are. I took the opportunity, after the ceremony was concluded and the parties were detained in church owing to a heavy shower of rain, of giving a word of advice to the young people. I asked them in the first place whether they had a place to live in. The girl answered, No; that they were for the present to live with her father (a wretched profligate fellow). I said they ought at least to have been as wise as the birds of the air, who made themselves nests before they brought up their young. The man, or rather the cad, said they could not wait for that. . . .

John Skinner (1772–1839)

April 12

ST ZENO OF VERONA (d. 380) was bishop there in confused times, when the church was threatened from within by Arianism and without by Goths and other barbarians. His writings, among the earliest to survive (127 of his sermons were among the first things printed at Venice) give interesting details of current practice, such as that baptism was by total immersion, but the water was warmed.

1930: . . . . refer to Rose's collection of distinguished feminists, giving [Lady B.] to understand that I know them all well and intimately, and have frequently discussed [marriage] with them. Lady B. waves her hand—(in elegant white kid, new, not cleaned)—and declares That may be all very well, but if they could have got *husbands* they wouldn't *be* Feminists. I instantly assert that all have had husbands, and some two or three. This may or may not be true, but have seldom known stronger homicidal impulse. Final straw is added when Lady B. amiably observes that *I*, at least, have nothing to complain of, as she always thinks Robert such a safe, respectable husband for *any* woman. Give her briefly to understand that Robert is in reality a

compound of Don Juan, the Marquis de Sade, and Dr
Crippen, but that we do not care to let it be known locally.
Cannot say whether she is or is not impressed by this.

E. M. *Delafield*, Diary of a Provincial Lady

April 13

Sᴛ Hᴇʀᴍᴇɴɢɪʟᴅ (d. 586) was the son of the Arian king of Spain,
the Visigoth Leovigild, but became an orthodox Trinitarian
Christian. He led a revolt against his father, appealing not very
successfully to the small Roman forces remaining in Spain, but
was captured and imprisoned. His father, angry at his refusal of
an offer of release if he would take communion from an Arian
bishop, ordered his execution. St Gregory the Great (*see March
12*) said that whatever guilt he had incurred by taking up arms
against his father was "expiated by his heroic virtue and death."

1861: .... Brett has been spending a year at Florence .... Able and intelligent as Brett is, his love of
paradox and his chivalrous proud devotion—self-opinion-
ated too—to unpopular causes is very pleasantly provoking.
Litchfield asked what he thought of Raffaelle after a year's
study: he replied calmly "I think he is the worst painter I
have known;" and proceeded to show *à la* Ruskin, that
Raffaelle was all wrong in colour and could not draw. ...

A. J. Munby (1828–1910)

April 14

Sᴛ Jᴜsᴛɪɴ (100–167, or some say 162) was an educated pagan
who felt a desire to find God. He went to a Stoic who
undertook to prove that this was not possible. He went to a
Peripatetic (rather debased follower of Aristotle) who haggled
about fees. He went to a Pythagorean who said well, that meant
beginning with music, astronomy and geometry. He went to a
Platonist, and, finding some hope in the doctrine of eternal
forms and ideas, became a seashore solitary, where he met an
old man who converted him in 133. He resolved to work for the

conversion of the intellectual heathen, and opened a school in Rome. He died as a martyr, and is regarded as the first of the Fathers of the Church.

1928: There are few good letter-writers, I fancy: as few as there are good sonnetteers: for the same reason: that the form is too worn to be easy, and there are too many who try. It is a less crowded profession, is epic poetry: and that's why there are few bad epics. . . .

T. E. Lawrence (1888–1935)

April 15

Sᴛ Rᴜᴀᴅʜᴀɴ, a 6th-century abbot of Lothra (Ireland), was said to have hidden one Odo, a refugee from King Dermot. The King however did seize Odo. Ruadhan and his monks pursued him, rang his bell, and drew themselves up in a square singing psalms. Dermot took no notice, but on the second night dreamt he saw a great tree falling down. Waking after this ominous warning, he heard the psalms still going on, and there followed what Baring-Gould calls a "truly Hibernian scene of mutual recrimination," ending with King Dermot saying: "You are a protector and fautor of lawlessness, but I endeavour to keep order in the country. You and the like of you are the confusion of my kingdom. However, as you are the elect of God, go your way, and take the man with you, but pay me his price."

1778: We breakfasted, dined, supped and slept again at home. Brewed a vessell of strong Beer today. My two large Piggs, by drinking some Beer grounds taken out of one of my Barrels today, got so amazingly drunk by it, that they were not able to stand and appeared like dead things almost, and so remained all night from dinner time today. I never saw Piggs so drunk in my life, I slit their ears for them without feeling.

James Woodforde (1740–1803)

April 16

Sᴛ Bᴇʀɴᴀᴅᴇᴛᴛᴇ (1844–1879) was the poor miller's daughter who, at fourteen, had the series of visions of the Blessed Virgin. Her claims (which had more or less to be dragged out of her) were greeted with great scepticism, not least by the Bishop of Tarbes and other ecclesiastical superiors, perhaps rightly disturbed by the original sensation caused by her story. She entered a convent at Nevers and bore both scepticism and increasing ill-health with extraordinary patience. Lourdes had become the most famous Marian shrine in the world, and beyond all official doubt in the church, long before she was canonized in 1933.

> *1814:* [My dearest Mother] .... We had yesterday a poor French prisoner of Ashbourne to dine with us, who was an officer of Buonaparte's guards. He damns the "ingratitude" of his countrymen to Buonaparte, and says if he was in his army now he would stick by him to the last. It has been from first to last a strange melodrame, and if it had not been so very bloody, would be very ridiculous. It is that mixture of the tragical and the farcical, which poor wretched human nature exhibits so often. ....
>
> *Thomas Moore (1779–1852)*

April 17

Sᴛ Sᴛᴇᴘʜᴇɴ Hᴀʀᴅɪɴɢ (d. 1134) was one of the three founders of the great Cistercian Order. Finding that the Benedictine monastery of Molesme passed from holy poverty to "sloth and irregularity" even in the time he was there, with his abbot, St Robert, and his prior, St Alberic he retired to the "marshy wilderness" of Cîteaux. They made a vow to return to the "utmost severity" of the Rule of St Benedict (*see March 21*) on that saint's feast day in 1098. St Stephen became the third abbot, after his companions. In spite of the severity of the rule, and his scholarliness, he was always, says William of Malmesbury "blithe of countenance". The Cistercian Order spread to his native England in his lifetime; and to it we owe such glories as

Rievaulx, Fountains and Tintern—not to mention much of new cultivation, soil draining and, in fact, the beginnings of scientific farming.

1870: The happiest, brightest, most beautiful Easter I have ever spent, I woke early and looked out. As I had hoped the day was cloudless, a glorious morning. My first thought was "Christ is Risen." . . . . There was a heavy white dew with a touch of hoar frost on the meadows, and as I leaned over the wicket gate by the mill pond looking to see if there were any primroses in the banks but not liking to venture into the dripping grass suddenly I heard the cuckoo for the first time this year. . . . It is very well to hear the cuckoo for the first time on Easter Sunday morning.

Francis Kilvert (1840–1879)

April 18

ST AYA, Countess of Hainault (not the one on the Central Line, but the original one in Belgium) (7th century), left all her property to the canonesses of the chapter at Mons. Some of her heirs claimed it also, and after a long lawsuit it was decided to let her settle the matter. Perhaps not surprisingly, a voice from her tomb declared for the canonesses. Since then "those who suffer, or fear suffering, injustice in a lawsuit, place themselves under her protection."

1717: For me, I am not ashamed to own I took more pleasure in looking on the beauteous Fatima, than the finest piece of sculpture could have given me. . . . Her maids' dance was very different from what I had seen before. Nothing could be more artful, or more proper to raise certain ideas. The tunes so soft!—the motions so languishing!— accompanied with pauses and dying eyes! half-falling back, and then recovering themselves in so artful a manner, that I am very positive the coldest and most rigid prude upon earth could not have looked upon them without thinking of something not to be spoken of . . .

Lady Mary Wortley Montagu (1689–1762)

April 19

S T ALPHEGE ("or properly Aelfheagh") (954–1012) was a monk in Gloucestershire, an abbot in Bath, bishop of Winchester in 984, and in 1006 archbishop of Canterbury. This was during the time of many Danish incursions. In 1008 another lot came, and 1011 they took Canterbury. The saint was attacked by a drunken mob of them when he refused to pay a ransom (having already spent some time in prison). Some accounts say that the man who actually gave the death blow was a Christian who only did it to save him longer torment. Lanfranc said he was not a true martyr, but St Anselm (*see April 21*) said he was, and he was venerated as such.

1781: Sowed a great many seeds in the nursery that Archibald had brought from England. Received a large quantitie from Sir Joseph Banks of those brought home by the Descovery Ships which went out with Captain Cook the 10th Feby 1776 and likewise some Seeds from Mr Morison with a great many other ever green tree seeds; made a compleat Nursury; the only thing wanted was a Hottehouse for several sorts of seeds from the friendly Islands and Ottahiette (Otahiti)

Thomas Blaikie (1750–1838)

April 20

S T JAMES "of Sclavonia or Illyricum" (d. 1485) became a cook for the Franciscans at Bitecto, near Bari; and a most unusual one. "One morning whilst he was making ready a mess of beans for his community's dinner, he happened to be thus ravished in spirit, and stood for a considerable time motionless and entirely absorpt in God, and tears streaming from his eyes, fell into the vessel of beans before him." The Duke of Atria, who was a guest passing through, had seen this; and when James came to himself he went to ask the duke what he would like for dinner. " 'I will eat nothing,' said the duke, 'but some of the beans which have been seasoned with your tears.' The duke took every occasion of testifying his extraordinary veneration for his sanctity."

1690: [Coventry] In the morning I went to the great church, which is fifty paces broad and ninety long. There I heard Mr Fox preach and received the sacrament from him. In the afternoon I preached on Luke i.28, and after prayers went to see the cross, which is a very rich and glorious structure, having all the Kings of England in effigy round it, with some other images. Near the top, at the gate end, stands the image of an old man looking out of the window, being kept in memory of a fellow who peeped out there when the queen rode naked through the town.

Dean Rowland Davies (1649–1721)

April 21

ST ANSELM (1033–1109), Italian by birth, was the second post-Conquest archbishop of Canterbury. His chief fame is as the proponent of one of the few truly original, obvious, maddeningly ambiguous, sublimely bold and endlessly fascinating ideas in philosophy (which in his time meant theology; his was the famous dictum *credo ut intelligam*, "I believe that I may understand"). Thousands of profound pages have been written about his ontological proof of the existence of God, which is brutally summarized as "God is the greatest *existing* reality the mind can conceive of, therefore He exists." They range from the monk Gaunilo ("if we can conceive of our own non-existence, why not God's?") to Descartes and Spinoza with different versions of the same idea, to Kant with his statement that "you cannot predicate existence," and G. E. Moore with his criticism of *that* statement—

But he was also the type of the dreamy, unworldly thinker who miraculously survives among tough thugs. He was originally invited over from his beloved abbey at Bec in Normandy by Hugh the Fat, first Earl of Chester, a thug if ever there was one but with a corner of his mind that *respected* people like Anselm and was glad they existed. William Rufus, at a time when he was ill and feeling rather sorry for himself, made Anselm a very unwilling archbishop, then had tremendous rows with him about revenues and about which of two rival popes he should receive the official *pallium* from. Anselm was more or less an exile in Rome for three years, during which he wrote *Cur Deus Homo?*, "Why a Man-God?," a profound exposition of the whole doctrine of the Atonement. Then came William's death, return to England and more rows with Henry I over the king's right to appoint bishops and abbots

Once a hunted hare took refuge underneath St Anselm's horse. The soldiers and hunters closed in with their dogs, laughing and shouting. But St Anselm wept. "You laugh, but for the poor unhappy creature there is nothing to laugh at or be glad for. Its mortal foes are pursuing it and it flies to us for life, in its own way beseeching for shelter. *You see the image of the departing soul of man.*" He forbade the dogs to touch the hare, "which escaped joyfully to the woods."

"To a child-like singleness and tenderness of heart," says Baring-Gould, "was joined an originality and power of thought which rank him, even to this day, among the few discoverers of new paths in philosophical speculation." Curiously, he was not canonized till 1720.

1765: Of all the towns in Italy, I am least satisfied with Venice. . . . Old, and in general, ill-built houses, ruined pictures and stinking ditches dignified with the pompous denomination of canals, a fine bridge spoilt by two rows of houses on it, and a large square, decorated with the worst architecture I ever saw.

Edward Gibbon (1737–1794)

April 22

S T LEONIDES was beheaded for the faith in Alexandria in 202, in the persecution under Severus. He was a Christian philosopher, but in this he was eclipsed—like everyone else who preceded him, by the eldest of his seven sons, the great Origen (c. 185–264), of whom the German theologian Harnack wrote "by proclaiming the reconcilation of science with the Christian faith, he did more than any other man to win the Old World to the Christian religion." Immensely learned in Greek and Hebrew Origen was also deeply ascetic, and made himself a eunuch to avoid temptation when teaching the young (afterwards admitting this to be wrong). He made a powerful defence of Christianity against one Celsus. He had broad sympathies with Platonism, and expounded the doctrine of Christ as Logos, the Eternal Word. He was imprisoned and tortured under the persecution of Decius, but survived. Certain heretical views (one of which, that the punishment of Satan, let alone merely the damned, was not eternal, seems to confirm his essential broad tolerance) were imputed to him, and he was suspected—probably wrongly—of Gnosticism, of which a crude view is that Truth is reserved for a few chosen intellectuals. Origen was not finally "condemned" as a voice of the church till the 5th century, and probably not wholeheartedly or by everyone even then. He deserves to be remembered on his father's feast day.

1897: [Cimïez, Nice] After a quiet day on the 22nd Sarah Bernhardt gave a lovely little piece, in the drawing-room before the Queen and she acted it with the greatest feeling and her voice was lovely. . . . the Queen had at first been reluctant to allow Sarah Bernhardt to appear before her and one likes to think it was Lady Lytton who persuaded her to give herelf this pleasure. Certainly it was a triumph, for the general opinion of her among "ladies" was expressed by the Empress Frederick in a letter to her daughter Sophie in 1893: "It must have been interesting to see Sarah Bernhardt she is an extraordinary actress from all I have heard. I hope you did *not* make her acquaintance, as alas no *lady* can, she is so very bad, and has an awful reputation. It is a pity those immoral pieces are always given, such as you saw."

Lady Lytton's Court Diary (ed. Mary Lutyens)

April 23

UNTIL 1960 the Catholic *Daily Missal* gave the feast of ST GEORGE, martyred in 273 under Diocletian, as a double of the first class, with octave. Subsequently he was reduced to a name briefly mentioned in the office of the day. The trouble of course is the immense overlay of legend. There clearly *was* a Saint George, who was much venerated in the east (and of whom Crusaders would have heard, although he became patron saint of England before his formal adoption as such in the reign of Edward III). His shrine at Lydda was near the traditional site of the rescue of Andromeda by Perseus; hence *that* legend, although the Latin Acts place it near Silene in *Libya*.

1715: I have heard such a strange story from England; I wonder if it is true? I heard that the Prince of Wales saw a play where some actress, supposed to be impersonating the late Queen Anne, pretended to get drunk, and flung herself into a chair. Then a milord climbed on to the stage and laid about the actors with his sword, and the Prince is supposed to have ordered his guards to shoot him down. The entire pit shouted that if a single shot was fired they would do away with the King's whole party, and the captain of the guards is supposed to have said to the Prince that shooting might be the thing in Hanover, but in England it just wasn't done.

Elisabeth Charlotte (Liselotte) Princess Palatine & Duchess of Orleans (1652–1722)

April 24

St Mellitus (d. 624) was a Roman abbot sent by Pope Gregory to assist St Augustine in his mission to England. There still exists a letter which St Gregory sent him instructing him to show respect for the sacred places of the heathens, merely removing the idols and purifying with holy water for the services of Christianity. After three years in Kent he went to London, where Sibert, king of the East Saxons, was converted. It was Sibert who built the first church where Westminster Abbey now stands.

1824: No one was in the house but Fletcher, of which I was glad. As if he knew my wishes, he led me up a narrow stair into a small room, with nothing in it but a coffin standing on trestles. No word was spoken by either of us; he withdrew the black pall and the white shroud, and there lay the embalmed body of the Pilgrim*—more beautiful in death than in life. The contraction of the muscles and skin had effaced every line that time or passion had ever traced on it; few marble busts could have matched its stainless white, the harmony of its proportions, and perfect finish; yet he had been dissatisfied with that body, and longed to cast its slough. How often had I heard him curse

*Byron

82

it! He was jealous of the genius of Shakespeare—that might well be—but where had he seen the face or form worthy to excite his envy?

E. J. Trelawney (1792–1881)

April 25

ST MARK THE EVANGELIST was converted by the Apostles, probably by St Peter, of whom he was a constant companion. He accompanied St Paul on some of his journeys, but is said to have written his Gospel at the request of the Romans, who wished to have in writing what St Peter had spoken to them. Afterwards he took the faith to Egypt, and the tradition is that he was martyred by being dragged about at the end of a rope. Various reasons are given for the adoption of the lion as his symbol. It is the royal beast, standing for the dignity of Christ. It was the beast in the vision of Ezekiel which made the desert echo with its roaring, and St Mark's Gospel begins with St John the Baptist, the "voice crying in the wilderness."

1775: The town [Paris] is lighted in the night by lamps which is suspended upon a cord fixed across the street; the lamp is fixed upon a pully and another rop to descend it when lighted or cleaned; as it is hung in the middle of the street the end of the cord to tht pully is fixed in an iron box in one side of the street which the lamplighter opens and shuts with a key; there is always two people to light a lamp one to let it down and hold the cord while the other lights it; those lamps is placed at a great distance from one another and by reason of there reverberetoirs lights the streets tolerable well.

Thomas Blaikie (1750–1838)

April 26

ST CLETUS, whose name occurs in the canon of the Mass, was one of St Peter's immediate three successors, the others being St Clement and St Linus (also in the canon), although there is some doubt as to the order in which they came. He is also known as St Anacletus, and is venerated as a martyr.

1786: "Le Nozze di Figaro" is being performed on the 28th [April] for the first time. It will be very surprising if it is a success, for I know that very powerful cabals have ranged themselves against your brother. Salieri and all his supporters will again try to move heaven and earth to down his opera. Duschek told me recently that it is on account of the very great reputation which your brother's exceptional talent and ability have won for him that so many people are plotting against him.

Leopold Mozart (1719–1787) to his daughter.

April 27

Sᴛ Pᴇᴛᴇʀ Cᴀɴɪsɪᴜs (1521–1597) is a Counter-Reformation saint. Born at Nijmegen in Holland, he became a Jesuit, in a time when a clear, almost schematic articulation of the Catholic faith seemed called for as an answer to Luther's catechism. St Peter's *Summa Doctrinarum* supplied this need, and he was a principal theological adviser to the Council of Trent (1545–63) which moulded the church into a shape from which it has only broken in our own time. St Peter refused the bishoprics of Vienna and Cologne, founded many schools and colleges and maintained the interest of the church at the Diet of Augsburg and the Conference of Worms; he is in fact one of the main reasons why south Germany remained Catholic. He is said always to have been courteous, tolerant and humble in his personal style.

1859: [To E. B. Cowell.] . . . I sent you poor old Omar who has *his* kind of Consolation for all these Things. I doubt you will regret you ever introduced him to me. And yet you would have me print the original, with many worse things than I have translated. The Bird Epic might be finished at once; but "cui bono?" No one cares for such things; and there are doubtless so many better things to care about. I hardly know why I print any of these things, which nobody buys; and I scarce now see the few I give them to. But when one has done one's best, and is sure that best is better than so many will take pains to do, though far from the best that *might be done,* one likes to make an end of the matter by Print. I suppose very few People have ever taken such Pains in Translation as I have: though certainly not to be literal. But at all Cost, a Thing must *live*: with a transfusion of one's own worse Life if one can't retain the Original's better. Better a live Sparrow than a stuffed Eagle. I shall be very well pleased to see the new MS. of Omar . . .

Edward Fitzgerald (1809–1883)

April 28

S᙭ PAUL OF THE CROSS (1694–1775) was a mystic with an intense devotion to the Passion and sufferings of Christ. A short career as a soldier in the Venetian army was followed by a period of solitude and reflection, and he was ordained in 1727. He founded the Passionist Order. "The Congregation of Discalced Clerks of the Most Holy Cross and Passion of Our Lord Jesus Christ" had its rule approved by Pope Benedict XIV in 1741. Devoted to mission and revival work, they first came to England exactly a hundred years later; and four years after *that,* in 1845, one of them, Fr Dominic Barberi, received into the church her most famous and influential convert—John Henry, later Cardinal Newman, himself now a candidate for canonization.

1923: This is a superb town! The raging wind has gone down, and the sky is completely blue. We have just seen the great mosque. One is allowed inside, for in 1840, the French stabled their horses inside, and so defiled the mosque for good. It is far more beautiful than Cordova, with a vast marble courtyard outside surrounded by a colonnade of marble pillars, which I think were taken from Carthage. Lytton has been buying leather morocco skins in the souks this morning. They are absurdly cheap, even although we are swindled, I expect, by these crafty Moslems. Yesterday we had coffee outside a little Moorish coffee house, and watched the sun go down. The good Moslems eat nothing from sunrise to sunset now for 40 days. It's very simple and rather extraordinary to see them sitting in rows outside the eating houses with oranges and cakes in their hands waiting until the muezzin from the minaret cries out. Then they all fall on their food, and drink up their cups of coffee. Kairouan is far more Eastern than Biskra. There are only 500 Europeans in the whole population, and no French buildings, and only this one hotel.

Carrington (1893–1932)

April 29

S⊤ Peter of Verona (1205–1252), also known as St Peter Martyr, came from a family inclined to the doctrine of the Cathari, the Manichaean sect who believed the physical world to have been created by evil forces. Educated by orthodox Catholic teachers, St Peter became a Dominican and preached so successfully against the Cathari, being greeted "in every place by a cross, banner, trumpet and drums" that they hired two assassins to kill him on the road between Como and Milan. One of them, Carinus, afterwards repented of this and ended his life as a Dominican lay-brother.

1891: . . . . Bath ready—could scarcely bear it so hot. I persevered, and got in; very hot, but very acceptable. I lay still for some time.

On moving my hand above the surface of the water, I experienced the greatest fright I ever received in the whole course of my life; for imagine my horror on discovering my hand, as I thought, full of blood. My first thought was that I had ruptured an artery and was bleeding to death, and should be discovered, later on, looking like a second Marat, as I remember seeing him in Madame Tussaud's. My second thought was to ring the bell, but remembered there was no bell to ring. My third was, that there was nothing but the enamel paint, which had dissolved with boiling water.

George and Weedon Grossmith, The Diary of a Nobody

April 30

S⊤ Catherine of Sienna, the youngest of twenty-five children of Giacomo di Benincasa, a dyer, was attracted to austerities and the ecstasies of the solitary from early life (she is said to have experimented with sleep till she found she could manage with half an hour in every twenty-four). She received the stigmata (the marks of the wounds of Christ's passion) but her prayer that they should not be visible was answered. She was however drawn into the centre of bitter public controversies. She persuaded Pope Gregory XI to return from Avignon in 1376; the last of the popes in the "Babylonian captivity of the church." She was in Florence trying to make the people there make peace with him when he died. She spent her last years trying to restrain the impatient temper of his successor, Urban VI, in Rome, although in fact there were now French anti-popes in Avignon till 1418. She died in 1380.

1753: *Avoir du monde* is, in my opinion, a very just and happy expression for having address, manners, and for knowing how to behave properly in all companies; and it implies very truly, that a man that has not these accomplishments, is not of the world. Without them, the best parts are inefficient, civility is absurd, and freedom offensive. A learned parson, rusting in his cell at Oxford or Cambridge, will reason admirably well upon the nature of man; will profoundly analyse the head, the heart, the reason, the will, the passions, the senses, the sentiments, and all those subdivisions of we know not what; and yet, unfortunately, he knows nothing of man, for he has not lived with him, and is ignorant of the various modes, habits, prejudices and tastes, that always influence and often determine him. He views man as he does colours in Sir Isaac Newton's prism, where only the capital ones are seen; but an experienced dyer knows all their various shades and gradations, together with the result of their several mixtures. Few men are of one plain colour; most are mixed, shaded and blended; and vary as much from different situations, as changeable silks do from different lights.

Lord Chesterfield (1694–1773) to his son

MAY

May 1

Ss Philip and James the Less, Apostles. Although St Philip, of Bethsaida in Galilee, was called by Jesus the day after St Andrew, he is named the first disciple because he followed Jesus more or less immediately, whereas the others returned to their trade of fishing for a year before becoming permanent followers. After the Resurrection his mission was to upper Asia, and he was martryed by crucifixion at Hierapolis in Phrygia (towards the west of modern Turkey). He was married, and had several daughters. St James the Less is called "the brother of the Lord," and he was related by blood to Jesus. It was he who presided over the Synod in Jerusalem at which it was decided that Gentile converts were not bound by Mosaic law, and it was to him that St Paul first went after his conversion. Also known as James the Just, he was thrown from the roof of the temple by the scribes and pharisees, but this did not kill him, the final death-blow being delivered by a fuller's club, with which he is often represented in art.

1871: Up early, breakfast at 7 and the dog cart took me to the station for the 8 train. It was a lovely May morning, and the beauty of the river and green meadows, the woods, hills and blossoming orchards was indescribable. At Hereford two women were carrying a Jack in the Green about the High Town. In the next carriage a man was playing a harp and a girl a violin as the train travelled.

Francis Kilvert (1840–1879)

May 2

St Athanasius (d. 373) is an absolutely key figure in the inevitable progress of the church from the original small band of followers who simply "knew" that Jesus was both man and God to its historical status as a worldwide body which had to produce its formulation of the subtle and profound doctrines of the Incarnation and the Trinity—its *dogma*, (this word, which most people seem to think is a put-down, is only the Greek for "teaching.") At the Council of Nicaea in 325 St Athanasius, then a young deacon, was eloquently victorious over Arius and his heresy, that Jesus was only a good man, *could* have sinned, etc. Easier to believe, of course, and perhaps more in accord with a basic eastern tendency to think of the real God as spiritual abstraction. Anyway the emperor Constantius soon turned away from the Nicene creed, Athanasius, having been made bishop of Alexandria, was banished to Gaul. He enjoyed recognition by the western emperor Constans, and was enthusiastically welcomed back to Alexandria after eight years' exile, then had to flee to the desert when Arianism gained the ascendancy again, and also later under Julian the Apostate. He is a Doctor of the Church.

1859: Went to the Working Men's College to hear Ruskin's "talk" about Switzerland. The room was full, many of the teachers there. Ruskin had brought one or two of his best Turners, and photographs & maps. He spoke well and in his normal free pleasant way: with as usual a little too much *infant school* humour—like the funny papa telling stories to the good boys. His lecture was historical and geographical chiefly—without book, he standing before the fire with hands under coat tails, or whisking about in his airy way.

A. J. Munby (1828–1910)

May 3

ST ALEXANDER (d. 117), a martyr, was also Pope Alexander I. His is one of the names in the Canon of the Mass. It was he who prescribed that water should be mixed with the wine "on account of the blood and water that flowed from the side of Jesus." In the Latin Mass, after the Council of Tibur, the water was held to represent the faithful, about to be united with the blood of Christ, and this is preserved in the modern vernacular; "by the mystery of this water and wine may we come to share in the divinity of Christ, who humbled himself to share in our humanity."

1974: I once purchased, in the Grand Bazaar of Istanbul, and at ruinous expense, an elderly musket about five feet long and with a stock riddled with woodworm. I wrapped it most carefully in copies of an airmail

91

edition of *The Times* and drove home with it. Of course, it arrived in one piece. But I was even more impressed by the fact that at the innumerable border posts on the journey, from a Turkish Nissen hut to a wet and crowded Dover at four in the morning, *The Times* seemed to insulate it from more than a cursory glance from a comprehensive selection of Europe's customs officers. I cannot say, sir, what might have happened had I sought the protection of a lesser journal.

N. D. J. Lane, in a letter to The Times

May 4

S⊤ MONICA (332–388) was the mother of St Augustine (*see August 28*). She lived at Tagaste in North Africa, married to Patricius, a pagan of choleric (and sometimes unfaithful) temper, who was eventually converted, by her patience as much as her prayers, before his death. She did not "succeed", to outward appearances, during his youth, in making a Catholic Christian, let alone the pillar of Christian philosophy that her son eventually became. On the contrary he became attracted by Manicheism. He became a professor of rhetoric at Rome, and later at Milan. There, contact with St Ambrose and Neoplatonism changed his mind. He finally gave in to St Paul on reading the Epistle to the Romans, but his conversion has always been ascribed as much to the constant tears and prayers of his mother. He wrote that she "brought me forth, both in the flesh, that I might be born to this temporal light, and in heart, that I might be born to Lights eternal." There is a very moving description in Chapter IX of his *Confessions* of how, when she knew she was going to die at Ostia on their way back to North Africa, they sat in the window of the house and passed beyond admiration of natural beauty into a kind of shared ecstasy, so that "the very highest delight of the earthly senses, in the very purest material light, was in respect of the sweetness of that life, not only not worthy of comparison, but not even of mention. . . ."

1856: The music of *La Traviata* is trashy; the young Italian lady cannot do justice to the music, such as it is. Hence it follows that the opera and the lady can only

92

establish themselves in proportion as Londoners rejoice in a prurient story prettily acted.

The Athenaeum

May 5

S<small>T</small> P<small>IUS</small> V (1504–1572) is not the kind of saint likely to have an ecumenical appeal, for it was he who excommunicated Queen Elizabeth I, and the last efforts of his life were directed to organizing a league against England. Extremely zealous in promoting the decrees of the Council of Trent (and a keen supporter of the Inquisition), he was passionately devout and sternly opposed to any corruption detectable in a Rome grown fairly used to it over the centuries. It was he who organized a reluctant Christian west to oppose the advances of the Turks under Selim II—A saint for a barbarous age, one might say, until one remembered that our own age could show any other a thing or two about barbarity. By his organization and the public prayers which he commanded, he was the spirit behind the famous victory of Don John of Austria at Lepanto.

1824: [To Bernard Barton] What is the reason we do not sympathize with pain, short of some terrible surgical operation? Hazlitt, who boldly says all he feels, avows that not only does he not pity sick people, but he hates them. . . .

Charles Lamb (1775–1834)

May 6

S<small>T</small> J<small>OHN</small> D<small>AMASCENE</small> (d. about 780), although a Christian, was made governor of Damascus when that city was already under Mohammedan rule, but abandoned an evidently brilliant career to become a monk in Palestine. He became a great apologist and poet. His Exposition of the Orthodox Faith was a schematic theology of the kind later adopted in the west by St Anselm. A stout opponent of the Iconoclasts, he was known as the Doctor of Christian Art. Although also skilled in mathematics he wrote: "without assiduous prayer, reasoning is a great dissipation of the mind." His feast, once this day, appears to have been moved to March 27.

✏ *1937:* [Mrs Patrick Campbell] talked a great deal about "flight" in acting as being the first quality of a great actor. For four hours I listened to chatter about everything, from Moses to Schnabel. About the former: "He probably said to himself, 'Must stop or I shall be getting silly.' That is why there are only ten commandments." She described Schnabel's playing of Beethoven as being "like the winds of the air and the waves of the sea, without shape.". . . about an American actress: "she has a Siamese forehead and a mouth like a galosh." About another actress: "She is the great lady of the American stage. Her voice is so beautiful that you won't understand a word she says." About the same actress: "She's such a nice woman. If you knew her you'd even admire her acting."

James Agate, My American Journey

May 7

Sᴛ Sᴛᴀɴɪsʟᴀs (1030–1079) after studying at Gnesna (the first university in Poland) and Paris, became bishop of Cracow, that frontier post of western Christendom, in 1072. He incurred the enmity of the cruel and lustful king, Boleslaw II, who was always stealing the wives of his nobles. In the end the king sent soldiers to kill him, but at the last moment they dared not strike, until the king himself dealt the first blow.

✏ *1644:* Fontaine Bleau . . . is nothing so stately and uniforme as Hampton Court.

John Evelyn (1620–1706)

May 8

Sᴛ Pᴇᴛᴇʀ ᴏғ Tᴀʀᴇɴᴛᴀɪsᴇ (1102–1175) founded the Cistercian monastery of Tamie, in the Alps and became widely known for his unassuming charity. Among other things he rebuilt the famous Little St Bernard hospice. When the faction called the Frangipani in Rome put up one Octavian, as Pope Victor IV, in opposition to Alexander III, legitimately elected by the majority of the cardinals, Octavian had the support of the emperor, Frederick Barbarossa. St Peter was one of the few to stand out against him, eventually bringing the entire Cistercian Order behind him.

1940: What can Neville [Chamberlain] do now? He can reconstruct his Government: he can resign; but there is no doubt the Government is seriously jarred and all confidence in it is gone. Hitler will be quick to take advantage of our divided councils.

What changes does that fatal division portend? Neville may survive but not for long: Oh, the cruelty of the pack in pursuit . . . shall I too crash when the Chamberlain edifice crumbles?

I am disgusted by politics and human nature and long to live like Walpole, a semi social—semi literary life in a Strawberry Hill (only not Gothic) of my own. Perhaps one day I will.

"Chips" Channon (1897–1958)

May 9

ST GREGORY NAZIANZEN (312–391) was born at the town of that name in Cappadocia. By nature shy and retiring, he looked back to the period when St Basil and he were hermits as the happiest in his life ("my hut is so placed on the summit of the mountain that I overlook the extensive plain . . . shall I speak of the lovely singing of the birds, and the profusion of flowers?") He was, however, more or less forcibly ordained priest by his father, who was bishop of Nazianzen; and then, only slightly less forcibly, made bishop of Sasima, near Caesarea. Later a recluse again, and famous for his eloquent defence of Catholic doctrine against Arianism, he was installed by the emperor Theodosius as the unwilling bishop of Constantinople, a post he left for solitude again as soon as his conscientiousness would allow him.

1836: . . . physical science, if studied at all. seems too great to be given a secondary place in one's studies:

wherefore, rather than have it the principal thing in my son's mind, I would gladly have him think that the sun went round the earth, and that the stars were so many spangles set in the bright blue firmament. Surely the one thing needful for a Christian and an Englishman to study is Christian and moral and political philosophy, and then we should see our way a little more clearly without falling into Judaism, or Toryism, or Jacobinism, or any other *ism* whatever.

Thomas Arnold (1795–1842)

May 10

S<small>T</small> I<small>SIDORE</small> <small>THE</small> L<small>ABOURER</small> was at the opposite end of the intellectual and social scale from St Isidore the Doctor of the Church (*April 4*). He was a farm labourer from just outside Madrid (d. about 1130) of the kind about whose obvious, feeding-birds-in-the-snow simple goodness legends accumulate. He is the patron saint of Madrid.

1637: There came in my time to the Coll; Balliol one Nathiel Conopios out of Greece, from Cyrill the Patriarch of Constantinople, who returning many years after was made (as I understand) Bishop of Smyrna. He was the first I ever saw drink coffe, wch custom came not into England till 30 years after.

John Evelyn (1620–1706)

May 11

S<small>T</small> M<small>AMERTIUS</small> (d. about 480) is a characteristic saint of the period when Rome was decaying and at the same time sowing mysterious seeds of religion and culture in the wild north. He was bishop of Vienne at time when Goths and Huns were ravaging Gaul; there had been earthquakes, fires and crop failures, and he is chiefly remembered as the initiator of the Rogation (literally "asking") processions.

1943: Churchill's broadcast last night, in which he announced that the Germans had already lost more men on the Russian front than they lost in the whole of the last war, and that the Russians had evidence that the Germans might use gas, gave my stomach a twist, and made me think rapidly and desperately all last night.

James Lees-Milne (1908–   )

May 12

S⊤ Pancras, of whom nothing certain is known except that he was martyred around 304 and buried on the Aurelian Way, was also the dedicatee of the first church consecrated in England by St Augustine. "A curious legend is to the effect that when St Augustine said Mass on the altar, the devil flew away, leaving the impression of his claws on the stone. The fragment of wall containing the impression still remains."

1801: . . . I am proud to say that I have a very good eye at an Adultress. for tho' repeatedly assured that another in the same party was the *She*, I fixed upon the right one from the first.—A resemblance to Mrs Leigh was my guide. She is not so pretty as I expected; her face has the same defect of baldness as her sister's, & her features not so handsome;—she was highly rouged, & looked rather quietly & contentedly silly than anything else.

Jane Austen (1775–1817)

May 13

S⊤ John the Silent (454–558) was born at Nicopolis in Armenia. Made bishop of Colonia, he later retired to the *laura* or hermitage of St Sabas in Palestine, where he at first worked as a labourer. St John later returned to the desert "conversing only with God, and subsisting only on wild roots and herbs", but he "did not refuse instruction to those who resorted to him." During Saracen raids other monks retired to a fortified monastery, but he remained alone (guarded, it was said, by a lion) and lived to the age of 104.

1801: I cannot anyhow continue to find people agreeable;—I respect Mrs Chamberlayne for doing her hair well, but cannot feel a more tender sentiment.—Miss Langley is like any other short girl with a broad nose & wide mouth, fashionable dress, & exposed bosom.—Adm: Stanhope is a gentlemanlike Man, but then his legs are too short. . . .

Jane Austen (1775–1817)

May 14

S⊤ Pachomius (about 290–346) has a prominent place in the history of monasticism, for he was the first to produce a written rule for the community he founded at Tabenna, or Tabennisi, in Egypt. St Benedict was influenced by it in writing his own rule. Although St Pachomius (like St Benedict) himself led a life of the highest possible asceticism, his rule insisted that each should only undertake the fasts and tasks of which he was capable, and 'each brother was allowed to eat and drink as much as he thought fit". There were high standards, though, in what was thought fit. Observing once the funeral procession of one who had been "a tepid monk" he ordered the ceremonial to be cut short and the corpse's clothes to be burned, hoping that a little humiliation even after death might yet earn him some of the grace unearned on earth.

1907: The ladies [Sargent] paints, according to Meynell, generally bore him so much that he is obliged to retire every now and then behind a screen and refresh himself by putting out his tongue at them

Wilfrid Scawen Blunt (1840–1922)

May 15

ST John-Baptist de la Salle (1651–1719) was the founder of a pioneer teaching order, the Brothers of the Christian Schools. The De la Salle brothers are not ordained but take religious vows. I once knew one of them who was determined to write a school song but had never got past the first line, which occurred to him when he realized that the signature tune of the radio programme *Much Binding in the Marsh* exactly fitted the words "St John Baptist de la Salle."

1869: . . . a cold May, and in fact no such hot weather as we had in April till the beginning of June and the haymaking, and then again cold winds.

Br. Wells calls a grindstone a *grindlestone*.

To *lead* north-country for to *carry* (a field of hay etc.) *Geet* north-country preterite of *get*: 'he geet agate agoing.'

Trees sold 'top and lop': Br. Rickaby told me and suggests *top* is the higher, outer and lighter wood good for firing only, *lop* the stem and bigger boughs when the rest has been lopped off used for timber.

Br. Wells calls white bryony Dead Creepers, because it kills what it entwines. . . .

Gerard Manley Hopkins (1844–1889)

May 16

ST Brendan the Navigator (about 486–578) was born in Kerry. He founded the monastery of Clonfert and visited Iona and Scotland and probably Brittany. The legend of his seven-year voyage in search of the Land of Promise to the Saints, although dismissed by Kingsley as "a monkish Odyssey" . . . nevertheless contained enough specific detail (a coracle of wattle, covered with hides tanned in butter) for a modern expedition to prove such a voyage, through ice-floes and storms to America, physically possible.

1717: Sir, coming last week into a Coffee-house not far from the *Exchange* with my Basket under my Arm, a

Jew of considerable Note, as I am informed, takes half a Dozen Oranges of me, and at the same Time slides a Guinea into my Hand. I made him a Courtesy and went my Way: He followed me, and finding I was going about my Business, he came up with me, and told me plainly, that he gave me the Guinea with no other intent but to purchase my Person for an Hour. Did you so Sir? Says I: You gave it me then to make me wicked, I'll keep it to make me honest. However, not to be in the least ungrateful, I promise you I'll lay it out in a Couple of Rings, and wear them for your Sake.

Your humble Servant,
'Betty Lemon'
The Spectator

May 17

ST MADERN, a Cornish hermit of uncertain date, whose chapel near the Madron named after him was partially destroyed in Cromwell's time, had the unusual distinction of the Protestant Bishop Hall of Exeter's testifying to the miraculous cure of a cripple at his well. Another miracle, reported to Charles I when he was at Oxford, involved a boy of twelve who playing football "not far from the Land's End, snatching up the ball ran away with it; whereupon, a girl in anger struck him with a thick stick on the backbone, and so bruised or broke it, that for sixteen years after he was forced to go creeping on the ground." Cured at the well, "he grew so strong, that he wrought day-labour among other hired servants; and four years after listed himself a soldier in the king's army."

1877: The ways of the Royal Academy are to me unaccountable—not that it is unaccountable they should reject six of my drawings; but that they should hang those two which I thought far least likely. I expected they would reject the *"Whole kettle and boiling"*, as they have for these two years, and intended, with the patience of an ox, to prepare eight colour'd pictures for their rejection next season; and if *they* were refused, a like dose on the year succeeding.

Samuel Palmer (1805–1881)

May 18

S⊤ Eric (d. about 1160) was king of Sweden. "An old table of kings denominates him the Lawgiver, and the rights of Swedish matrons to the place of honour and housewifedom, to lock and key, to the half of the marriage-bed, and the legal third of the property, as the law of Upland expresses it, are said to have been conferred by the law of St Eric." After his death in battle against the Danes he was venerated as the national saint of Sweden.

1875: One day at *table d'hôte* I began to talk in French to my neighbour, a nice quiet-looking girl. I soon found out that she was American; she said she could talk English if I liked, but she would rather talk French, so we talked French most of the time. Her home was close by the Falls of Niagara, and she had been travelling all this last year, spending most of it at Berne. She said how much more beautiful American scenery was than Swiss. Swiss was very nice on a small scale.

Florence Sitwell (1858–1930)

May 19

S⊤Dunstan (925–988) was born near Glastonbury and educated there. After a taste of life at the court of Athelstan he retired to a hermitage at Glastonbury. Under Athelstan's son Edmund he became abbbot there (and rebuilt the abbey). When Edmund (also a saint, though not *the* St Edmund martyred by the Danes) was murdered, St Dunstan got on very well with Edmund's son Edgar. On one occasion of debate—the anti-celibacy opposition being led by a Scottish bishop—St Dunstan appealed to Heaven for judgment, whereupon the roof fell in on his opponents who "escaped from the ruins with broken bones;" a story perhaps as apocryphal as the one about his catching the devil by the nose with a pair of pincers. But he *did* become archbishop of Canterbury, and he was an accomplished musician and metal-worker.

1780: The Duke of Chartres carried me to his petite Maison at Moussow (near Paris), where we dined a pretty numerous, noisy company, there being some Females of the Party. After Dinner we amused ourselves in flinging one another into the water, at last by stripping naked and hunting the Hare through Wood, Water etc.

Lord Herbert

May 20

ST ETHELBERT of the East Angles was murdered at Sutton Wall(i)s in Herefordshire, where he had gone to seek the hand of Offa's daughter, Alfreda. But, according to Matthew of Westminster, Offa's queen, Quendritha, with her eyes on Ethelbert's kingdom, "placed a richly adorned chair in the bedroom of the young king, over a trap door which gave way, and he was precipitated into a vault where some servants of the queen were stationed, and they suffocated him with the silk cushions." Hereford Cathedral is dedicated jointly to St Mary and to him.

1920: Then I went with L.† to dine with the Coles* in Chelsea—The Coles are Webbs in embryo—with differences of course. I'm used to being at ease with clever young men, & to find myself stumped, caught out, leg before wicket at every turn is not pleasant. Never was there such a quick, hard, determined young man as Cole; covering his Labour sympathies, which are I suppose intellectual, with the sarcasm & sneers of Oxford. Then there's a bust of W(illiam) Morris on the side board, too much to eat, Morris curtains, all the works of all the classics, & Cole & Mrs hopping on the surface like a couple of Cockney sparrows incapable of more than pecks and sips which they do too skilfully for my taste. The whole effect as of electric light full in the eyes—unbecoming at my age. . . . One can seen Mrs Cole rapidly becoming the cleverish elderly fox terrier type of intellectual woman—as it is not a shade or valley in her mind. Cole, grinning like a guttersnipe demon took us to the door—so spry, alert, virile, & ominous.

Virginia Woolf (1882–1941)

† Leonard Woolf
* G. D. H. Cole and his wife Margaret

102

May 21

S⊤ GODRIC (d. about 1170) was born in Norfolk, and began life as a travelling pedlar. He became a sailor and merchant. His biographer, Reginald, a Durham monk who used to come and say Mass for him, attracted by the deep asceticism of his life as a hermit, says that by now "he may have done things which lay heavy on his conscience . . . it was getting time to think about his soul." Returning from a pilgrimage to Jerusalem, however, he next became steward to a Norman baron, whom, fairly unsurprisingly, he left when he found himself involved with the other servants in stealing from and bullying the local peasants. Then he went on a pilgrimage to Rome, somehow more surprisingly with his mother, before becoming a hermit near the shrine of St Cuthbert (*see March 20*) whom he greatly venerated. His austerities, which included a hair shirt, and sitting half the night in the river Wear, and keeping his food till it decayed before eating it, are, says Butler, "rather to be admired than imitated."

1727: [To the Countess of Mar] . . . My cure for lowness in spirits is not drinking nasty water, but galloping all day, and a moderate glass of champagne at night in good company; and I believe this regimen, closely followed, is one of the most wholesome that can be prescribed, and may save one a world of filthy doses, and more filthy doctor's fees at the year's end. . . .

Lady Mary Wortley Montagu (1689–1762)

May 22

S⊤ JULIA (5th century) was a Christian girl of Carthage who was sold as a slave to a Syrian merchant called Eusebius after Genseric the Vandal had taken the city. Taking her with him on a voyage he went ashore for a pagan festival at Corsica, where the governor, Felix, was simultaneously angry at her refusal to take part and so anxious to buy her that he offered Eusebius four female slaves in exchange. Eusebius refused, but

103

the governor captured her while he was drunk. Persisting in her refusal, she was "beaten on the mouth and then crucified."

1884: I was dreadfully puzzled when we got to Edinburgh. It is always so if one has a clear idea of a place one has not seen. I knew exactly what the different places were like, the Carlton (sic) Hill, Arthur's Seat, the Castle, but I had fitted them together all wrong. But I am anything but disappointed with the real form. . . .

Beatrix Potter (1866–1943)

May 23

ST DESIDERIUS OF VIENNE (d. about 608), otherwise Didier, was one of the bishops to whom St Gregory wrote commending St Augustine to them on his way to England. He fell foul of Queen Brunhilda (otherwise Brunehaut), the grandmother of King Theodoric (otherwise Thierry), who had "like the rest of the race of Clovis, degenerated from the old Teutonic virtues and plunged headlong into Roman licence. In vain his subjects had attempted to wean him from his countless mistresses by a marriage with the daughter of the Visigothic king. Neglected, mortified, persecuted by the arts of Brunehaut, the unhappy princess returned home." When St Desiderius upbraided him for this, "Brunehaut had no mind to see the king wakened from his lethargy and take the reins of government from her hands" and she got three assassins to waylay and murder him.

1845: I was at a party of modern wits last night that made me creep into myself, and wish myself talking away to any Suffolk old woman in her cottage, while the trees murmured without. The wickedness of London appals me; and yet I am no paragon.

Edward Fitzgerald (1809–1883)

May 24

S<small>T</small> V<small>INCENT</small> <small>OF</small> L<small>ERINS</small> (d. 450), who after a military career
retired to the island south of Antibes, is the putative author
of the *Commonitorium*, the kind of definitive statement of Christian doctrine that was periodically necessary as one or other
aspect of it was developed to the point of deviation from the *via
media* that becomes heresy. In this case it was the central nature-
and-grace controversy. The Pelagian position that man's good
works alone can merit salvation had been so effectively coun-
tered by St Augustine's soaring vision of the nothingness of
man, the greatess of God, and the infinite help of grace, that
there was some danger of that devaluing of nature and free
choice which has its logical end in Calvinistic predestination.
The Semi-Pelagians claimed that they had found the *via media* in
the doctrine that grace was dependent on a kind of built-in will
in man to obtain salvation, "whereas the Catholic doctrine is
that the will must receive its first incentive from God. It is God
who stimulates the will, and then leaves man by an act of free
will to resist or concur with grace." The *via media* is not so easy
as it looks, or sounds. Left is easy, right is easy; centre is difficult.
The combination of freedom with determination, of being able
to choose as well as or after being chosen, is a divinely simple
but humanly intensely complicated idea; anyone who articulates
it correctly has surely earned canonisation.

1875: This afternoon I walked over to Lanhill. As I
came down from the hill into the valley across the
golden meadows and along the flower-scented hedges a
great wave of emotion and happiness stirred and rose up
within me. I know not why I was so happy, nor what I was
expecting, but I was in a delirium of joy, it was one of the
supreme few moments of existence, a deep delicious
draught from the strong sweet cup of life. It came unsought,
unbidden, at the meadow stile, it was one of the flowers of
happiness scattered for us and found unexpectedly by the
wayside of life. It came silently, suddenly, and it went as it
came, but it left a long lingering glow and glory behind it
as it faded slowly like a gorgeous sunset, and I shall ever
remember the place and the time in which such great
happiness fell upon me.

Francis Kilvert (1840–1879)

May 25

GREGORY VII (1025–1085) was the stern pope who received the legendary homage of the emperor, Henry IV at Canossa in 1077, after keeping him waiting in the snow for three days. This was the most famous, but by no means culminating point in the career of the man who, starting as the monk Hildebrand, fought sternly all his life for two basic objectives; removal of the right of princes and kings to elect bishops and abbots, and celibacy of the clergy. Had the general improvement in the spiritual tone of the church, which the latter was meant to help promote, taken place before he was (by popular acclaim) elected pope, the former might not have been quite so well entrenched. It was because of such scandals as the nepotistic appointment of a twelve-year-old boy, to be consecrated as Benedict IX, his subsequent attempt to marry (his first cousin), his subsequent sale of the papacy to one John Gratian ("Gregory VI"), the instant appearance of the rival Sylvester III, and his own reappearance, so that there were *three* popes, that led the earlier emperor, Henry III, to appoint rather better men, and for his right to do so to be half accepted even by the Romans. Gregory died in exile at Salerno.

1829: We shall certainly never become reconciled to either the first or last movements of this, Beethoven's Seventh Symphony both being full of asperities and almost unbearably whimsical.

Harmonicon, editor William Ayrton

May 26

NOTHING IS known of ST AUGUSTINE (d. 605) before his historic mission with his forty monks to England in 596 save that he was prior of the monastery of St Andrew, on the Coelian Hill, of which the pope who sent him, St Gregory, had been abbot. His primary mission was of course to the Kentish Saxons, in which he was, as everyone knows, highly successful, converting thousands, from King Ethelbert downwards. He went to Arles to be consecrated archbishop, with power to appoint twelve bishops in southern England, and with primacy over the see of York. He had less success in "converting" the British Christians who had been driven into the west and north by the Saxon and other invaders. In the old Catholic Missal his feast is on May 28.

1720: Mr John Seyliard & Mr ffra̅ Howlet came past my house wth a gunn & shot at the Rooks & the paper fell upon the mault house & began to smoke & blaze, but by God's great mercy & providence my sonns & 2 or 3 other boyes had got a ladder on that side of the house goeing to get a Rook's nest, & so rann up & pulled down the fire, in all likelyhood it would have done a mischief before a ladder could have been fetched. For this & all other thy great mercyes my soul doth magnify thee O Lord. (*See also June 4*)
William Coe of Mildenhall (1680–1729)

May 27

ANOTHER GREAT English saint. THE VENERABLE BEDE (672–734), who was educated at Wearmouth abbey and spent the whole of his adult life in the monastery at Jarrow, is regarded as "the father of English history." He wrote several other works, such as a treatise on metre, a natural history, and a "universal chronology of the Christian era" based on astronomical studies; but it is his *Ecclesiastical History,* embarked on at the request of Albinus, abbot at Canterbury, which is his great glory. The French critic Emile Legouis wrote, "his direct narration of facts, and the marvels of an artless faith in which he clothes them, are far more eloquent than all the effusions and paraphrases of the poets . . . one scene has been quoted over and over again. It occurs in the account of the conversion of Northumbria in 633 . . . one noble spoke as follows . . . 'so, O king, does the life of man on earth seem to me, in comparison with the time which is unknown to us, as though a sparrow flew swiftly through the hall, coming in by one door and going out by the other, and you, the while, sat at meat with your captains and liegemen, in wintry weather, with a fire burning in your midst and heating the room, the storm raging out of doors and driving snow and rain before it. For the time for which he is within, the bird is sheltered from the storm, but after this short while of calm he flies out again into the cold and is seen no more.' (Thus the life of man is

107

visible for a moment, but we know not what comes before it or follows after it. If, then, this new doctrine brings something more of certainty, it deserves to be followed." Nowhere else is there anything at once so exact and so ample. The image is as great as it is intimate, precise although mysterious. Shakespeare never produced one which was more striking or which better conveyed the feeling of life's strangeness. Nothing equal to it is to be found in the whole of Anglo-Saxon poetry.")

1857: . . . I called on Mrs Byles—She put into my hands a tale by Anthony Trollope, which I have since read. *The Warden* A singular history. It is a sort of controversial tale with no object clearly made out. It is founded on Whiston's attack of the Deans and Chapters. . . . There is a sharp satirical description of *The Times* newspaper, called *Jupiter*, and of *The Times* office, called *Olympus*. It is a singular book—a sort of "wild-goose" flight—

Henry Crabb Robinson (1775–1867)

May 28

ST THEODOULOS THE STYLITE (d. about 410) was a prefect at Constantinople who was seized with a desire to become a hermit. His wife of two years, Procula, asked if he really meant to divorce her, to which he suggested that they should live separately, in poor clothes, on a mean diet, in the same house. Shedding her finery she went weeping to her room, where she was found dead the next morning. Theodoulos then went and lived on top of a pillar. After forty-eight years he thought he must be near a heavenly crown when God appeared to him in a dream and said "Cornelius the Clown." Descending from his pillar, he found after much search Cornelius "capering with double pipes in his mouth, and a hideous mask, before a laughing crowd." St Theodulos asked him what he had done to inherit eternal life, saying ". . . I have given up houses and land and a dear wife, I have spent forty-eight years on a pillar, exposed to the glaring sun by day, and to the numbing frost by night."

"I have done nothing," answered the clown humbly, "I cannot compare with thee."

"But thou hast done something," said Theodoulos roughly,

108

shaking him; "I know thou wilt be accounted great in heaven, tell me what hast thou done?" Then the clown reddening said, "There is one little thing I did but it is not worth mentioning. Some time ago there was a virtuous young wife in this town who had been married only two years, when her husband fell into the debtor's prison. She, poor thing, was constrained to beg for food and money to keep him and herself alive . . . and I was grieved, for I had piped and danced in the court of her house for a few coppers not many months before. Then I asked her how much her husband owed, and she said 'four hundred pieces of silver.' I ran home, and turned out my money box, and found therein two hundred and thirty pieces. So I took a pair of gold bracelets and some brooches which had belonged to my dear dead wife, and they were worth seventy pieces of silver. But that was not enough. So then I got together some of my silk theatrical dresses, and I rolled them all up in a piece of linen, and I took it to the woman, and I said to her, 'There, take all, and release your husband from jail.' Then I ran away. And this, I believe is the only good thing I have ever done."

Theodoulos saw how this man had sacrificed himself for a strange woman, bound to him by no tie, whereas he had cast away his own wife, and had broken her heart, seeking only his own self.

Then the old hermit smote his breast, and lifted his hands to heaven and blessed the poor clown, and thanked God, and went back to his pillar and re-ascended it, and there, not many years after, he died.

1802: There is yet one primrose in the orchard. The stitchwort is fading. The wild columbines are coming into beauty. The vetches are in abundance, Blossoming and seeding. That pretty little waxy-looking Dial-like yellow flower, the speedwell, and some others whose names I do not yet know. The wild columbines are coming into beauty—some of the gowans fading. In the garden we have lilies and many other flowers. The scarlet Beans are up in crowds. It is now between 8 and nine o'clock. It has rained sweetly for two hours and a half—the air is very mild.

Dorothy Wordsworth (1771–1855)

May 29

ST MARY MAGDALEN DEI PAZZI (1566–1607) was a mystic and contemplative. Daughter of a famous Florentine family (its name will recall to most people who have seen Florence the austerely elegant Pazzi Chapel by the cloisters of Santa Croce) and christened Catherine, she took the name of Mary Magdalen as a Carmelite nun. In 1585 she entered a five-year period of terrible dryness, her mind "troubled with the most hideous images of hellish monsters, and seemed abandoned like Job to the power of hell; and her soul was plunged into a state of darkness in which she was able to see nothing but horror in herself and in all things about her." It suddenly ended in 1590 when the *Te Deum* was being intoned on Whitsunday, and she fell into a rapture; "now winter is passed with me; assist me to thank and glorify my good Creator."

1803: West knows Fulton who has invented the machine for diving and blowing up ships . . . the Boat can be kept under water 8 Hours at a time, & when raised to procure fresh air, it is only necessary to allow Her to rise so High as that the valves which are to receive the air may be above water; the vessel may then again be sunk to any depth, 40 fathom or more: he has also a means of obtaining light. This most dangerous & dreadful contrivance is said to be fully understood only by Fulton. . . .

Joseph Farington (1747–1821)

May 30

ST FERDINAND (1199–1252) was the son of Berengaria and Alfonso IX of Castile, who were later divorced on grounds of consanguinity. When, through a blood relationship she became queen of Castile after a fatal accident to its child king, she gave the sovereignty to Ferdinand, who had to fight for it during many years against his father. He eventually not only united the kingdoms of Castile and Leon but captured Cordova, Jaen and Seville and liberated most of Andalusia from the Moors. He founded the great university of Salamanca and was respon-

110

sible for the codification of Roman and Gothic laws called the *Forum Judicum*. He was canonised in 1671.

1891: Mrs James arrived and, as usual, in the evening took the entire management of everything. Finding that she and Carrie were making some preparations for table-turning, I thought it time really to put my foot down. I have always had the greatest contempt for such nonsense, and put an end to it years ago when Carrie, at our old house, used to have seances every night with poor Mrs Fussters (who is now dead). If I could see any use in it, I would not care. As I stopped it in the days gone by I am determined to do so now.

I said: "I am very sorry, Mrs James, but I totally disapprove of it, apart from the fact that I receive my old friends on this evening." Mrs James said: "Do you mean to say you haven't read *There is No Birth?*" I said: "No, and I have no intention of doing so." Mrs James seemed surprised and said: "All the world is going mad over the book." I responded rather cleverly: "Let it. There will be one sane man in it, at all events."

George and Weedon Grossmith, The Diary of a Nobody

May 31

ST PETRONILLA is one of the few saints of the first century not recorded as a martyr. The bearer of this mellifluous name, a diminutive of Peter, was said to have been his daughter (others say merely "spiritual daughter"). It was near her tomb in St Peter's that the daughter of Pepin le Bref was baptised, and she was always specially honoured by the kings of France.

1782: . . . I went by myself and gave a peep into St Pauls Church this aft: To a Barber this Afternoon for shaving &c. gave 0.1.0 For 2 Places in the Salisbury Coach pd 2.2.0. For 1 outside Place Do. pd 0.10.6. Paid and gave at the Bell Savage for all of abt. 1.15.0. They were very civil People at the Bell Savage Inn by name Barton and a very good House it is. About 10 o'clock at Night we set of in the Salisbury Coach from the same Inn for Salisbury, and the Coach guarded. I was bit terribly by the Buggs last Night, but did not wake me.

James Woodforde (1740–1803)

JUNE

June 1

Sᴛ Aɴɢᴇʟᴀ ᴏꜰ Bʀᴇꜱᴄɪᴀ, born at Desenzano, on the shores of Lake Garda in 1474. "The disorders of society," she said, "are caused by those in families; there are few Christian mothers, because the education of young girls is neglected." After a vision she founded a teaching order (which at first had no community life, habit, or vows), the first for women: The Ursuline nuns.

1941: The big news this morning is clothes rationing. Oliver Lyttelton is only going to allow us 66 coupons per annum. A suit takes 26. Luckily I have 40 or more. Socks will be the shortage.

"Chips" Channon (1897–1958)

June 2

Sᴛ Nɪᴄᴇᴘʜᴏʀᴜꜱ (d. 828) lived a couple of centuries before the final separation of the Orthodox church from the Catholic (in 1054). The early Christian church used only *symbols*, such as the fish, the dove, the palm-branch. The 6th Council of Constantinople (692) allowed the representation of Christ as a man, and the 2nd Council of Nicaea allowed sacred images in the churches, making a distinction between veneration and worship. Several eastern emperors, however, were strict Iconoclasts or image-breakers, whereas Rome always leaned towards the use of the representational in religious art, if only for instructional purposes. St Nicephorus was an *eastern* follower of the representational line, and was deposed from the see of Constantinople for these views.

1865: Walked about by moonlight in the evening. Wondered what woman, if any, I should be thinking about in five years" time.

Thomas Hardy (1840–1928)

June 3

S⊤ KEVIN (or Coemgen), "the Fair-begotten," *pulchrum genitum*, (d. 618, said to have been born in 498 and therefore lived to 120) founded the famous monastery of Glendalough in Wicklow. He was dissuaded from going on a long pilgrimage in old age, being wise enough to take the advice of a hermit who said "birds do not hatch eggs whilst on the wing." There is an accretion of legends to the story of his life, as with all Irish saints of the period. One of them is consolingly unsaintlike and human. To a raven which stole his milk he said, "bad luck to thee! When I am dead there will be a famous wake, but no scraps for thee and thy clan. Whilst all the mourners are making merry below thou wilt be croaking round the mountain supperless."

1802: Yesterday morning William walked as far as the Swan with Aggy Fisher. She was going to attend upon Goan's dying Infant. She said "There are many heavier crosses than the death of an Infant," and went on, "There was a woman in this vale who buried 4 grown-up children in one year, and I have heard her say when many years were gone by that she had more pleasure in thinking of those 4 than her living Children, for as Children get up and have families of their own their duty to their parents *'wears out and weakens'*."

Dorothy Wordsworth (1771–1855)

June 4

S⊤ PETROC (6th century) is the saint who gave his name to Padstow in Cornwall. He is another magnet for legends, such as that when he was in India (!) he was taken in a shining bowl to an island where he lived for seven years on one fish that always grew whole again, then an angel told him to go back, and there was a wolf waiting to greet him and his bowl and guide him.

1699: I had like to have swallowed a large spider in my beer & what effect it would have had vpon me God onely knows *(see also June 23).*

William Coe of Mildenhall *(1680–1729)*

June 5

I T SEEMS extraordinary that the main apostle of Germany should have been an Englishman from Crediton, in Devon. But that is where ST BONIFACE (about 680–755) came from. His first mission, to Friesland, was abortive, as it was in the throes of war. But returning in 719, with a mission from Gregory II, he began his great work in Bavaria, Thuringia, Hesse and Saxony. He became bishop of Mainz in 745, then founded the great monastery of Fulda in 746, and brought many monks and nuns over from England to consolidate his work. Yet he always felt an urge to work on the outer fringe of the now ever-growing Christendom, and it was in the still obstinately pagan Friesland that he met a martyr's death.

1791: Sunday .... I read Prayers, Preached, and gave notice of Sacrament on Sunday next being Whitsunday, this morning at Weston Church. ... We had Green Peas for supper this Evening being the first pulled this Season by us. Also cut the first Cucumber and gathered the first Strawberries.

James Woodforde, *(1740–1803)*

June 6

ST NORBERT (c. 1080–1134) from a noble Rhineland family, until his mid-thirties lived a courtly and luxurious life, although he was in minor orders. Then he had an experience similar to St Paul's; in this case, lightning striking the ground immediately in front of him. He became an idealistic preacher, which did not please his fellow canons at Xanten. Pope Calixtus II then asked him to reform the abbey at Laon (where one sees today that majestic cathedral crowning the hill) but here again this did not please the local canons. Having a vision of white-robed men carrying tapers, in a pleasant valley of Prémontré, he founded the Premonstratensian Canons, who took the rule of St Augustine and were a kind of halfway house between the monks of that and the friars of the following century.

1817: . . . I have read two pages of "Lalla Rookh" or whatever it is called. Merciful Heaven! I dare read no more, that I may be able to answer at once to any question. "I have but just looked at the work. . . . .

Samuel Taylor Coleridge (1772–1834)

June 7

ST ROBERT OF NEWMINSTER (d. 1159) was first of all a priest in York. Then he took the Benedictine habit there. Then, finding the life not strict enough, he was one of the twelve men from there, led by the prior Richard, who went to the wild Skelldale "thick set with thorns, fit rather to be the lair of wild beasts than the home of human beings." Their first winter was spent sheltering under an elm. They obtained permission to embrace the Cistercian rule; and this was the origin of what today is the most beautiful and moving monastic ruin in Britain—Fountains Abbey.

1665: This day, much against my will, I did in Drury Lane see two or three houses marked with a red cross upon the doors, and "Lord have mercy upon us" writ there—which was a sad sight to me, being the first of that kind that to my remembrance I ever saw. It put me to an ill conception of myself and my smell, so that I was forced to buy some roll-tobacco to smell and chaw—which took away the apprehension.

Samuel Pepys (1633–1703)

June 8

Sᴛ Mᴇᴅᴀʀᴅ (d. 545) became bishop of Noyon, and later of Tournai simultaneously; an uncanonical practice, but no one else suitable could be found. He instituted the festival of the "Rosière" at Salency, in which the *seigneur* had the right to nominate the most virtuous of three girls presented to him. The girl was given a crown of roses and a purse. "In the chapel of St Medard," says Baring-Gould, "is a board on which are inscribed the names of all the Rosères; a few of the names have been effaced, because they have misconducted themselves since they received the crown of St Medard."

1775: .... the weather much changed rain and thunder in the Vallys although a clear day upon the Mount; this makes a most singular effect to see the storm raging under your feet and the thunder roaring but it soon cleared up. Saw several trees tore with the lightning, and the echo of the Rocks makes the noise awfull . . .

Thomas Blaikie (1750–1838)

June 9

Sᴛ Cᴏʟᴜᴍʙᴀ, the Apostle of the Picts and the founder of the famous Christian centre of Iona (about 521–597) was of royal birth in Ireland, and to the end of his life had enormous nostalgia for it, particularly for Derry. A poet, and a learned man, main repository of culture, as monks were in those days, he was said to have made 300 copies of the Gospel and Psalter. This was the passion, in fact, which led to his mission. Still young and fiery, he is said to have objected to a judgment given against him by King Diarmid that he could not keep a copy he had made of another monk's book. He was on the other side in a subsequent civil war, and had laid on him the duty of converting as many heathen as there had been Christians killed in the battles. He left Ireland, never to return. It was he who consecrated the Scottish king Aidan (it is said on what later became the Stone of Scone). Over the years the passionate and revenge-seeking young man mellowed into the gentle old saint.

118

1826: [To Dibdin] I never knew an enemy to puns who was not an ill-natured man. Your fair critic in the coach reminds me of a Scotchman who assured me that he did not see much in Shakespeare. I replied, I daresay *not.* He felt the equivoke, look'd awkward and reddish, but soon return'd to the attack by saying that he thought Burns was as good as Shakespeare: I said that I had no doubt he was— to a *Scotchman.* . . .

Charles Lamb (1775–1834)

June 10

ONE OF Scotland's most famous saints was English. ST MAR-GARET (d. 1093) was niece of Edward the Confessor and sister of Edgar Atheling, whom many regarded as rightful heir to the English throne. Fleeing to Scotland from the Normans, they were hospitably entertained by King Malcolm III, who fell in love with and married her. She became famous both for her personal sanctity, rising at midnight for Matins, and her charity, never sitting down to table "without having first fed nine little orphans and twenty-four poor people." She died a few days after her husband had been treacherously killed by the Normans at Alnwick. In Scotland her feast is on November 16 (*q.v.*)

1813: [To John Constable] Do my dear Son exert yourself, or you must pine away your prime,—and fret away the aged remnant of your Parents' lives. Your heart is so kind and good—& your mind is well furnished, so that you have great advantages if you would but improve them. You need never want for friends, if you will but be a friend to yourself. Your Mother has a peculiar claim to tell you the truth & you would treat her with unkindness, not to believe her; and know her motive to be good.

Would you but make yourself independent, how much would you exalt my heartfelt anxieties on your account. Your valuable Uncle D. P. W. is kind and good but the best friend will tire of giving and lending, without they see great industry and a desire to gain—which must be in such times and such a world as this, but we are fast travelling to another and a better—if we live & act uprightly.

Ann Constable (1748–1815)

119

June 11

S<small>T</small> B<small>ARNABAS</small>, by birth a Cypriot Jew, had been a fellow student, with Saul, of Gamaliel, the rabbi who later dissuaded the Sanhedrin from killing St Peter and the other Apostles, and it was he who brought the newly converted Saul to the Christians at Jerusalem. It was while Barnabas, whose name means "son of consolation and exhortation", was at Antioch that the term "Christian" was first used. After the big dispute over circumcision, SS. Paul and Barnabas were "the Apostles of uncircumcision;" this new religion was not just for Jewish converts, but for the world. He undertook several missionary journeys with St Paul. St Barnabas made many converts in Tarsus, in Syria, but was martyred, by stoning, at Salamis in his native Cyprus.

1799: Dr Gardiner was married yesterday to Mrs Percy and her three daughters.

Jane Austen (1775–1817)

June 12

S<small>T</small> E<small>SKIL</small> (d. about 1080) was an Englishman who went to assist St Sigfried of York in the conversion of Sweden. At a big festival in honour of Thor it was he who brought down a great storm of thunder and hail. This did not have the same effect as the rain brought down by Elijah in somewhat similar circumstances, for the pagans killed him on the spot.

1951: Sir: If at breakfast a kipper is spread out on your plate with its tail on the right, the backbone is found sometimes on one side, sometimes on the other. Does this mean that—for want of a better term—some kippers are left-handed?

Letter to *The Times* from John Christie

June 13

Sᴛ Aɴᴛʜoɴʏ ᴏғ Pᴀᴅᴜᴀ (1195–1231) had a strong mind in a frail body. Ill health having thwarted his desire to go to Morocco and convert the Moors, if necessary dying in the attempt, he returned to humble status in a Franciscan friary at San Paolo, near Bologna. There he was discovered, almost by accident, to have a gift for the kind of preaching that prompted people to secure places in the church by sitting there all night before he was due to speak. He is the St Anthony to whom people pray for the recovery of lost things.

> 1770: . . . I used to imagine that a French audience durst not hiss to the degree I found they did upon this occasion. Indeed quite as much, mixt with horse laughs, as ever I heard at Drury Lane, or Covent Garden. In short it was condemned in all the English forms, except breaking the benches and the actors heads; and the incessant sound of *hish* instead of *hiss*
>
> Charles Burney (1726–1814)

June 14

Sᴛ Bᴀsɪʟ (about 331–379) is one of the four Doctors of the Eastern church. Called from the solitude he loved (and which he had shared with the friend of his youth St Gregory Nazianzen, May 9) to be bishop of Caesarea, he led a life of anxious controversy particularly difficult for the kind of man who said "quiet is the first step to sanctification." He felt deeply the dissension beginning to arise between east and west. Many of his own clergy withdrew their support, and in 377 he wrote sadly "I seem, for my sins, to be unsuccessful in everything." But when he died "the very Pagans and Jews wept with the Christians, lamenting the death of the common father of all, and the great doctor of the world. Those that knew him, took a pleasure in recounting his minutest actions, and every expression they had heard from his mouth."

121

1896: Dear Mrs Compton [organising a bazaar, she had asked famous people to name their favourite flower and sign the card to be attached to it], I only know the names of 2 or 3 flowers: so I have to take one of them. I had decided after a sleepless night on the *white carnation* and if it will relieve your pressure (which I deeply commiserate) to know so slight a thing I rejoice to be able to help you. I feel, blissfully, far from bazaars. I enclose signed the luggage-tags—with as much curiosity for your dénouement (with them) as we could have wished all the plays I haven't written to excite. Yours with all good wishes.

Henry James (1843–1916)

June 15

ST BERNARD OF MENTHON (923–1008), on the lake of Annecy, was known as the Apostle of the Alps (over which he fled from a marriage which would have united his to another noble house, that of Miolans). He became archdeacon of Aosta, but most of his work was done among the still pagan mountains. It is after him that the famous hospices, and the passes themselves, of the Great and Little St Bernard are named.

1801: . . . Now what I object to in Scotch philosophers in general is that they reason upon man as they would reason upon x; they pursue truth, without caring if it be useful truth. They are more fond of disputing on mind and matter than on anything which can have a reference to the real world inhabited by real men, women and children; a philosophy which descends to the present state of things is debased in their estimation: in short a Scotchman is apt to be a practical rogue upon sale, or a visionary philosopher.

Sydney Smith (1771–1845)

June 16

ST BENNO (d. 1106) was abbot of Hildesheim and later bishop of Meissen. Several nice stories. One is that a fish which had swallowed the keys of his minster during a time of trouble was caught lower down the Elbe when the trouble had ended. The other relates how the croaking of some frogs disturbed his evening prayer, but when he got to the verse "O ye whales and all that move in the waters, bless ye the Lord" he was full of shame, and thinking that the praises of the poor frogs might be as acceptable as his own he returned to the marsh and said "O frogs, sing on to the Lord your song of thanksgiving."

1873: I looked at the pigeons down in the kitchen yard and so on. They looked like little gay jugs by shape when they walk, strutting and jod-jodding with their heads. The two young ones are all white and the pins of the folded wings, quill pleated over quill, are like crisp and shapely cuttle-shells found on the shore. The others are dull thunder-colour or black-grape-colour except in the white pieings, the quills and tail, and in the shot of the neck. I saw one up on the eaves of the roof: as it moved its head a crush of satin green came and went, a wet or soft flaming of the light.

Sometimes I hear the cuckoo with wonderful clear and plump and fluty notes: it is when the hollow of a rising ground conceives them and palms them and throws them out, like blowing into a big humming ewer.

Gerard Manley Hopkins (1844–1889)

June 17

FOR A SAINT so popular in medieval England, and with so many churches named after him, from London (four, one of them near Liverpool Street), Colchester, Culpho and North Cove in Suffolk, not to mention the town of Boston ("Botolph's stone"), ST BOTOLPH (d. 655) is not very well documented. He is said to have sought outlandish and solitary places and to have founded a monastery at "Ikanhoe," thought to be Boston but, after recent discoveries, the more obvious-sounding Iken, near Aldeburgh.

1915: [Korytin] To our left, the artillery park of our division was stationed; the men were busy over their fires; the whinnying of the tired, hungry horses resounded plaintively through the glades. Refugees were still streaming down the road. One old man hobbled by leaning on a stick, driving three heifers before him; a number of *telezhki* (small truck-carts), drawn by small puny-looking horses, or "cats" as the soldiers called them, rumbled along; they were packed tightly with boxes, barrels and household furniture; the heads of the children and very old men and women were often to be seen protruding from the midst of these loads. Women and children walked by in large parties, all carrying bundles of varying dimensions. One woman, with a sleeping infant in her arms, was bowed almost double by a large wicker-basket containing poultry, which was strapped on her back.

Florence Farmborough (1897–1958)

June 18

S⊤ Ephraim (about 306–373), a deacon, who lived mostly at Edessa in Mesopotomia, wrote many treatises (and is in fact a Doctor of the Church) but is chiefly famous as the first great writer of hymns. They were rather different from what we now understand by "hymns," being lyrico-epic-dramatic elaborations of Biblical and hagiographical stories; an introductory strophe (*koukoulion*) followed by "a great row of generally long strophes of identical rhythm (*oikos*)," showing "subtlety and considerable pathos" and only surpassed by "the grandiose closing strain" (says Paul Lang in *Music in Western Civilisation*). They were fundamentally oriental, "a kind of lyrical preaching;" but in so far as they were in strophic form they *were* (unless you count the Psalms) the first hymns.

1935: At lunch Oliver Stanley told Honor that Lord Halifax had recently heard the word "Pansy" and had to send for one of his Secretaries to ask the meaning of the word.

"Chips" Channon (1897–1958)

June 19

Ss GERVASE AND PROTASE (2nd century) are regarded as the protomartyrs of Milan. When St Ambrose was archbishop there it was he who discovered their relics after a dream. The story of their martyrdom (which involves a time-lapse not covered with such documentary certainty as that of many early martyrs, though their names are in the Litany of Saints) is that they were twin brothers who suffered under a Roman general called Astasius. Gervase was scourged to death, and Protase was beheaded.

1815: The first thing I did, of course, was to put out my hand and congratulate [the Duke of Wellington] upon his victory. He made a variety of observations in his short, natural, blunt way, but with the greatest gravity all the time, and without the least approach to anything like triumph or joy.—"It has been a damned serious business," he said. "Blucher and I have lost 30,000 men. It has been a damned nice thing—the nearest run thing you ever saw in your life . . ."

Thomas Creevey (1768–1838)

June 20

St ADALBERT OF MAGDEBURG (d. 981) was a monk from Trier who was among those sent as missionaries by the emperor Otto into Russia. This was at the request of St Olga of Kiev; but some of them were killed by her heathen son Sviatoslav. St Adalbert returned safely, however, and after doing much to encourage learning among the monks of his monastery at Weissenberg he became, in 968, the first archbishop of Magdeburg.

1887: [During preparations for Queen Victoria's Golden Jubilee] . . . we were very busy arranging our fairy lights, on each of the nine front window sills, seven in each length, five white above and three blue at the top. The

Square are mostly hanging bottles and paper lanterns, the latter very pretty but most unsafe. . . .

As to illuminations, a house without, is remarkable. Stucco houses don't lend themselves to decoration, the effect is more curious than beautiful. . .

Beatrix Potter (1866–1943)

June 21

S⊤ Eusebius (d. 380) was bishop of Samosata (the modern Samsat, in eastern Turkey), and his life was lived in the context of the struggle with the Arians—one of whom comes out with credit for a change. Having refused to depose St Meletius from the see of Antioch at the request of the Arian-sympathizing Constantius, he was himself deposed under the aggressively Arian emperor Valens; but his people ostracized his Arian successor, and emptied the public bath after he had been in it, as impure, whereupon, being a gentle soul, he resigned. Reinstated after the death of Valens and the end of the persecution, Eusebius was killed by a tile thrown from the roof by an Arian woman.

1845: I confided to you *as a secret and in my trust in you*—that I had indeed . . . after a struggle . . . seen Mr Browning—but then, writing about poetry and criticism, in a correspondence we had, had made us personal friends, in a manner, before he came—and I honour his genius and could not refuse a request he thought it worth while to press so kindly on me . . . when the circumstance of his *living seven miles out of London* made him exceptional, in itself,—and when he promised, in all faith, that the fact of his having seen me should never escape his lips.

Elizabeth Barrett (1806–1861)

June 22

ST ALBAN (d. about 287) is venerated as the first British martyr. During the persecution by Diocletian he sheltered a priest and when the soldiers came he put on the priest's cloak and took his place. Recognized by the governor as the wrong man, he affirmed his faith, for which he was first scourged and then beheaded. The great church which bears his name today was founded by Offa, king of the Mercians.

1824: ... Had a letter from Paris. Mr Arrowsmith informed me of the safe arrival of the pictures & how much they were admired. The letter shall be sent to you [his wife Maria]—he talks of coming again in the end of this month. I shall be ready for him. His letter is quite flattering, but I do not hope to go to Paris as long as I live.
John Constable (1776–1837)

June 23

ST ETHELDREDA or Audrey (about 630–679), born at Exning in Suffolk, was twice married; once to Tonbrecht, who on his death three years after had settled on her the isle of Ely, and subsequently to King Egfrid of Northumbria. This marriage certainly, and probably the first one, was not consummated. She established a double monastery at Ely, presiding over the convent herself and leading a life of great austerity. Many miracles were attributed to her, and the place became a great shrine.

1713: I was riding with Mr John ffenn of Wisbech in Cambridg̃ street going to Hasleingfield & Mr ffenn's horse stood still at something & jostled against mine (wch was the horse I call Delph) & thrust him against a low piece of dirt wall & he fell over it with me upon his back. I fell ag^t a window wth my elbow & broke as much glass as I pd 6d for, but I thank Almighty God who dayly preserves us that I gott not ye least harm, it was God's great mercy he did not fall upon my legg or Chrush me ag^t the house side. For this

& all other thy great mercyes towards me & mine my soul doth magnify thee O Lord (*see also July 31*).

William Coe of Mildenhall (1680–1729)

June 24

S<small>T</small> J<small>OHN THE</small> B<small>APTIST</small> lived in the desert on locusts and honey, he saw the Holy Ghost and heard the voice of God the Father when he baptised Jesus, he was beheaded for preaching against the corruption of the world, as typified by Herod's court. His words inspired the opening music of the *Messiah*; "every valley shall be exalted" . . . . and the vespers hymn for this feast gave us the very names of the notes of the scale. *Ut* queant laxis *re*sonare fibris/*Mi*ra gestorum *fa*muli tuorum/*Sol*ve polluti *la*bii reatum/Sancte Johannes ("that your servants may sing full-throatedly the marvels of your works, purify the guilt of their polluted lips, blessed John"). The italicized syllables, it was noticed, are a successive note higher in the melody; ut, re, mi, fa, sol, la . . . . it was the Italians who substituted *doh* for *ut*.

1876: Midsummer Day, and the cuckoo singing from Gipsy Hill. Walked to sweet green Dulwich and visited the picture gallery. Rembrandt's immortal servant girl still leaned on her round white arms a-smiling from the window as she leaned and smiled for three hundred years since that summer's day when her master drew her portrait and made her immortal, imperishable and ever young. St Sebastian still raised his eyes to heaven with the sublime pathetic look of tender submission and gentle resignation. The strange solitary white angel still hovered down through the gloom in Jacob's Dream. The Oriental-looking Spanish flower girl still offered her flowers for sale. The Spanish boys still laughed audibly and went on with their game, and Albert Cuyp's cows grouped on a knoll at sunset stood or lay about in the evening glow chewing the cud and looking placidly over the wide level pastures of Holland.

Francis Kilvert (1840–1879)

June 25

ST PROSPER OF AQUITAINE (d. 455) was a lay theologian who became deeply involved in the controversy about will and grace, in which the towering figure was of course St Augustine. It was partly because of St Prosper's writings that Pope St Celestine wrote a letter to the bishop of Marseilles containing nine articles on grace remarkable for their middle-of-the-road temperateness, the crucial one being that "none can use free-will aright except by the help of grace through Jesus Christ." Perhaps the most encouraging thing about all this is that there were saints on both sides. St Prosper also wrote a history of the world, from the Creation to (naturally) 455.

1828: After dinner I went into Longland field, where the remainder of the hay is tything, having been summoned thither by the misconduct of the farmer, who will not suffer my men to remove my tythe cocks till his own is carried. He was very insolent because I happened to make use of the the word "fellow" when speaking of him, which word he could not comprehend.

John Skinner (1772–1839)

June 26

TODAY IS the feast of SS JOHN and PAUL, martyrs at Rome 362, St Vigilius, bishop of Trent (405), St Maxentius, abbot in Poitou (515), St Perseveranda, virgin of Poitou (6th century), St David, hermit of Thessalonica (650), St Babolen, abbot of St Maur des Fosses (7th century), St Corbican, confessor in the Low Countries (8th century), St John of the Goths (800), St Salvius, bishop and martyr at Valenciennes (8th century), St Pelagius (not the heresiarch, but a boy killed by Moors), martyr at Cordova (924), St Anthelm, bishop of Bellay (1177) and St Dionysius, archbishop of Bulgaria (1180), among others.

1804: . . . . My reception at Philadelphia was extremely flattering: it is the only place in America which can boast any literary society. I felt quite a regret in leaving

129

them; and the only place I have seen, which I had one wish
to pause in, was Philadelphia.

Thomas Moore (1779–1852)

June 27

S^T LADISLAS (1047–1095) is, or was, greatly venerated in
Hungary, a kingdom which he had to defend—first to save
his elder brother Geiza's slightly doubtful title to it (his uncle,
King Andrew, having rescinded his gift of it to Geiza in favour
of a son, Solomon, later born to him)—and in various wars
against Huns, Bohemians and Poles. On Geiza's death Ladislas
was elected king, and is said to have been a just and virtuous
ruler.

1591: Arthur wounded on his hed by his own wanton
throwing of a brik-bat upright, and not avoyding the
fall of it agayn, at Mr Harberts abowt sonn-setting. The half-
brik weighed 2½ lb.

Dr John Dee (1527–1608)

June 28

S^T IRENAEUS (d. 202) is a classic figure in the Mediterranean
seeding of Christianity. Born in Asia Minor, probably
Smyrna, a pupil of St Polycarp, he was deeply versed in Greek
philosophy and poetry, especially Homer and Plato. This enabled
him to criticize from the inside, as it were, the Gnostics, who
thought that the way to God was open only to some kind of
intellectual élite. St Irenaeus became bishop of Lyons and was a
powerful light of the Gospel to the Gauls. He was a moderating
influence in the battle about the date of Easter between the
Eastern church (sixteen days after the moon after the spring
equinox) and the western (the *Sunday* following the fourteenth
day). The tradition is that he died a martyr.

1782: A troop of Morrice dancers headed by the
buffoon; but to me, their mummery appeared tedious,

and as little enjoy'd by the performers as the spectators; the genius of the nation does not take this turn.

Lord Torrington

June 29

THE FEAST OF SS PETER and PAUL. The fisherman and the tentmaker, the first Vicar of Christ and the missionary, surely, of all time. There is a marvellous rightness about their juxtaposition; St Peter, whose weeping at the sound of the cock-crow after his denial of Jesus was so mysteriously counterbalanced by the encounter by the shore of Tiberias, the great catch, the fish cooked over the fire, the three times repeated "Simon, son of Jonas, lovest thou me?," and the command, so valiantly obeyed, "Feed my sheep," the story of his meeting Jesus at the gate of Rome, asking Him *quo vadis* ("where art thou going?"), receiving the reply "to Rome, to be crucified again," overcoming fear again, returning to be crucified upside-down, as not worthy to die the same way as his master; and St Paul, the archetypal convert, yet boasting, as everyone knows, not of his strength but his weakness.

1875: . . . . the air seemed all breathed up. But I heard a boy whistling one of Moody and Sankey's hymns down the street; which made one really feel that one was in England again! Mother, Aunt Minnie and I had breakfast together in our funny little sitting-room. Aunt Minnie, delighted with a sign of English life, seized up the toast and kissed it.

Florence Sitwell, (1858–1930)

June 30

ST RAYMOND LULL, or Lulli (1235–1315), patron saint of Majorca, was by any reckoning a remarkable man. Converted in youth from a lady-killing career evidently advanced by a considerable skill in music, he conceived a tremendous plan to convert the Moors, and learnt Arabic in North Africa, but failed to persuade one pope after another to get oriental languages seriously taught in monasteries. He also became, obviously partly through his Arab contacts, skilled in alchemy. The "enlightened doctor" died from the effects of stoning on a last mission in Tunisia.

1914: There has been another assassination, this time of the heir of the Austrian Emperor. I do not quite know how it affects the political situation.
Wilfrid Scawen Blunt (1840–1922)

JULY

July 1

ST SERF or Servan (5th century) seems to have been a saint so legendary that there may even have been two of him. One story is that he was Pictish on his mother's side, another is that he was a prince of Arabia, bishop of Jerusalem and *pope* for seven years before coming to Scotland, where he was both missionary and hermit.

1762: The journeymen carpenters, like the cabinet makers, have entered into an association not to work unless their wages are raised; and how can one complain? The poor fellows, whose all the labour is, see their masters advance their prices every day, and think it reasonable to touch their share.

Horace Walpole (1717–1797)

July 2

SS PROCESSUS and MARTINIAN were soldiers of the guard at the Mamertine prison, where they were converted to Christianity by two prisoners, Ss Peter and Paul, whom they released. It was from this escape the St Peter returned voluntarily to his martyrdom after the *quo vadis* episode (*see June 29*). A few days later Processus and Martinian were arrested, tortured when they would not venerate an image of Jupiter, and beheaded.

1784: [To Mrs Thrale on her marriage to Mr Piozzi] Madam: If I interpret your letter right, you are ignominiously married; if it is yet undone, let us once more talk togather. If you have abandoned your children and your religion, God forgive your wickedness: if you have forfeited your fame and your country, may your folly do you no further mischief. If the last act is yet to do, I who have loved you, esteemed you, reverenced you, and served you, I who long thought you the first of womankind, entreat that, before your fate is irrevocable, I may once more see you. I was, I once was, Madam, most truly yours, Sam: Johnson.
I will come down, if you will permit it (*see also July 6*).

Samuel Johnson (1709–1784)

July 3

S T Leo II (d. 683) a native of Sicily, was pope for the last two
years of his life, shortly after the Sixth Council (or the Third
of Constantinople) in 680. He ratified and strongly upheld its
condemnation of the Monothelete heresy, which asserted that
Christ had only one will—in the case of this particular heresy,
the divine one. All the early heresies could be said to take a
simplistic view of one aspect of the uniquely Christian doctrine
that a man was God but that God was not only that man.

1824: ... Mr Appleton the tub maker, Tottenham
Court Road, called to know if I had a landscape *damaged*
that I could let him have cheap—as he was fitting up his
room one pair stairs.

John Constable (1776–1837)

July 4

S T Odo (d. 958) made the transition from the paganism of his
Danish parents to the Christianity of Alfred, to one of whose
nobles he fled as a child. As a bishop he was with King Athelstan
at the battle against a combined northern host at Brunanburgh
in 937, and subsequently became archbishop of Canterbury.

1757: ... three or four gentlemen [at Durham] put me
in mind of the honest man at London, who was so gay
and unconcerned, while Dr Sherlock was preaching concerning the day of judgment. One asked, "Do you not hear
what the Doctor says?" He answered, "Yes, but I am not of
this parish!"

John Wesley (1703–1791)

July 5

Sᴛ Pʜɪʟᴏᴍᴇɴᴀ ᴏꜰ Sᴀɴ Sᴇᴠᴇʀɪɴᴏ (date uncertain) was discovered, as an incorrupt body, with an inscription saying who she was, in the place of that name in 1527. Her cultus is now also regarded as "unsatisfactory." It is a significant name; *philomena* means "being loved."

> *1820:* [To Lady Mary Bennet] You see revolutions are spreading all over the world,—and from armies.* Would Mr.—be pleased with an improvement of public liberty, which originated from the Coldstream Guards? . . .
>
> *Sydney Smith (1771–1845)*

July 6

Sᴛ Mᴀʀɪᴀ Gᴏʀᴇᴛᴛɪ (1890–1902) died resisting rape. When she was canonized in 1950 her attacker, who had undergone a change of heart eight years after the event, and was released from prison twenty-seven years after it, was present at the ceremony. He had received communion side by side with the saint's widowed mother on Christmas Day 1937.

> *1784:* [To Dr Johnson] Sir, I have this morning received from you so rough a letter in reply to one which was both tenderly and respectfully written, that I am forced to desire the conclusion of a correspondence which I can bear to continue no longer.
>
> The birth of my second husband is not meaner than that of my first; his sentiments are not meaner; his profession is not meaner, and his superiority in what he professes acknowledged by all mankind. . . . The religion to which he has always been a zealous adherent will, I hope, teach him to forgive insults he has not deserved; mine will, I hope, enable me to bear them at once with dignity and patience. . . . God bless you (*see also July 8*).
>
> *Mrs Thrale (1741–1821)*

---

* Alluding to the military revolt at Naples in 1820. Mr.—is probably Mr Bennet.

July 7

St Willibald (about 700–786) was the first known pilgrim to the Holy Land, among other things. His father, a Wessex man, sold his goods to finance this, and died with him on the way, in France. He saw Jerusalem and Bethlehem and the place of St Paul's conversion near Damascus. He smuggled balsam out of Palestine, and stopped off at Constantinople. Then he stayed at Monte Cassino. Later he was s _nt to assist his kinsman St Boniface (see June 5) in the conversion of Franconia. Ordained in 739, he was later made bishop of Eichstadt, where he died at a great age.

1971: Lunch yesterday with Eric Roll—just back from Paris and off to Vienna. He is a keen European and was interested in the latest developments on the Common Market. . . . The argument has been used that the Six must be helpful to us, otherwise Her Majesty's Government would be unable to carry the British public with them. This argument will do for Greeks or Portuguese but is not one we have to descend to so far.

Cecil King (1901–   )

July 8

St Elizabeth of Portugal (1271–1336) was christened after her great-aunt, St Elizabeth of Hungary. A natural ascetic and almsgiver, she was married at twelve to King Dionysius (Denis) of Portugal, whom she spent a great deal of her life converting, although he did quite early on rule well and found hospitals, etc. He was perhaps the kind of unfaithful husband who welcomes accusations, however unfounded, of unfaithfulness on the other side. Later St Elizabeth managed to persuade her son Alfonso to make peace with his father, and died during a mission to achieve the same thing in a war between him and Castile.

1784: [To Mrs Thrale] Dear Madam: What you have done, however I may lament it, I have no pretence to

137

resent, as it has not been injurious to me: I therefore breathe out one sigh more of tenderness, perhaps useless, but at least sincere.

I wish that God may grant you every blessing, that you may be happy in this world for its short continuance, and eternally happy in a better state; and whatever I can contribute to your happiness I am very ready to repay, for that great kindness which soothed twenty years of a life radically wretched. . . .

I am going into Derbyshire, and hope to be followed by your good wishes, for I am, with great affection. . . .

Samuel Johnson (1709–1784)

July 9

S s Thomas More (1478–1535) and John Fisher (1469–1535). A leading statesman and a leading churchman who had the courage, unto death, to know where to say no to a tyrant. St Thomas was a marvellously robust character (Aubrey's *Brief Lives* story of how he whipped the bed-covers off his sleeping daughters to show them to a suitor, who said when they quickly turned over on their backs "now I have seen both sides" would doubtless confound some people's idea of a saint). Famous author of *Utopia*, Lord Chancellor of England, Robert Bolt's *Man for All Seasons*, he died, as every one knows, for refusing the oath denying papal supremacy which would pave the way to Henry VIII's divorce from Katharine of Aragon. It is difficult to select his most heartening saying. On the scaffold he said, "I die the king's good servant—but God's first." He also said to his daughter, "we shall all meet merrily in heaven."

St John was Chancellor of Cambridge as well as bishop of Rochester, it was he who invited Erasmus to teach there (St Thomas More's "darling Erasmus"). In days when the phrase "treason of the clerks" is heard a great deal, these were two clerks who knew where they stood. St John was beheaded at Tower Hill in April 1535; St Thomas died in the same way in the following July.

1763: Sir, I was once in company with [Adam] Smith, and we did not take to each other; but had I known that

he loved rhyme as much as you tell me he does, I should have *hugged* him.
Samuel Johnson (1709–1784), in Boswell's Life.

July 10

Ss Januarius, Felix, Philip, Sylvanus, Alexander, Vitalis and Martial (2nd century) were seven martyrs, who were later said to be the seven sons of St Felicitas. Of these martyrs Januarius was flogged to death, Felix and Philip clubbed, Sylvanus was cast down a precipice, and the other four died by the sword.

1826: [To Eduard van Bauernfeld] I cannot possibly get to Gmunden or anywhere else, for I have no money at all, and altogether things go very badly with me. I do not trouble about it, and am cheerful.
Franz Schubert (1797–1828)

July 11

St James, bishop of Nisibis in Mesopotamia (d. 350) was a doctor of the Syrian church, a typical hermit-renowned-for-sanctity-dragged-into-public-life. When Nisibis was besieged by the Persian king Sapor, St James was not willing to pray for the destruction of the enemy but said, "Lord, thou art able by the weakest means to humble the pride of thy enemies; defeat these multitudes by an army of gnats," upon which "whole clouds of gnats and flies came pouring down upon the Persians, got into the elephants' trunks, and the horses' ears and nostrils, which made them chafe and foam, and put the whole army into confusion and disorder.

1841: [Dalmally] As there was no place of this name in our route, you will be surprised to see it at the head of this present writing. But our being here is a part of such moving accidents by flood and field as will astonish you. If you should happen to have your hat on, take it off, that your hair may stand on end without any interruption.

Charles Dickens (1812–1870) to John Forster.

July 12

S^T Veronica is not in the old Roman (pre-Vatican II) missal; but she does still figure in the service of the Stations of the Cross, for the Sixth Station is "The Face of Jesus is wiped by Veronica." She is not mentioned in the Gospels, but there was a very early tradition of the woman so moved by compassion at the sight of Our Lord on the way to Calvary that she offered him a clean cloth which received the image of His Face.

1884: Oscar Wilde was there. I thought he was a long lanky melancholy man, but he is fat and merry. His only peculiarity was a black choker, and his hair in a mop. He was not wearing a lily in his button hole, but to make up for it, his wife had her front covered with great water-lilies.

Beatrix Potter (1866–1943)

July 13

S^T Eugenius (d. 505) was bishop of Carthage when that city was ruled by Hunneric, son of Genseric the Vandal. Many of the Vandals were Arians, and before open persecution broke out there was a public disputation—rigged from the start, and to which the king expected one result only—between the Arians and the Catholics. When the Catholics could not be beaten in debate real trouble began. Anyone not in Vandal dress entering a church was seized. "A favourite torment was to twist little knotted sticks into the hair, and then tear them from the head, bringing away often large pieces of scalp. Women, with their heads thus torn, were conducted round the city by a public crier." Thousands were sent into exile in the desert, St Eugenius among them. He died in exile in Gaul.

1789: Think but of the surprise of his Majesty when, the first time of his bathing, he had no sooner popped

140

his royal head under water than a band of music, concealed in a neighbouring machine, struck up "God save great George our King."

One thing, however, was a little unlucky: when the Mayor and burgesses came with the address, they requested leave to kiss hands. This was graciously accorded; but, the Mayor advancing in a common way, *to take the Queen's hand*, as he might that of any lady mayoress. Colonel Gwynn, who stood by, whispered: "You must kneel, sir!" He found, however, that he took no notice of this hint, but kissed the Queen's hand erect. As he passed him, in his way back, the Colonel said: "You should have knelt, sir!"

"Sir," answered the poor Mayor, "I cannot."

"Everybody does, sir."

"Sir—I have a wooden leg!"

Poor man! 'Twas such a surprise! And such an excuse as no one could dispute.

Fanny Burney (1752–1840)

July 14

S^T BONAVENTURE (1221–1274) is one of the great saints of the high medieval period, and the greatest intellectual of the Franciscan Order. He was called the Seraphic Doctor, and sometimes he is simplistically contrasted as giving the will and heart precedence over the intellect, in "opposition" to St Thomas Aquinas. In fact his philosophy, though less Aristotelian and more Platonic than St Thomas's, is founded on a very subtle concept of the way God illuminates the human mind (and of the relation of that mind to the body it inhabits).

1690: We marched to Carlow, and baited on our way at Hungerlins Bush. As we passed two of the Enniskillen dragoons hung by the way-side with papers on their breasts exposing their crime, and thereby our march was very regular, without any such excursions or pillaging as before. (*See also July 23*)

Dean Rowland Davies (1649–1721)

July 15

S⊤ SWITHIN (d. 862) is about the only saint whose feast day is known by everyone, together with the legend that it will rain for forty more days if it is raining then (origin uncertain). Under the patronage of King Egbert of Wessex, who defeated the Mercians and then the Northumbrians and "in a council at Winchester, enacted that his kingdom should ever after be called England, and all its subjects Englishmen," he became bishop of Winchester.

1918: You guessed rightly that the Arab appealed to my imagination. It is the old, old civilisation, which has refined itself clear of household gods, and half the trappings which ours hastens to assume. The gospel of bareness in materials is a good one, and it involves apparently a sort of moral bareness too. They think for the moment, and endeavour to slip through life without turning corners or climbing hills. In part it is a mental and moral fatigue, a race trained out, and to avoid difficulties they have to jettison so much that we think honourable and grave: and yet without in any way sharing their point of vew, I think I can understand it enough to look at myself and other foreigners from their direction, and without condemning it: but I cannot believe them worse.

T. E. Lawrence (1888–1935)

July 16

ACCORDING TO LEGEND, S⊤ HELIER (6th century) was the child promised to the hitherto childless pagan couple, Sigebard and Lusegarde, at Tongres in modern Belgium, by a hermit called Cunibert, if they would allow him to bring it up as a Christian. Later, alarmed by his son's unworldliness and attachment to Cunibert, Sigebard killed the latter. "Helier, alarmed by the noise, rushed into the church, where he found his friend and tutor dead, with his bloody finger resting on the last line he had sung 'When shall I come to appear before the presence of

142

God?' " He eventually settled in a cave in the bay of Jersey that bears his name, and was killed by pirates.

1666: A wonderful dark sky and shower of rain this morning. At Harwich a shower of hail as big as walnuts.
Samuel Pepys (1633–1703)

July 17

EVEN MORE legendary than the story of yesterday's saint is that of today's. ST KENELM (d. 819) was heir to the throne, at the age of seven, of his father Kenwulf of Wessex. His sister bribed Askbert, his guardian, to murder him so that she could be queen. When Askbert began to dig a grave in the forest, Kenelm said, "I shall die in another spot; in token whereof see this rod blossom." He put a stick into the ground, and it instantly took root, and later became a great tree called St Kenelm's Ash.

1857: [Beaumaris] I had a strange experience last Sunday. Standing by the roadside near the sea, I saw a shabby carriage with two horses and postillion approaching. It passed close by me, so that I looked clearly in at the window and saw—what the men saw of forty-two years ago: Napoleon flying from Waterloo. Fat, yellow, dirty, dust-covered, but the same unmistakeable, incommunicable face. For a moment the world seemed to roll back, like a watch that runs down. Walking into the village, I found it all agog with the unexpected arrival of "Prince Napoleon". . . .
Sydney Dobell (1824–1874)

July 18

ST CAMILLUS DE LELLIS (1550–1614) was a soldier of fortune who lost everything because of a passion for gambling. When working as a labourer in a Franciscan friary he experienced his conversion and joined the Order, but had to leave because of a leg ulcer which troubled him all his life. His subsequent work in hospitals convinced him of the need for a religious nursing order. He determined to study for the priesthood, a grown man (in fact a very large one) among boys who laughed at him; but he outdistanced them and was ordained in 1584. His Order, the Servants of the Sick, pioneered such notions as fresh air and isolation of contagious cases, and was the first to send a nursing unit to troops in the field. He is patron saint of nurses and the sick.

1894: . . . Appearance of Hamilton who had forgotten something. Mild pleasant gentleman with wooden leg. Pony arrived. Much amused with tameness of birds, sparrows in dining-room and swallows' nests all round house. The Hamiltons are said to be fond of mice, and a robin was seen stealing butter in the larder. . . . The river is swarming with trout and small fry. The gamekeeper is a curiosity, such a buck, with most extraordinary whiskers, it is thought it must be done with curling tongs. Anyway they are quite overpowering. His name is Turnbull. The gardener speaks English, but most of them are Scotch, especially the coachman.

Beatrix Potter (1866–1943)

July 19

Sᴛ Vɪɴᴄᴇɴᴛ ᴅᴇ Pᴀᴜʟ (about 1580–1660) is one of the most famous names in the church when it comes to practical charity. The son of a small farmer in the Landes, he was educated by the Franciscans and became a priest in 1600. Captured by Barbary pirates on a voyage, he was sold into slavery in North Africa but afterwards escaped. This experience made him a good choice for one of his later tasks as chaplain to the galleys, where he did his best for the convicts. His natural sympathies lay with the underdogs and the rejected; but he combined this with a marvellous gift for *organizing*. In 1625 he founded the Lazarists for mission work—and, with St Louise de Marillac, as Mme le Gras eventually became (*see March 15*), the Sisters of Charity, originally for nursing the sick poor. The Society of St Vincent de Paul, founded by Fredric Ozanam in 1833, is still the most active and practical charitable organization in a good Catholic parish. Anouilh was co-writer of the film about him made in 1948, *Monsieur Vincent*.

1872: To Correspondents
Little Beggar—We do not understand your question.
Silver trays are only covered when not in use.

7.8.9. is informed that it is against our rules for two
correspondents to use the same pseudonym, and that no
communication from her has been received in this depart-
ment for "Pax Vobiscum".

Jelly—They are made of tin or of pewter and are procurable
at any first-rate ironmonger's.

B.A.J.—There is no other remedy but to have it re-stuffed.

The Queen, The Lady's Newspaper

July 20

S^T WILGEFORTIS (date unknown). "The story of this Saint is
almost too absurd to be given." She was the daughter of a
king of Portugal, who desired her to marry the king of Sicily;
but she had taken a vow of perpetual virginity. She therefore
prayed, and a beard, moustache and whiskers appeared on her
face, not surprisingly repulsing the king of Sicily, whereupon
her father had her crucified. "A preposterous tale," says Attwater.

1867: . . . the two principles of Berlin architecture
appear to me to be these—On the housetops, whenever
there is a convenient place, put up the figure of a man; he
is best placed standing on one leg. Whenever there is room
on the ground, put either a circular group of busts on
pedestals, in consultation, all looking inwards—or else the
colossal figure of a man killing, about to kill, or having
killed (the present tense is preferred) a beast. . . .

C. L. Dodgson (Lewis Carroll) (1832–1898)

July 21

S^T BARHADBESCIABAS (d. 354) has some claim to be the most
unpronounceable saint in this book. A deacon in the city of
Arbela, he was tortured on the rack and, when he remained

constant, a Christian apostate called Aghaeus was ordered to behead him. He did this so unsteadily that seven blows of the sword were not enough, and he finally ran him through the body.

1799: Turner told me he has no systematic process for making drawing. He thinks it can produce nothing but manner and sameness. Turner has no settled process but drives the colours about till He has expressed the Idea in his mind.

Joseph Farington (1747–1821)

July 22

ST MARY MAGDALEN. *Dic nobis Maria, quid vidisti in via,* the monks used to sing in that dawn-fresh, dewy, joyful Sequence, *Victimae Paschali,* of the Mass for Easter Sunday; tell us, Mary, what you saw in the way? Her tears are the most moving in the Gospel. She stood at the foot of the cross, she was in the faithful-to-the-last group that took spices to the tomb. In St Luke, all the women see the vision of the angels; in St John, she alone. It was to her that Jesus spoke the first words after the Resurrection; "woman, why weepest thou?," and, surely with a terrible gentleness, "touch me not; for I am not yet ascended to my Father . . ."
Her name comes from Magdala, on the Sea of Tiberias. She was the woman from whom Jesus had cast out seven devils.

1800: We took a long hot walk to the village of Murry [Staffordshire] to see a tape manufactory, of which seven gentlemen of that neighbourhood are proprietors. The noise of the machinery is hardly to be borne, tho' the workpeople told us they themselves hardly heard the noise! Such is use!

Mrs Philip Libbe Powys (1739–1817)

146

July 23

ST JOHN CASSIAN (early 5th century), who was born in Scythia—
that vaguely defined territory beyond Greece which reached
up to Russia—played a major part in bringing the monastic
tradition from the east to the west. He made two journeys to the
Nile desert hermits and was in Constantinople and Rome before
settling at Marseilles, where he set up two monasteries, one for
men and the other for women. St Benedict drew on his
Institutions when devising his famous rule, and he also wrote an
account of his seven years with the eastern monks. Some of his
writings were attacked by St Prosper of Aquitaine (*see June 25*)
as being "semi-Pelagian" or devaluing the power of divine
grace.

1690: The garrison of Waterford sent this day very
saucy proposals in a capitulation, but were assured by
the King that he would give them no other terms than
Drogheda had, and accordingly the heavy cannon were
drawn over the hill, in order to begin the attack on Friday
morning.

Dean Rowland Davies (1649–1721)

July 24

ST LUPUS (d. 478), although he did not actually convert Attila,
can nevertheless stand as a symbolic figure in that mysterious process of the Christianization of the west, where time and
again some howling mob of barbarians is met on the road by
some quiet old man with nothing but a cross and suddenly
everything is different. He was at first married, then he and his
wife took vows of continence and he joined the famous monastery at Lerins (*see May 24*) and subsequently became bishop of
Troyes. When that city was threatened by Attila he went out to
meet him. He spoke first "and asked him who he was. 'I am,'
said Attila, 'the scourge of God.' 'Let us respect whatever comes
to us from God,' replied the bishop; 'but if you are the scourge
with which heaven chastises us, remember you are to do nothing
but what that almighty hand, which governs and moves you,

permits.' Attila, struck with these words, promised the prelate to spare the city."

✒ *1860:* Found my housekeeper Miss Mitchell and a policeman in anxious talk: my rooms, at 4 p.m., had been broken open and robbed.

It is curious to observe one's own behaviour under a new sensation. My first impulse was to laugh; and I accompanied the friendly peeler upstairs with a cheerful calmness which was perfectly heroic. . . . I feel magnanimous pity for the wretched miscreant: I will enjoy my triumphs over him, if he is caught: and if not, I know—blessed thought! that he will suffer for his doings in a future world.

A. J. Munby (1828–1910)

July 25

S<small>T</small> J<small>AMES THE</small> G<small>REAT.</small> With his brother John and, of course, Peter, he had a kind of primacy among the Apostles. James and John, sons of Zebedee, were fishermen, called by Jesus on the same day that he called Simon (Peter) and Andrew and told them He would make them fishers of men. Jesus gave the brothers the surname "Boanerges," meaning "sons of thunder." They had burning and impetuous natures. It was they who asked Jesus if they should command fire to come down and consume the unwilling Samaritan villagers "as Elias did," they who asked if "we may sit, one on thy right hand, and the other on thy left hand, in thy glory," to receive the reply "you know not what you ask. Can you drink the cup that I drink of?" They were chosen to be present both at the Transfiguration and the Agony in the Garden. St James's Epistle is a passionate and profound short exposition of the entire Christian faith, which can make its reader wonder how all that argument about faith and works could later became so divisive. There it is, perfectly plain. "Thou believest there is one God; thou dost well: the devils also believe and tremble. But wilt thou know, O vain man, that faith without works is dead?" St James died by the sword, under Herod Agrippa. He is the patron saint of Spain.

✒ *1868:* . . . as the Interlaken Frenchman said, the mountain summits are not the places for mountain views, the things do not look high when you are as high as they are; besides Monte Rosa, the Lyskamm, etc did not make themselves; shape as well as size went: then the cold feet, the spectacles, the talk, and the lunching came in. Even with one companion ecstasy is almost banished: you want to be alone and to feel that, and leisure—all pressure taken off.

Gerard Manley Hopkins (1844–1889)

July 26

Sᴛ Gᴇʀᴍᴀɴᴜs ᴏғ Aᴜxᴇʀʀᴇ (about 378–448) was a noble who changed his life for one of great asceticism when he became bishop of Auxerre. In 429 with St Lupus (*see July 24*) he came to Britain, sent by Pope Celestine to combat the heresy of Pelagianism. Among other things he was successful in a public disputation at St Albans. During a Saxon attack he showed he had not forgotten his military skills. "He led his little army into a vale between two high mountains, and ordered his troops to send forth the same shout for which he would give them a sign. When the Saxon pirates came near them, he cried out thrice, *Alleluiah*, which was repeated by the whole British army; and the sound was often repeated by the echo from the hills with as dreadful a noise as if the rocks had been rent asunder. The barbarians, in a sudden fright, judging that they were falling upon the swords of a mighty army, flung down their arms and ran away, leaving all their baggage and a great booty." In later calendars his feast is on July 31.

1889: [At Covent Garden] box after box is thrown away on inveterate dead-heads whose mission in life is to pester impresarios for free admissions. And they impose on the management impertinent sumptuary regulations by which I, for instance, am compelled to attend the opera in the cheapest, ugliest, and least wholesome suit of clothes I possess: regulations which are supposed to afford me a guarantee of high personal character and perfect propriety in appearance, manners, and conversation of my neighbors. The guarantee is worth nothing. I shall not pretend that the average stallholder is in any of these respects a specially offensive person; but I unhesitatingly affirm that the average pittite is at no disadvantage whatever compared to him and is, on the whole, better company.

George Bernard Shaw (1856–1950)

July 27

THERE ARE many forms of the legend of the Seven Sleepers. In the original Christianization of this piece of folklore they were seven boys who fled to a cave from the persecution of the emperor Decius. Edward the Confessor was said to have astonished his courtiers when, abstracted during a banquet, he burst out laughing at his vision of the Seven Sleepers all turning over together. The feast is no longer kept.

1907: Lady Paget was here today and talked very pleasantly, telling amongst other things the latest spiritualistic story according to which the late Lord Carlingford has re-entered into communication with the living and is carrying on a correspondence in his own handwriting with one of his friends, principally on Irish politics, of which he has found a new devolutionary solution. He is in daily intercourse with Gladstone and has converted him to the doctrine of protection!

Wilfrid Scawen Blunt (1840–1922)

July 28

ST SAMSON (d. about 450) was a monk, educated originally by St Illtyd in Wales. There were enough signs of his eminence for two other monks to be jealous of him, so they poisoned his cup, but he gave some to the cat first, and it died. He retired to an island (possibly Caldey) near the monastery, where lived also Piro "a holy priest and excellent man." However Piro died through falling into a well when coming back to his cell drunk. He later founded the monastery of Dol in Brittany.

1783: ... This has been the hottest day this year, and I believe the hottest that ever I felt, many say the same.

We fully expected a Tempest today, but thank God had none.

James Woodforde (1740–1803)

July 29

S<small>T</small> M<small>ARTHA</small>, the sister of Mary and Lazarus of Bethany, is of course the one who was "cumbered about with much serving," and is regarded as the patron of those who work practically to assist the needy. It was to her that Jesus said, "I am the Resurrection and the Life," before the raising of Lazarus. There was a legend that she and Mary Magdalen came miraculously to Gaul and evangelized the Rhone valley and Provence.

1843: [To Frederic Tennyson] . . . You would rave at this climate which is wetter far than that of England. There are the Wicklow hills (mountains we call them) in the offing—quite high enough. In spite of my prejudice for a level, I find myself every day unconsciously verging towards any eminence that gives me the freest view of their blue ranges. One's thoughts immmediately take wing to the distance, I fancy that moderately high hills (like these) are the ticket—not to be domineered over by Mont Blancs, etc. But this may be only a passing prejudice. . .

Edward Fitzgerald (1809–1883)

July 30

T<small>HE UNUSUALLY</small> named SS A<small>BDON</small> and S<small>ENNEN</small> were in fact of Persian birth. They were martyred, about 252, in the persecution under Decius, being first scourged and then beheaded.

1821: Poor ELIA, the real, (for I am but a counterfeit,) is dead. The fact is, a person of that name, an Italian, was a fellow clerk of mine at the South Sea House, thirty (not forty) years ago, when the characters I described there existed, but had left it like myself many years; and I having a brother now there, and doubting how he might relish

certain descriptions in it, I clapt down the name of Elia to
it. . . .

Charles Lamb (1775–1834)

July 31

Don Inigo Lopez de Recalde, better known as St Ignatius
Loyola, the founder of the Jesuits (1491–1556) was the
greatest of all the Counter-Reformation saints. After a military
career (he was wounded in both legs in the defence of Pamplona)
he experienced a spiritual rebirth at Montserrat, that amazing
monastery perched on the jagged heights above Catalonia which
is one of the mysterious sacred places of Spain. The Jesuit Order
was approved conditionally in 1540, completely in 1543. Its
"Bible" has always been St Ignatius's *Spiritual Exercises* in which
the truths of religion are systematically presented in a manner
appealing to both head and heart. The Jesuit Order, dispensing
with the choir office of some older Orders, completely mobile
and completely centralized, and having utter obedience as its
keystone, attracted men of high intellectual calibre and courage,
producing not only missionaries to China who compiled Chinese
dictionaries and discussed astronomy, but the missionaries
martyred by Canadians whose feast is also kept today. Some
people thought they were *too* clever. Largely to please the
French, Pope Clement XIV actually suppressed the Order
throughout the world in 1773. The ban was lifted again by Pius
VII in 1814.

1716: My son Thō fell into a Quagmire in Frecknam
Fen up to the wast, but God be thanked got noe harm.
(see also October 18) William Coe of Mildenhall (1680–1729)

AUGUST

August 1

S<small>T</small> E<small>THELWOLD</small> (about 925–984) was a co-student with St
Dunstan at Glastonbury (*see May 19*). He was made abbot of
Abingdon and, later, bishop of Winchester, where he consecrated the rebuilt cathedral in 980. He was associated with St
Dunstan in replacing married canons and other clergy with
monks. He found his cathedral "served by secular married
priests, canons under no strict rule, living with their wives and
families near the great church, feeding well, and sometimes
taking the convivial glass, chirpy, jovial, worthy souls. He
replaced them with some of his monks from Abingdon." Like St
Dunstan he was skilled in mechanical arts and music, and
himself cast two of the bells for Abingdon. The writing for which
he was best known was his translation of the Rule of St Benedict
into Anglo-Saxon.

1908: The young swallows in the bathroom have
flown, but they still come back to their nest at night. It
has been a great pleasure watching them, the old swallows
having come in and out of the room while I was in the bath
quite undisturbed though the nest was just above it, built
on a curtain rod. There were four young ones hatched and
all have flown.

Wilfrid Scawen Blunt (1840–1922)

August 2

S<small>T</small> A<small>LPHONSUS</small> L<small>IGUORI</small> (1696–1787) was the founder of the
Congregation of Missionaries of the Holy Redeemer—the
Redemptorists. In his old age "he boasted that he had never
once in his long life sent away a penitent unabsolved. He never
imposed heavy penances, wisely saying, 'If the sinner is really
contrite, he will punish himself; but if you impose on him a
penance, he will neglect the penance and cleave to the sin.' " He
also said "I have never preached a sermon which the poorest old
woman in the congregation could not understand." Canonised
1839.

1721: [To Alexander Pope] I have found time to read some parts of Shakespeare which I was least acquainted with. I protest to you in a hundred places I cannot construe him: I do not understand him.

Francis Atterbury, Bishop of Rochester (1662–1732)

August 3

ST WALTHEOF (d. 1160) was the son of the Maud whose second marriage, after that to his father, Simon of Senlis, Earl of Huntingdon, was to King David of Scotland. He was a gentle soul; prior of Kirkham and eventually abbot of Melrose. He showed a "reverence for life" which is quite up to anything told of St Francis (or Schweitzer). Once, after repeatedly brushing off a persistent fly with his sleeve, he killed it. Then "he confessed his sin in having killed a creature of God, which he was unable to restore to life again. The abbot smiled, and gave him a very light penance."

1770: Venice has ... been one of the first cities in Europe that has cultivated the musical drama or opera; and, in the graver stile, it has been honoured with a Lotti and a Marcello. Add to these advantages the *conservatorios* established here, and the songs of the *Gondolieri*, or Watermen, which are so celebrated, that every musical collector of taste in Europe is well furnished with them, and it will appear that my expectations were well grounded. The first music I heard here was in the street, immediately on my arrival, performed by an itinerant band of two fiddles, a violoncello, and a voice, who, though unnoticed here as small-coal-men or oyster-women in England, performed so well that in any other country of Europe they would not only have excited attention, but have acquired applause, which they justly merited.

Charles Burney (1726–1814)

August 4

Sᴛ Dᴏᴍɪɴɪᴄ (1170–1221) was the founder of the Order of Preachers which also bears his name, the Dominicans ("the dogs of God," *Domini canes* was the obvious Latin pun on their name). Pope Innocent III is said to have had a vision of the church tottering to its fall and being held up by two men whom he later recognized as St Dominic and St Francis (the two did meet in Rome, and their greeting was commemorated in an annual ceremonial re-enactment). He matured at a time when the laxity of the clergy had made the pure-living, flesh-despising (but Christ's-divinity-denying) Albigensian heretics and their doctrines attractive to the people of Languedoc. St Dominic, hitherto a canon at Osma in the Spain of his birth, conceived a desire to convert them by preaching when he first came across them on an official royal-marriage-arranging trip to Denmark. He rebuked the luxuriously appointed Papal mission, and in 1215 his Order of preaching friars bound to poverty was approved. He had no part in the bloody and cruel military "crusade" against the Albigensians, although later Dominicans were associated with the Inquisition. He personally was a man of the utmost asceticism and charity. Although the Dominican Order has produced some of the greatest intellectuals in the church, from St Thomas Aquinas downwards, he is credited with the creation of the Rosary, in which the fifteen deepest mysteries of the Christian faith are incorporated in a system that involves only the three prayers known by heart to every Catholic; the Our Father, the Hail Mary and the Doxology.

1784: About 10 o'clock this Night a Clergyman by name Campbell (Vicar of Weasingham in this County and formerly of Oriel Coll: Oxford and afterwards Fellow of Worcester Coll: in the same University) came to my House and he supped and slept here—himself and horse. I remember him at Oriel Coll: but not so intimate as to expect that he would have taken such freedom especially as he never made me a Visit before. He slept however in the Attic Story and I treated him as one that would be too free if treated too kindly. It kept me up till after 12 o'clock.

James Woodforde (1740–1803)

156

August 5

S^T AFRA (d. 303) was martyred by being burnt to death at Augsburg when the persecution of Diocletian had reached to this fringe of the empire. A tradition grew that she was a converted prostitute; but the name suggests an African origin, and troops from Africa are known to have served here, so she may have been simply a member of a soldier's family.

1837: Lady Sefton has a letter from Lady Cowley of her dinner at *Viccy's* one day this week . . . the Queen, she said, was excessively civil to everyone, had excellent manners, but was *Royal* (and quite right, little Vic, too, I say again); then Lady Cowley adds that in the evening the Queen relaxed, and that nothing could be more amiable and agreeable than she was. Can you wish for a better account of a little tit of 18 made all at once into a Queen?

Thomas Creevey (1768–1838)

August 6

P^{OPE} S^T S^{IXTUS} II (d. 258) began his pontificate many years before the first emperor became Christian (Constantine, in 311). The emperor in his time was Valerian, who began by being quite tolerant of Christians, but was gradually turned against them, it was said by one Macrianus, a follower of the Persian Magi; and in the subsequent persecutions Sixtus was executed.

1906: [To his mother, when he was 17, from Dinard] Please give my kindest regards to Father and the rest and *don't work too hard*: do nothing rather than too much; you are worth more than the house; love to all: hope you are all well: I have not been bilious yet; don't expect to be. A flock of sheep disappeared in the sands round the Mont St Michel this spring and so I will not try to find them. Ta Ta. Love. love. love. love. love. love. NED

T. E. Lawrence (1888–1935)

August 7

S⊤ Cajetan (Gaetano), 1480–1547, lived in troubled times for the church. The notoriously profligate Alexander VI had been succeeded as Pope by the temporally ambitious Julius II (1503–13), and many of the higher clergy were worldly men, to say the least. St Cajetan at first joined the Society of Divine Love. He urged, among other things, far more frequent reception of Holy Communion than the three or four times a year then common. Later with four friends he founded the Clerks Regular (or Theatines, named from the diocese of one of those friends), who were not only without property but not even allowed to beg, Cajetan trusting, correctly as it turned out, that their work for the poor and the sick would automatically attract help.

1664: While we were talking, came by several poor creatures, carried by constables for being at a conventicle. I would to God they would either conform or be more wise and not be ketched.

Samuel Pepys (1633–1703)

August 8

S⊤ John-Baptist Vianney (1786–1859) was better known as the Curé d'Ars. From obscure peasant origins, a poor scholar, he studied for the priesthood, interrupting this period by fourteen months in hiding to avoid military service, and became parish priest of Ars-en-Dombes from 1818 till his death. The fame of his powers as both preacher and confessor spread, so that he sometimes spent eighteen hours a day in the confessional. It was of him that his bishop made the well-known remark, when some complained that he was mad, "I wish all my clergy had a touch of the same madness!" In 1929 he was made the patron of parish priests.

1930: Conversation very, very literary and academic, my own part in it being mostly confined to saying that I haven't read it, and, It's down on my library list, but hasn't come, so far. After what feels like some hours of this, Miss

P. becomes personal, and says that I strike her as being a woman whose life has never known fulfilment. Have often thought exactly the same thing myself, but this does not prevent my feeling entirely furious with Miss P. for saying so. She either does not perceive, or is indifferent to, my fury, as she goes on to ask accusingly whether I realize that I have no *right* to let myself become a domestic beast of burden, with no interests beyond the nursery and the kitchen. What, for instance, she demands rousingly, have I read within the last two years? To this I reply weakly that I have read *Gentlemen Prefer Blondes*, which is the only thing I seem able to remember. . . .

E. M. *Delafield*, The Diary of a Provincial Lady

August 9

ST OSWALD OF NORTHUMBRIA (about 925–992) must be distinguished from St Oswald of Worcester (*see February 28*) and it was he whose name became known and adopted in Europe. Brought up in exile in Scotland, he regained his father's kingdom of Northumbria from the Briton Cadwallon at a battle under Hadrian's Wall, at a place that became known as Heaven's Field. He was associated in the Christianization of his kingdom with St Aidan, the founder of Lindisfarne.

1773: [To the Countess of Ossory] My poor Rosette is dying. She relapsed into her fits the last night of my stay at Nuneham, and has suffered exquisitely ever since. You may believe I have too; I have been out of bed twenty times every night, have had no sleep, and sat up with her till three this morning; but I am only making you laugh at me; I cannot help it—I think of nothing else. Without weaknesses I should not be I, and I may as well tell them as have them tell themselves.

Horace Walpole (1717–1797)

August 10

St Lawrence (258), who is named in the canon of the Mass, was one of the seven deacons of Rome. Ordered to produce the treasures of the church, in the persecution under Valerian, he pointed to the crowd of poor and sick and said, "these are the treasures." The tradition is that he was martyred in a gridiron placed over a slow fire, and made the famous request to be turned over as he was done on one side. He is always represented with his gridiron. Attwater says, "it is more likely that in fact he was beheaded."

1936: [To her sister] I was sorry you missed Dick Sheppard on the wireless. . . . He really did make goodness sound like an urgent and desperately important job to be tackled; his idea was that we should all tackle it for 24 hours, on Monday, just to try it. I wonder how many people did! And what were the results. Perhaps huge gifts of money to useful things; perhaps businesses ruined through a day of honesty. . . .

Your loving *E.R.M.*

I am asked to sign a petition for voluntary euthanasia. Is this right? No hurry; send a p.c. sometime, yes or no.

Rose Macaulay (1881–1958)

August 11

Ss Tiburtius and Susanna. Tiburtius was the son of Chromatius, said (doubtfully) to have been a prefect at Rome. He suffered from gout, and one St Tranquillinus, a Christian who also suffered from it, "brought on by immoderate use of the bottle in his old pagan, jovial days," told Chromatius that he had never suffered from it since his baptism. After three weeks' preparation he was baptised "and broke all his idols. Under the new regimen imposed by his faith, the twinges of gout ceased to make themselves felt. His baptism had been preceded by severe fasting." Tiburtius, his son, was baptised at the same time, and, betrayed by an apostate called Torquatus, was beheaded on the Lavicanian Way. Some ten years later St Susanna, who had

160

refused to marry the son of Diocletian, Galerius Maximus, was beheaded.

1804: ... Lady Hamilton is grown prodigiously large & exposed her fat shoulders & breast manifestly having the appearance of one of the Bacchantes of Rubens.

Joseph Farington (1747–1821)

August 12

ST CLARE (1194–1253) was a girl of noble family who, already admiring St Francis of Assisi and all that he stood for, experienced a "consecration" on Palm Sunday when the bishop at Assisi personally brought her a palm seeing that she had now joined the congregational procession. She founded the Order of the Poor Clares, with a rule (of considerable austerity) supervised and approved of by St Francis. Like most good abbesses, she had a mind of her own. When the friars were forbidden to enter the convent for their normal ministrations, such as saying Mass, she said, "very well, if the holy friars may not feed us with the bread of life, they shall not minister to us the bread that perishes" and left the food collected outside for the convent untouched. The authorities relented.

1822: About seven this morning Dr Bankhead was called by Lady Londonderry's maid, who said my Lord wished to see him. The Doctor immediately rose and went into the bedroom, when he found Lord Londonderry had just gone into the dressing-room. He followed him, and saw him standing with his face to the window (and of course his back towards the Doctor) in his dressing gown, with his head leaned back, and his eyes fixed on the ceiling. "My dear Lord" said he, "why do you stand so?" "O Bankhead," he said, "I am glad you are there, let me fall into your arms; it is all over": and he fell back into Bankhead's arms, who then, for the first time, saw in his right hand a small-bladed pen-knife, with which our unhappy friend had just divided by a deep cut the carotid artery, and with a sudden effusion of blood the body fell forward on the face, and Castlereagh expired without a struggle.

John Wilson Croker (1780–1857)

August 13

S⊤ CASSIAN OF IMOLA (d. about 320) was a Christian schoolmaster who during a persecution was handed over to his pagan pupils who stabbed him to death with their iron pens. Butler and Baring-Gould tell this story without comment, but Attwater (who was a civilian lecturer to H.M. Forces but not a schoolmaster) thinks the manner of death (though there certainly was a martyr of that name) is fictitious.

🖉 *1788:* Of all *sombre* and *triste* meetings a French *table d'hôte* is foremost; for eight minutes a dead silence, and as to the politeness of addressing a conversation to a foreigner, he will look for it in vain.

Arthur Young (1741–1820)

August 14

THERE ARE two saints named EUSEBIUS commemorated today. The first, after being tortured demanded an interview with the emperor Maximian, to whom "his venerable old age seemed to breathe an air of courage above what is human. The emperor fixed his eyes on him, as if he beheld in him something divine" and, though "the most brutish and savage of men . . . desired to save the servant of Christ. However, like Pilate, he would not give himself the hazard of incurring the displeasure of those whom on all other occasions he despised," so Eusebius was beheaded. The other Eusebius, in the 4th century, was imprisoned in his room by the emperor, and died after seven months of solitary prayer.

🖉 *1916:* [Khutanova] They say that the young Grand Duke Alexei is far from well, and we were interested to hear from one of them who had recently returned from Petrograd that a monk, well-known in social circles, but regarded by many with suspicion, had worked his way into the affections of the Imperial Family to such an extent that he was able to influence both the Tsar and the Tsarina. It seems he had found favour with them by reason of some special treatment which had had a beneficial effect on the health of the young Alexei. There was much dissatisfaction both in Petrograd and Moscow at this man's growing power and it was whispered that because of him the Tsarina herself was becoming increasingly unpopular, for people were reminding each other that she was of German birth and would, therefore naturally uphold the cause of Germany rather than that of Russia. We were shocked and grieved to hear this, but paid little attention, realizing that it could be only sheer gossip, for we well knew that the Tsarina was devoted to Russia and the Russian people.

Florence Farmborough (1897–1958)

August 15

S t Alypius was a native of Tagaste in North Africa, where he was a slightly younger contemporary and lifelong friend of St Augustine. His conversion followed the other's and they were baptized on the same day by St Ambrose. He became bishop of Tagaste in 393. He is mentioned by St Augustine in a letter in 429 and probably died soon after.

Today is also of course the great feast of the Assumption of the Blessed Virgin into heaven.

1813: My dearest Mother: It is very late, and I have been obliged to leave you last of half a dozen letters, so that you will come off very badly. We dined out today at the Ackroyds, neighbours of ours. You would have laughed to see Bessy and me going in to dinner. We found, in the middle of our walk, that we were near half an hour too early for dinner, so we set to *practising country dances*, in the middle of a retired green lane, till the time was expired. Ever your own, Tom.

Thomas Moore (1779–1852)

August 16

Sᴛ Rᴏᴄʜ (14th century) is a fairly legendary saint. It seems to be agreed that he died, after having been gaoled as a spy and/or vagrant, in his native Montpellier, in about 1350. After that the story blossoms out. He was the nephew of the governor of Montpellier, he had gone on a pilgrimage to Rome, he cured people miraculously of the plague in northern Italy, and was himself miraculously cured of it by the touch of an angel. . . . The other figure often seen with him is a dog with a loaf in its mouth, since a dog is said to have fed him when he was ill with plague at Piacenza.

1915: . . . The other day a member of the staff of the Lister Institute called to see me on a lousy matter and presently drew some live Lice from his waistcoat pocket for me to see. They were contained in pill boxes with little bits of muslin stretched across the open end thro' which the Lice could thrust their little hypodermic needles when placed near the skin. He feeds them by putting these boxes into a specially constructed belt around his waist and all night sleeps in Elysium. He is not married.

W. N. P. Barbellion (1889–1917)

August 17

Sᴛ Hʏᴀᴄɪɴᴛʜ ᴏꜰ Cʀᴀᴄᴏᴡ (1185–1257) became known by an alteration of his name as St Jacko (diminutive of Jacob). When he was already a canon and "a doctor of divinity" he met St Dominic (*see August 4*) on a visit to Rome, and became a friar-missionary. He went preaching through Prussia and the Scandinavian countries, founding several friaries, and then went to Russia. He was later involved in some predictably fruitless attempts to get the Russians to abandon Orthodox for Roman Christianity in return for a western crusade against the Mongols.

1938: [To the Times] In your issue of July 30 you employed *rhinoceri* as the plural of rhinoceros. This is surely a barbarism, although in referring to the New Oxford Dictionary I find to my surprise and regret that it is one of the usages cited.

This plural has given writers of English considerable trouble. Besides rhinoceros, rhinoceroses, and the above-mentioned rhinoceri, the N.E.D. quotes, rhinocerons, rhinoceroes, rhinocerotes, and rhinocerontes.

Rhinoceroses would appear to be the least objectionable, but even this still has a pedantic sound. Has not the time come when we can discard our etymological prejudices, accept the usage of the ordinary man, and frankly use "rhinos"? Confusion will not arise, since the slang use of rhino for money is moribund, if not dead.

Julian Huxley (1887–1975)

August 18

Sᵀ Helena (d. 328) the wife of the emperor Constantius Chlorus, and the mother of Constantine, the emperor who pronounced Christianity the state religion, was very active in spreading the Christian faith. Her work for and with the people of Palestine was traditionally rewarded with the finding of the True Cross on the hill of Calvary.

1715: Mr Whatley knocked at my chamber door and called me up when I was in bed. He came to go with me to the cold bath. Went with him fully designed not to go in. When came there was company. He undressed and went in first. It appeared a very small matter as he performed it. When he came out and was dressed I resolved to go in too and went to the brink of the bath and jumped in head forward with a great deal of resolution and swam about and went out and went in again. It is indeed a very small matter, the cold does not affect one at all and is scarce perceptible while in the water. I applauded myself mightily when I came out for my resolution and courage.

Dudley Ryder

August 19

S T MOCHTEUS OF LOUTH (d. 535) belongs to that happy time
when a Briton could be an Irish saint; he was the youngest
and last surviving disciple of St Patrick. His life, says Baring-
Gould, "a late composition, is a collection of marvels." It relates
how as a child he learned letters from an angel who brought him
a waxed slate for the purpose from heaven. This slate the saint
afterwards presented to the Pope. Also how, when he sailed
with his disciples for Ireland, one who had been left behind tore
off a green bough and was carried over the waters on it to the
retreating ship of Mochteus.

> *1772:* . . . I do not think it answers any good purpose
> to send our Country People up to Town. The Change is
> so great that not one in ten can stand it without being
> ruin'd or spoild or being seized with the Swiss disorder. . . .
> *Josiah Wedgwood (1730–1795)*

August 20

S T BERNARD (1090–1153) was associated with the Cistercian
Order almost from its beginnings. From the monastery
which he founded in the "Valley of Wormwood" at Clairvaux in
incredibly Spartan conditions nearly seventy others, including
our own Rievaulx, were established. His European reputation
for sanctity meant the acceptance of Pope Innocent II against the
rival Anacletus II (Peter Leoni) who had been accepted by the
French king and the Cluniac monks. His opposition to these
latter went to unedifying lengths in his violent opposition
(successful) to a Cluniac appointment to the see of Langres. He
also preached the disastrous Second Crusade, the failure of
which clouded the latter part of his life. He was a prolific
correspondent, writing "to persons of all classes, on all subjects,
ranging from the most spiritual raptures on the welfare of the
soul down to the stealing of pigs." Of undoubted personal
asceticism and sanctity, he was a classic medieval figure, and
was called *Doctor Mellifluus,* "the honey-tongued doctor." Attwa-

166

ter remarks that "as a theologian he belongs to the pre-Scholastic era, and he is sometimes spoken of as 'the last of the Fathers.' "

1944: [To Stalin] We are thinking of world opinion if anti-Nazis in Warsaw are in effect abandoned. We believe that all three of us should do the utmost to save as many of the patriots there as possible. We hope that you will drop immediate supplies and munitions to the patriot Poles of Warsaw, or will you agree to help our planes in doing it very quickly?* We hope you will approve. The time element is of extreme importance (*See also August 22*)

Roosevelt and Churchill

August 21

ST JANE FRANCES DE CHANTAL (1572–1641) was the foundress of the Visitation Order of nuns. Left a widow at twenty-eight, with four children, she lived a somewhat difficult life with her father-in-law, but her vocation for the religious life was strengthened by her deep spiritual tutelage under St Francis de Sales (*see January 29*). Her Order, originally designed to some extent for late vocations such as her own (although she had always herself been deeply spiritual) faced early criticism; but there were eighty Visitation houses before her death. Her son, Celse-Benigne, opposed her departure, lying across the doorway and saying "if I cannot keep you back, you will at least have to pass over the body of your son." She nevertheless made her tearful departure. This son's daughter grew up to be Mme de Sevigné.

1770: I too am still alive and, what is more, as merry as can be. I had a great desire today to ride on a donkey, for it is the custom in Italy, and so I thought I too should try it. We have the honour to go about with a certain Dominican, who is regarded as a holy man. For my part I do not believe it, for at breakfast he often takes a cup of chocolate and immediately afterwards a good glass of strong Spanish wine; and I myself have had the honour of lunching with

*The Russians refused the RAF landing rights, and planes dropping supplies to the doomed resistance army under General Bor had to make the double journey to and from Allied lines.

this saint who at table drank a whole decanter and finished up with a full glass of strong wine, two large slices of melon, some peaches, pears, five cups of coffee, a whole plate of cloves, and two full saucers of milk and lemon. He may, of course, be following some sort of diet, but I do not think so, for it would be too much; moreover, he takes several little snacks during the afternoon. *Addio*. Farewell. Kiss Mamma's hands for me. My greetings to all who know me.

Wolfgang Amadeus Mozart (1756–1791)

August 22

S^T SYMPHORIAN (d. about 180) died in the persecution which darkened the name of the noble stoic thinker, the emperor Marcus Aurelius. Refusing, at Autun, to sacrifice to an image of Bercynth (Cybele) St Symphorian was beaten with clubs, and two days later taken out to execution by the sword. His mother shouted encouragement to him as he passed; he is one of several martyrs of whom this is told.

1944: [To Roosevelt] The message (*see August 20*) from you and Mr Churchill has reached me. I should like to state my views.

Sooner or later the truth about the handful of power-seeking criminals who launched the Warsaw adventure will out. Those elements, playing on the credulity of the inhabitants of Warsaw, exposed practically unarmed people to German guns, armour and aircraft. . . .

Stalin (1879–1953)

August 23

S^T SIDONIUS APOLLINARIS (about 431–488), "patrician turned churchman, a little," says Helen Waddell in *The Wandering Scholars*, "like John Donne, against his will, and, again like Donne, misliking the poetry of his youth, shepherding his people against the shock of the Burgundian invasion, prisoner among the barbarians for two years and thereafter adored by them, a little to his own embarrassment . . . holding at Clermont the last stronghold of Roman culture in Auvergne, and dying at last in his cathedral, with the wailing of his people in his ears." The cathedral was Arvernum, now Clermont. His exile occurred under Alaric, but he was eventually allowed back.

1712: Sir, Having a little Time upon my Hands, I could not think of bestowing it better, than in writing an Epistle to the SPECTATOR, which I now do, and am,
Sir,
Your humble Servant,
BOB SHORT
P.S. If you approve of my Stile, I am likely enough to become your Correspondent. I desire your Opinion of it. I design it for that Way of Writing called by the Judicious the *"Familiar."*

The Spectator

August 24

THERE IS a tradition identifying the Apostle ST BARTHOLOMEW with the Nathanael who was brought to Jesus by St Philip, in the account in St John's Gospel (very near the beginning, immediately after Our Lord's baptism by St John and the calling of St Peter). He said to Philip disbelievingly "can any good come out of Nazareth?" but, recognized by Jesus as "an Israelite in whom there is no guile", said, "Rabbi, thou art the Son of God." He was among those to whom Jesus appeared on the shore of Galilee after the Resurrection. He was martyred, probably in Armenia (some writers credited him with having preached as far as India); he was said to have been flayed alive.

1824: In the course of the last week the tame pigeon died, which my children have had for nearly eight years. . . . Owen and Joseph prepared a grave, and asked me to give them an inscription for his tombstone . . .
> *Hic jacet in Tumba*
> *Formosa Columba*
> *Thomas vocata*
> *Dolore humata*

For their faithful dog Myrtle, they also prepared a

monumental record to be placed over his grave, comme-
morating his attachment and the catastrophe which occa-
sioned his death, in these words.

Hic jacet Myrtelis
Canis fidelis
Cum sit venatus
Plumbo necatus

These are trifling things in themselves, yet if they tend to
encourage feeling and affection, ought to be attended to in
the education of young people.

John Skinner (1772–1839)

August 25

Sᴛ Lᴏᴜɪs (1214–1270) became king of France (as Louis IX) at
the age of twelve. Recovering from a serious illness in 1244
he resolved on a Crusade, although many of his people tried to
dissuade him. After an easy capture of Damietta, his soldiers,
weakened both by disease and the fleshpots of the east, were
heavily defeated. Louis was taken prisoner and only released
with the surrender of Damietta and payment of a large ransom.
He cared deeply about the physical and moral welfare of his
men but was no general. Back in France he was a just and well-
loved ruler. He organized yet another Crusade in 1270—this
time by way of the North African coast; and died of dysentery at
Tunis. Two tributes from men neither of whom were exactly
sympathetic to the medieval ideal: Gibbon said, "he united the
virtues of a king, a hero and a man;" Voltaire said "never has it
been accorded to man to push virtue further."

1892: ... old Mr McInroy became insolvent, under
Trust, as the Scotch say, ... there are five daughters. ...
and the eldest son and heir, a morose person in white
flannel trousers, who has 'let it be known'. ... that he
intends to do nothing. He spends the whole day wandering
to and from the Recreation Ground with a tennis racquet,
doesn't play, but sits on a bank, visibly waiting for his
father's demise. He is a great nuisance to meet round
corners, but reduces the embarrassment to a minimum by
scowling constantly at his toes.

Beatrix Potter (1866–1943)

170

August 26

S⊤ ZEPHYRINUS, the fifteenth Pope (from 199 to 217), was yet
another figure in the great debates and controversies before
the final formulation of the Dogma of the Trinity. He had to
condemn the doctrine of Sabellianism, which said that the
Father, the Son and the Holy Spirit were the same person. He
also abolished the use of wooden chalices in the Mass, replacing
them with glass ones, and prescribed that all should receive
Communion at Easter. He died a martyr.

1766: In the west part of Kent from every eminence
the eye catches some long winding reach of the Thames
or Medway, with all their navigation; in the east, the sea
breaks in upon you, and mixes its white transient sails and
glittering blue expanse with the deeper and brighter greens
of the woods and corn. This last sentence is so fine, I am
quite ashamed.

Thomas Gray (1716–1771)

August 27

S⊤ JOSEPH CALASANCTIUS (1557–1648) came from a noble Ara-
gonese family. After graduating in law and divinity in Spain
he became a priest. In Rome, "shocked," says Attwater, "by the
ignorance and moral and physical squalor of the common
people," he founded the Order of the Poor Clerks of the Pious
Schools of the Mother of God (known as the Piarists); the first
priests to teach in elementary schools.

1890: . . . Carrie prepared a little extemporized supper, consisting of the remainder of the cold joint, a small
piece of salmon (which I was to refuse, in case there was
not enough to go round) and a *blanc-mange* and custards.
There was also a decanter of port and some jam puffs on the
sideboard. Mrs James made us play rather a good game of
cards, called "Muggings." To my surprise, in fact disgust,
Lupin got up in the middle, and, in a most sarcastic tone,

171

said: "Pardon me, this sort of thing is too fast for me. I shall go and enjoy a quiet game of marbles in the back-garden."
George & Weedon Grossmith, The Diary of a Nobody

August 28

S⊤ A∪gustine (354–430) was a *passionate* man. With all the uninhibited ardour of a hot-blooded North African nature he wrestled with the mighty problems of the dual nature of man, of his insatiable desire for perfection in a world which was not only obviously temporary but apparently contained a principle of evil as well as of good. His mother, St Monica (*see May 4*) was a Christian, his father a pagan who was converted shortly before his death. But in his youth Augustine resisted baptism. One of his many famous sayings is *"sero te amavi, pulchritudo tam antiqua et tam nova;"* too late have I loved Thee, O Beauty so old and so new! Reading Cicero, particularly the *Hortensius*, gave him a taste for philosophy, and it was as a teacher of rhetoric and philosophy, at Carthage and Rome, that he first distinguished himself. He was also coming under the influence of St Ambrose of Milan. His account of his conversion is of course classic, how he went restlessly into the garden, and heard from over the wall a child's voice saying the famous words; *"tolle, lege,"* take up and read. He took up the Epistle of St Paul, read, "Not in rioting and drunkenness. . . ." and the tears came. He was then baptized with his friend Alypius (*see August 15*) and his illegitimate son Adeodatus. There followed the community life at Tagaste, a seed of monastic life in the west, and his elevation as bishop of Hippo; but of course what mattered most were the great writings; the refutations of Manicheism, the fifteen treatises against Pelagianism with their stern insistence on the utter inadequacy of man's works, however good, without grace, and the even sterner words *"salus extra ecclesiam non est;"* no salvation outside the church. And above all, the famous *Confessions*. *"Fecisti nos ad te et inquietum est cor nostrum, donec requiescat in te."* Thou hast created us for Thyself, and our heart is restless till it finds quiet in Thee.

1675: Towards evening last night we discover a vessel belonging to the Tripolines thrust between two rocks, and many Moors lying behind the rocks to guard her: at which we made several great shot; but the evening coming suddenly on, caused us to stand off; till, in the morning early, having the *Roebuck*, a small ship come to us, which could go much nearer the rocks than we, we having beaten off the Turks, send in our pinnace, and carry away as much as we could to burn for our use. And, towards evening, we being bound to cruise Westward, drink to our friends in a lemonade.

Henry Teonge (1621–1690)

August 29

ST SEBBI (d. about 694) was an East Saxon king who, unlike his contemporary King Sighere, refused to see an outbreak of plague as a visitation from Woden and the old pagan gods, and held on to Christianity. He was, says Bede, "more fit to be a bishop than a king," and long desired to live the religious life, and had the not uncommon and not really surprising experience of his wife's objection to this course. After a serious illness however, with her consent he did take the religious habit. As death approached, says Bede, "he began to apprehend lest, when under pain, and at the approach of death, anything unbecoming might escape from his lips, or there might be want of dignity in the posture of his limbs. He therefore called to him the bishop of London, and entreated that none might be present at his death except the bishop and two of his attendants. The bishop consented. As Wladhere dozed by the king's bed, he thought he saw men in shining garments minister to the sick man, and promise him a painless death. Sebbi passed quietly away in slumber and was buried in St Paul's London."

1939: [To The Times] May I, through your columns, appeal to caricaturists and humorous writers to suspend during the present crisis the practice of making the dachshund a symbol of Nazidom or of the German nation? Absurd as it may seem, the prevalence of this idea in the popular imagination has produced a real risk of thoughtless acts of cruelty being committed against harmless little animals which are English by birth and often by generations of breeding.

Mr D. L. Murray

August 30

Two very interesting Christian (literally!) names today. SS FELIX and ADAUCTUS (about 304). St Felix was a Roman priest who, after torture on the rack, was being led out to execution. A stranger in the crowd was moved to call out, "I too am a Christian," upon which he was hastily tried and executed with Felix. As his name was not known he was called Adauctus, meaning that he was added on to St Felix. This is the feast day of St Happy and St Added.

> 1871: ... Grandmamma looks changed. She says—my father told me in the evening but I ought to have heard it from herself—that she has heard her grandfather say that he could remember an old man saying he had seen the soldiers going about the hedges in his part of the country in search of Charles I—after which battle?
>
> *Gerard Manley Hopkins (1844–1889)*

August 31

ST AIDAN (d. 651) was the great apostle of Northumbria. When the king-saint Oswald (*see August 9*) asked the Iona community to send someone to organize the task of re-Christianizing a region ravaged by the Saxon and Celtic wars, they at first sent one Corman who (says Baring-Gould) tended "to look on the gloomy side of affairs, to rebuke and threaten." When Corman reported back that he could make nothing of the Angles, Aidan suggested he might have tried a bit more tenderness, and this in fact made him the obvious candidate. He made his headquarters a kind of physical island replica of Iona itself—Lindisfarne. That tide-isolated outcrop, within sight of the coastal rock-fortress of Bamburgh, became the spiritual powerhouse of a region from Hull to Edinburgh. St Aidan practised what he preached—love and humility, making his immense missionary journeys on foot, to the astonishment of his horse-loving converts. Helping the poor and manumitting the many slaves still existing there, he founded schools and monasteries.

1798: In the morning we went to London a-shopping, and at Wedgwood's, as usual, were highly entertain'd, as I think no shop affords so great a variety. I there, among other things, purchas'd one of the new invented *petit soupé* trays, which I think equally clever, elegant, and convenient when alone or a small party, as so much less trouble to ourselves and servants.

Mrs Philip Lybbe Powys (1739–1817)

SEPTEMBER

September 1

S<small>T</small> F<small>IACRE</small>, or Fiachra, was an Irish hermit who came to France; the town of St Fiacre-en-Brie is on the site where he built a hospice for travellers. "He was," says Attwater, "very strict in excluding women from his own enclosure, and stories are told of the misfortunes that befell those who trespassed. His intercession was invoked especially by persons suffering from haemorrhoids. He is also looked upon as the patron saint of gardeners, because of the fine vegetables he grew around his hermitage. When cabs for hire first appeared in Paris in 1620 their stand was close by the Hotel Saint-Fiacre: hence the name *fiacre* for the French four-wheeler."

1554: The elephant (which some call an oliphant) is the biggest of all four-footed beasts, his forelegs are longer than his hinder, he hath ankles in the lower part of his hinder legs, and five toes on his feet undivided, his snout or trunk is so long, and in such form, that it is to him in the stead of a hand: for he neither eateth nor drinketh but by bringing his trunk to his mouth, therewith he helpeth up his master or keeper, therewith he overthroweth trees. Of all beasts they are the most gentle and tractable, and are of quick sense and sharpness of wit. They love rivers, and will often go into them up to the snout, wherewith they blow and snuff and play in the water. They have continual war against dragons, which desire their blood because it is very cold: and therefore the dragon lieth in wait as the elephant passeth by.

Richard Hakluyt (edited by) (1552–1616)

September 2

S<small>T</small> S<small>TEPHEN</small> (Istvan) of Hungary (975–1038), son of the pagan Magyar Geza, relied on linked fortress towns containing many Germans in his avowed campaign to convert the roaming, restless, still pagan Magyars of the countryside, and his successful battle against Kupa (grandson of Arpad, leader of the original Magyar invaders) at Veszprem "was stained by no acts of cruelty," although later "every Magyar found worshipping under the sacred oaks, by fountains, or before lichened rocks, was ordered to be put to death by drowning." He was crowned first King of Hungary in 1000. He abolished the old tribal system and divided the land into counties. He was tough but also just and charitable. "Finding that the morals of his subjects were not quite what they should be, he peremptorily ordered every man in his kingdom to be married, excepting only ecclesiastics and idolaters." He was once set upon by a crowd of beggars when giving alms, and "he was particularly anxious to wash the feet of poor men and cripples in public, but found the attempt dangerous. The haughty nobles were unable to appreciate the virtues of such an act, and before their sneers and suppressed laughter he was obliged to retreat, and perform the operation in private."

1841: [To Bernard Barton] I came to this house a week ago to visit a male friend, who duly started to England the day before I got here. I therefore found myself domiciled in a house filled with ladies of divers ages—Edgworth's wife, aged—say 28—his mother aged 74—his [step] sister (the great Maria) aged 72. . . . I am now writing in the Library here: and the great Authoress is as busy as a bee making a catalogue of her books beside me, chattering away. We are great friends. She is as lively, active and cheerful as if she were but twenty; really a very entertaining person.

Edward Fitzgerald (1809–1883)

September 3

Sᴛ Pɪᴜs X (1835–1914) became Pope in 1903, after 45 years in parish and diocesan work. His motto was *instaurare omnia in Christo*, to restore all things in Christ. He was indeed a reforming Pope; he reorganized the Curia, codified Canon Law, as well as condemning "Modernism." His *Motu Proprio* was written in 1904, in the days of brigand's-chorus masses: it re-established Gregorian chant as *the* church music.

1871: I went to Bettws in light rain and preached extempore on the Good Samaritan from the Gospel for

the day. A red cow with a foolish white face came up to the
window by the desk and stared in while I was preaching.

Francis Kilvert (1840–1879)

September 4

ST MARINUS is a saint of whom more than the birth date is
"uncertain." His story, though apocryphal, is delightful. He
was a Dalmatian peasant who worked for twelve years as a very
good stonemason on the walls and aqueduct at Rimini. Then "a
Dalmatian peasantess" appeared and announced that she was
his wife. No sooner did Marinus see her face peering in at the
entrance to the cave where he was now a hermit than he
slammed the door, and rolled stones against it. After six days he
ventured forth. His wife, devoid of provisions, had retired. He
seized the opportunity to go higher and ensconce himself on the
face of a cliff where no woman could reach him. There he
amused himself with taming a bear "to carry loads for him." It
is after him that the Republic of San Marino is named.

1930: Micky Thompson continues to show himself as
charming child, with cheerful disposition, good manners, and excellent health. Enquiry reveals that he is an
orphan, which does not surprise me in the least. Have often
noticed that absence of parental solicitude usually very
beneficial to offspring.

E. M. Delafield, Diary of a Provincial Lady

September 5

ST BERTIN (b. about 608 and said to have lived to be nearly a
hundred) led a monastic community at Sithieu in the Pas de
Calais, in the days long before it was drained, and many of what
are hillocks today were islands. He was a kinsman of St Omer,
who had summoned him to this work, and the modern town of
St Omer grew up round his monastery, which later became "the
noblest Gothic monument of French Flanders." It was suppressed during the Revolution, but was still standing (although

roofless and stripped) in 1830, when the magistrates of St Omer "barbarously pulled it down to afford employment to some labourers out of work."

1788: To Montauban. The poor people seem poor indeed; the children terribly ragged. . . . One-third of what I have seen of this province seems uncultivated, and nearly all of it is misery. What have kings, and ministers, and parliaments, and States, to answer for their prejudices, seeing millions of hands that would be industrious, idle and starving, through the execrable maxims of despotism or the equally detestable prejudices of a feudal nobility. Sleep at the Lion d'Or at Montauban, an abominable hole.

Arthur Young (1741–1820)

September 6

TWO RATHER confusing saints. ST CAGNOALD (d. about 635) was one of three children of Agneric, a noble at the court of King Dagobert. His brother Faro and sister Burgundofara also became saints. He was brought up under St Columbanus, the great Irish missionary of Europe, and became bishop of Laon. ST MAGNOALD (d. about 655) seems altogether more legendary. "An incident told of St Magnoald," says Baring-Gould, "is told verbatim of Cagnoald, the forger having only to change one letter." This, however, is not the incident of the bear. St Magnoald, a friend of St Gall after whom the great Swiss monastery is named, founded an abbey at Fussen, where a bear had shown him several iron veins in the mountains. Subsequently mines were worked there for centuries.

1896: There is something about the sentiment of a Quaker Meeting so exactly quaint and fine that a very little oversets the balance, and to an ordinary Philistine it is never comprehensible at all, but to those who can feel the charm, like Charles Lamb, it is exquisitely pleasant.

There was one child present, a little boy, who sat behind me on the women's side. He was very quiet, except for audibly sucking sweeties and sighing deeply at intervals. I fear, but do not wonder, that backsliders are numerous in the young generation.

181

I walked home with Miss Cochrane from the post-office, a fat, nice, yellow-haired, juvenile little person, a Quakeress from Kendal. She could not tell me much about the Colthouse meeting, except that her father had "told her where to go." We had much talk about the telegraph which is "worked by electricity," and gets stuck during thunderstorms. It is also said that Mr Foulkes can cook cutlets with the electric light.

Beatrix Potter (1866–1943)

September 7

S⊤ CLODOALD was one of three children of Clodomir, killed in battle against the Burgundians. Clodomir was one of the four sons of Clovis, the architect of the Frankish kingdom, and his orphaned children were brought up by their grandmother, Clotilda. Two brothers of Clodomir, Childebert and Clothair, jealous of the future claims of the children, murdered two of them, but Clodoald escaped, and lived to become a much-venerated hermit in Provence. Later he returned to Paris, where the wicked uncles no longer feared him, as a mere monk, and they allowed him to build a monastery in the place where he is now commemorated as St Cloud. "In art he is often represented with nails, as he is patron of the nail-makers, through an absurd pun on his name" (*clou* = nail).

1917: [To his mother, from Craiglockhart Hospital]. . . . Will you do a sacred task for me? Wrench open the Cupboard of my Desk and withdraw from the top-shelf right-hand side, three port-folios—two are khaki, one is Harold's gilt-stencilled velvet blotter. Upon your unimpeachable honour *do not inspect the contents either of the cupboard or of the portfolios.* But promptly pack off the portfolios under *secure wrappings and plain address.* I don't care if you damage the cupboard-door. But don't damage the hinges of your mind by wrenching the secrets of my portfolios. This sounds mysterious; but I am serious. Some of these verses will light my cigarettes, but one or two may light the darkness of the world. It is not a question of wheat and chaff, but of devils and angels. . . .

Wilfred Owen (1893–1918)

September 8

S<small>T</small> A<small>DRIAN</small>, or Hadrian (d. about 304) was an officer at the court of Maximian who was so impressed by the fortitude of some Christian martyrs that he announced that he too was a Christian; he was not in fact baptised, although his wife Natalia was. After a cruel flogging his legs were smashed by hammers on an anvil. Natalia, who had been present at all this, escaped a second marriage, to a tribune, by fleeing to Byzantium, where she died.

1927: Kenneth [Mozley] and I had tea, and he told me how he was the only true Augustinian in the church, much to the interest of the neighbouring tea tables. "I have no use at all, my dear Rose," he said, getting very loud and shrill, "for your weak, striving, well-meaning God, who has to rely on our encouragement of him for his success." Everyone looked at me with scorn, for having a God like that. I like to see a man so animated about religion. . . .
Rose Macaulay (1881–1958)

September 9

S<small>T</small> P<small>ETER</small> C<small>LAVER</small> (1580–1654) was the apostle of the slaves in the New World. Born in Catalonia, he became a Jesuit and in 1610 landed at Cartagena in what is now Colombia. His work in the mines and plantations and prisons and hospitals very often meant that his living conditions were as bad as for those to whom he ministered. The last four years of his life he spent alone, paralysed and in constant pain.

1778: . . . Mr and Mrs Custance are very agreeable people indeed, and both behaved exceedingly polite and civil to me. I there saw an Instrument which Mrs Custance played on that I never saw before. It is called Sticcardo pastorale. It is very soft Music indeed. It is several long pieces of glass laid in order in a case, and is played in the middle parts of the glasses by two little sticks with Nobbs at the end of them striking the glass. It is a very small Instrument and looks when covered like a working Box for Ladies.

James Woodforde (1740–1803)

September 10

Sт Sᴀʟᴠɪᴜs (d. 584) (St Sauve) was a monk who at one time was thought by his brethren to have died; but when being laid out for burial he suddenly recovered. For three days he ate nothing; "his mother came to see him, and at her persuasion he convoked the monks and told them what had befallen him. His soul had gone to heaven, and he had seen an ineffable light; but a voice had cried, 'Let this man return to earth; he is necessary to the church.' And then Salvius found that he was again in the body. After he had related this vision his tongue became covered with pimples, and swelled up as if to fill his mouth; he thought it was a punishment for having told what had befallen him." In 574 he became bishop of Albi. He was famous as a releaser of slaves.

1805: [To John Allen] . . . Lady Holland will find a very great difficulty in getting such a tutor as she wants; it must be some man so absorbed in discovering the difference between X and Y that the difference between dining in the parlor or out of it has never occurred to him. . . .

Sydney Smith (1771–1845)

September 11

Sт Tʜᴇᴏᴅᴏʀᴀ ᴏꜰ Aʟᴇxᴀɴᴅʀɪᴀ (5th century) is said to have been a married woman who after falling into sin was ashamed to face her husband and went to live in the desert as a *monk*, was later recognized by him in a mutual reconciliation, then returned to the desert, her funeral being attended by him. All very much more doubtful than some of her sayings, which have been preserved. E.g., "once a hermit said, 'I am so surrounded with temptations that I must leave this place and go elsewhere.' So he went out of his door, and put on his sandals, and he saw near him his double putting on his sandals, and preparing to journey. 'I am Self,' said the double, 'wherever you go, I go too.' "

1776: I spent about two hours in Mr Hoare's gardens at Stourton . . .Others were delighted with the temples, but I was not: 1. Because several of the statues about them were mean; 2. Because I cannot admire the images of devils, and we know the gods of the Heathens are devils; 3. Because I defy all mankind to reconcile statues with nudities, either to common-sense or common decency.

John Wesley (1703–1791)

(NB. *This entry is actually for Sept. 12, but seems more moveable than the diary extract actually chosen for tomorrow. It is the only entry in this book consciously so moved*)

September 12

Sᴛ Gᴜʏ, or Guido, or Wyden, of Anderlecht (about 950–1012) was a hermit who went on a pilgrimage to Jerusalem, in the company of the dean of Anderlecht whom he met on the way at Rome, each being delighted to hear the unexpected Flemish tongue there. A life written some time after his death, and therefore predictably full of marvels, tells how a horse, which struck his by then neglected tomb with its hoof, fell dead. Onulf, the lord of Anderlecht, at once put a hedge round it. Then two serfs laughed at the idea of Guido's being a saint, and *they* fell dead.

1908: To London for the Winston-Clementine wedding. It was quite a popular demonstration. Lord Hugh Cecil Winston's best man, and the great crowd of relations, not only the church full, but all Victoria Street. . . . The bride was pale, as was the bridegroom. He has gained in appearance since I saw him last, and has a powerful if ugly face. Winston's responses were clearly made in a pleasant voice, Clementine's inaudible.

Wilfrid Scawen Blunt (1840–1922)

185

September 13

S⊤ NotBURGA (about 1265–1313) was a kitchen-maid at the castle of one Count Henry in the Tyrol. Dismissed for giving to the poor some "broken food" that she had been told to give to the pigs, she later returned and spent the rest of her life there. She is the patron saint of hired hands in the Tyrol and Bavaria, if there are any left.

1803: The roads in Herefordshire are at least in many parts remarkably bad. Hoppner said that Christie [the auctioneer] told him that having an estate in Herefordshire to dispose of He had as usual set it off by a flowery oration, but before concluding He said that He felt bound to observe that Herefordshire was a county that had two peculiarities, viz.: "turnpikes without end,"—and "roads without bottom."

Joseph Farington (1747–1821)

September 14

S⊤ MATERNUS (4th century) is one of several saints concerning whom there is a cheerfully century-skipping legend that he was sent to Gaul and the north directly by St Peter, at the touch of whose staff he was miraculously restored after "dying" on the way. In fact he was bishop of Trèves (Trier) and Cologne in the fourth century, and was present at a council ordered at Arles in 314 by Constantine to deal with the Donatists, a kind of early puritans.

1804: I called yesterday morning (ought it not in strict propriety to be called yester-morning?) on Miss Armstrong and was introduced to her father and mother. Like other young ladies she is considerably genteeler than her parents. Mrs Armstrong sat darning a pair of stockings the whole of my visit. But I do not mention this at home, lest a warning be taken as an example. We afterwards walked together for an hour on the Cobb; she is very converseable in a common way; I do not perceive wit or genius, but she has sense and some degree of taste, and her manners are very engaging. She seems to like people rather too easily. . . .

Jane Austen (1775–1817)

September 15

ST CATHERINE OF GENOA (1447–1510) belonged to the patrician Fieschi family amongst whose privileges was that of minting the coinage of Genoa. Married, fairly ineffectively, to Julian Adorno, who was as luxury-loving as *she* was intensely ascetic, she was eventually separated. After he died "a reformed penitent in the Third Order of St Francis" she devoted her life to immensely practical and physical care of the sick, whilst never losing her mystical absorption. She left behind her two works; a dialogue between God and the soul, and one on Purgatory.

1921: It is the loveliest of evenings—still; the smoke going up straight in the quarry; the white horse & strawberry coloured horse feeding close together; the women coming out of their cottages for no reason & standing looking; or knitting; the cock pecking in the midst of his hens in the meadow; starlings in the two trees; Asheham fields shorn to the colour of white corduroy; Leonard storing apples above my head. & the sun coming through a pearly glass shade; so that the apples which still hang are palish red & green; the church tower a silver extinguisher rising through the trees. Will this recall anything? I am so anxious to keep every scrap, you see.

Virginia Woolf (1882–1941)

September 16

ST NINIAN (5th century) was the apostle of the southern Picts. He is said to have been born at Candida Casa, "White House," probably the modern Whithorn on the peninsula on the western side of Wigtown Bay. He became a bishop in Rome, and on his way back borrowed masons from St Martin of Tours (see November 11) and built the first stone church in Britain, dedicating it to St Martin on hearing of his death in 397.

1924:
Hudson gone.
Conrad gone.
Hardy very old: G. Moore gaga; D.H.L. ditto; whom have we to welcome year by year?
(Not Aldous Huxley, not a Sitwell, not J. Joyce, not Wyndham Lewis: somebody lovable).
E. M. Forster: very good; but is he quite great? I like him, but a little shamefacedly.

T. E. Lawrence (1888–1935)

September 17

Sᴛ Hɪʟᴅᴇɢᴀʀᴅ (1098–1179), abbess of Rupertsberg, near Bingen, was not only in the great tradition of visionary German mystics (known as "the Sybil of the Rhine" she wrote to four popes—Eugenius II, Anastasius IV, Adrian IV and Alexander III, and many other important figures) but stoutly practical, and a fearless castigator of the worldly and warlike German prince-bishops, quoting with approval a monk who said, "I can believe in any miracle and marvel except one—the possibility of salvation of a German bishop."

1712: I have known one Wench in this Town carry an haughty Dominion over her lovers so well, that she has at the same Time been kept by a Sea Captain in the *Streights*, a Merchant in the City, a Country Gentleman in *Hampshire*, and had all her Correspondence managed by one she kept for her own Uses. This happy Man (as the Phrase is) used to write very punctually every Post letters for the Mistress to transcribe. He would sit in his Night-Gown and Slippers, and be as grave giving an Account, only changing Names, that there was nothing in these idle Reports they had heard of such a Scoundrel as one of the other Lovers was; and how could he think she could condescend so low, after such a fine Gentleman as each of them? For the same Epistle said

188

the same Thing to and of every one of them. And so Mr
Secretary and his Lady went to Bed with great Order.

The Spectator

September 18

ST JOSEPH OF CUPERTINO (1603–1663) was no saint for the
inhibited. Slow and stupid-looking in youth (he was called
"the Gaper") he was taken on as stable boy at a Franciscan friary
at Martino, near Tarento. He was eventually admitted to holy
orders without examination (after the bishop had heard him
discourse on the text "blessed is the fruit of thy womb, Jesus")
and has been regarded as the patron of those sitting examina-
tions. He was extremely sensitive to music. One day, hearing
some nuns singing *Veni sponsa Christi,* "unable to restrain
himself, he ran across the choir, caught the confessor of the
convent in his arms, danced with him into the middle of the
church, and spun him round and round in the air. One day, in
the presence of the legate to Spain, uttering a shrill cry, he
jumped over the heads of those kneeling before the altar, twelve
paces to the feet of an image of the Blessed Virgin which stood
on the high altar, and jumped back over their heads 'with the
same noise.' " On another occasion he leapt up on to the altar
and embraced the tabernacle. Perhaps not surprisingly, he was
brought before the Inquisition as a suspected pseudo-Messianic
heretic, and sent to Rome for discipline. But he eventually
impressed everyone with his genuine sanctity, and became well
known as a spiritual adviser. "I like not scruples or melancholy,"
he would tell people who came to him, "let your intention be
right, and fear not." His leaping on to altars (or up into trees)
continued; and there were several testimonies to his levitation
while saying Mass.

1754: . . . Lord Brooke . . . has sashed the great Apartment (at Warwick Castle) and being since told that
square sash-windows were not Gothic, he has put certain
whim-whams within side the glass, which appearing
through, are to look like fretwork.

Thomas Gray (1716–1771)

September 19

S⊤ JANUARIUS (d. about 305), bishop of Beneventum, was a martyr under Diocletian. The famous liquefaction of his blood, kept in a glass phial in the cathedral at Naples, of which city he is patron saint, still occurs (and has never been satisfactorily explained) several times a year, during a ceremony at which the head of the martyr is brought near it. But the first mention of this is in the 14th century.

1938: Susan and I heard over the wireless on September 15th that Chamberlain was flying to Germany. From the moment I heard the news, I felt full of dismay and fear. . . .
Charles showed me today a most interesting letter from Lily's uncle written from Luxembourg. He said that last Wednesday things looked very bad but that Chamberlain's coup might stop war at the expense, as he put it very plainly, of honour.
Meanwhile the papers entirely back the Prime Minister. The one which is most independent and has the most news is the *Daily Telegraph*. *The Times* is induced to print on its leader page a letter from Lord Allen of Hurtwood [Chairman Independent Labour Party 1922–26] with the absurd heading *Justice with Security*.

Marie Belloc-Lowndes (1868–1947)

September 20

S⊤ AGAPETUS became pope in 535. He undertook a mission from the Gothic (and Arian) king Theodotus in Italy to dissuade the emperor Justinian from invading (otherwise Theodotus would burn Rome to the ground before he arrived, etc.). He was received with honour at Constantinople, and stood up to the emperor in opposing the appointment as patriarch of Constantinople of one Anthimus, suspected of the Eutychian heresy (doctrine that Christ had only divine nature). He died at Constantinople, but his body was taken to Rome for burial.

1806: [To Mary Godfrey]. . . . I was neither happy nor comfortable, and I did not like to throw the shade of my mind upon paper for you, though little bodies do not in general cast great shadows; yet you cannot imagine what an eclipse I spread around me whenever my orb becomes opaque with sorrow, or that the light of the heart does not shine pleasantly through me; and this has been the case all this fortnight past. I have had every possible *colour* of annoyance,—*brown* study, *blue* devils, not forgetting "*green* and *yellow* melancholy"—in short I have been a "rainbow ruffian" (as some sentimental poet styles a well-dressed soldier), and my *reflections* on paper would have been all of the prismatic kind. "Oh, this learning! what a thing it is!"

Thomas Moore (1779–1852)

September 21

Sᴛ Mᴀᴛᴛʜᴇw ᴛʜᴇ Aᴘᴏsᴛʟᴇ is named as Levi, the tax-gatherer, at the time of his calling by Jesus, after the cure of the man sick of the palsy, and before the disputation with the Jews about consorting with such outsiders ("I will have mercy, and not sacrifice: for I am come not to call the righteous, but sinners to repentance"). In his own gospel he gives himself the name Matthew. There are various traditions concerning the areas of his mission, but Ethiopia is included. He is venerated as a martyr, although some early authorities such as Clement, Origen and Tertullian say he died a natural death.

1778: Here is eassely seen the difference betwext Picardy and Normany all the country hearabouts is inclosed there houses later built and the inhabitants seems quitte another sort of people; nothing so remarkable as the differences where the two provinces join; this toun seems tolerable lively although small; there is a Cloth Manufactory; dined here and after set out to Neuchatell. All this road is inclosed pasture land and seems a very Rich Soil. Arrived in the evening at Neuchatell where we lodged; this toun is remarkable for Cheasse which is very rich; those cheeses are small and in form of a large cork about 2 inches long by about an inch or an inch and half diametre; this seems there principall comarse of this place.

Thomas Blaikie (1750–1838)

191

September 22

THE STORY OF ST LOLAN is, to say the least, both varied and unlikely. One story says that, being doorkeeper at St Peter's in Rome, in the 5th century, he left to follow his uncle St Serf who had gone to preach to the Scots so "one night he locked the church of St Peter as usual, left the key in a conspicuous place, and departed on foot for Scotland, which he reached after a weary journey." It was revealed to the people at Rome that the church could only be opened by the hand that had locked it. When St Lolan saw the deacon and subdeacon who were thereupon sent after him, he greeted them joyfully, and cut off his right hand with a sword, asking in return that they should send him, after re-opening the church with his hand, four ass-loads of earth from St Peter's cemetery for him to be buried in. Another story says he lived much later, and in 1039 was a councillor of the King Duncan who was killed by Macbeth. "It is probable, therefore, that there were two Lolans living at very different periods." There is, however, no doubt whatever about St Thomas of Villanova (1488–1555), who achieved the fairly difficult feat of living in utter poverty and simplicity as an archbishop, and having given everything else away, gave the bed in which he lay dying to the prison.

1689: About four in the morning, on the change of the moon, Mrs Patty fell into violent convulsions, whereon I was called and Dr Cotton sent for. By the time he came, she appeared to be apoplectic, whereon I had her cupped on each shoulder, which brought her a little to her senses. Then the doctor advised an application of pigeons to her head. . . . I despaired of anything but death suddenly. I went to church. As usual Mr Milbourn read prayers, and I preached in the morning, Luke xviii. 14, and in the afternoon I baptized seven children, and he preached in the evening. That evening I spent at home. (*see also September 23*)

Rowland Davies (1649–1721)

September 23

S<small>T</small> L<small>INUS</small> was the first bishop of Rome after St Peter; some say that he held that office for a time even before the death of St Peter. He is named as a martyr in the Canon of the Mass, although nothing definite is known about his death, which occurred around 67.

1689: In the morning I found Mrs Patty a little more lively than I expected. Nature having had some relief, and the doctor proposing some narcotics for her, I opposed it. (*see also September 26*)

Rowland Davies (1649–1721)

September 24

S<small>T</small> G<small>EREMAR</small> (d. about 658) was a Frankish noble with two daughters and a son. When the latter came of age he made over his estate to him and became a monk, eventually abbot of Pentale on the Seine. Some of the monks, finding his rule too strict, fixed a sharp knife so that it would kill him when he lay on it, but he discovered it, and retired, not surprisingly "disgusted at this attempt on his life, but without publishing abroad the reason lest it should cause scandal." His son died young, and he used the funds of his repossessed estate to build a large monastery at Flay, of which he became abbot.

1778: [To his son] As a lover of music you will not consider it beneath you to play the violin in the first symphony any more than does the Archbishop himself and also the courtiers who play with us. You would surely not deny to Haydn certain achievements in music? Has he, a Konzertmeister, become a court viola-player, because he plays that instrument in the chamber music concerts? Why, one does it for one's own amusement; and as the concert is short and only consists of four items, believe me that to play is a pleasant recreation, as one doesn't know what to do with oneself in the evenings. If something more important turns up, eh bien! one stays away—as others have done.

And I wager that rather than let your own composition be bungled—you will prefer to take part in the performance. It does not follow, however, that you will be regarded as a fiddler, while others enjoy themselves, and that you will have to play their trios and quartets. Not at all! My chief satisfaction in this arrangement is that your salary and my improved one will enable us to pay [our debts] and live in comfort.

Leopold Mozart (1719–1787)

September 25

ST SERGIUS (about 1314–1392) is a name, says Baring-Gould, "as dear to every Russian heart as is that of William Tell to a Swiss, or that of Joan of Arc to a Frenchman." But it is not only for his encouragement of Prince Demetrius (Dimitri)—to the extent of some of his monks fighting with coats of mail over their habits—that he is remembered. The Troitska monastery which he founded was a powerful centre of spirituality in Russia, and he himself embodied the simplicity, gentleness and earthy mysticism of Russian monasticism. Like St Seraphim of Sarov (*see January 2*) he was sometimes observed to be transfigured by light.

1660: I did send for a cup of tee (a China drink) of which I never had drink before.

Samuel Pepys (1633–1703)

September 26

ST JOHN DE BRÉBEUF (1593–1649) was one of the Jesuit martyrs canonized in 1930. On his second mission to the Huron Indians, more successful than the first, he was taken by the Iroquois in a raid and tortured to death. He shares this feast day with Sts Antony Daniel, Charles Garnier, of whom it was said "his very laugh spoke of goodness," Gabriel Lalemant, thin and delicate, who survived for a whole night the tortures that killed the burly John de Brébeuf in a few hours and was finally despatched with a tomahawk, John Lalande, Isaac Jogues (who penetrated 1000 miles inland up Lake Superior, and had lost the use of his hands through torture some years before his martyrdom), Noel Chabanel (who "had a natural repugnance to the Indians," suffered constantly from spiritual depression and therefore made a vow never to leave his post) and René Goupil (who, having had to leave the Jesuit Order through ill-health, had studied surgery and gone out at his own expense).

1689: In the morning Mrs Patty appeared somewhat better in her senses, and it was concluded to take off the pigeons, and, having washed her head with a decoction of warm and sweet herbs, and anointed it with aromatic oils, to put on a spiced cap by order of Dr Willis for amaurosis.

Rowland Davies (1649–1721)

September 27

Ss Cosmas and Damian, martyrs whose names come in the Canon of the Mass, are the patron saints of the medical profession, although they differed from most members of it, according to one tradition, in that they were styled in Greek *anargyri*, that is "without fees," because they took no money, and healed as much by the virtues of Christ as by natural methods. They were brought before the prefect Lysias in Cilicia (now part of Turkey) during the persecution of Diocletian, and after torture, were beheaded.

1796: [to Coleridge] My dearest Friend,—White, or some of my friends, or the public papers, by this time may have informed you of the terrible calamities that have fallen on our family. I will give you the outlines:—My poor dear, dearest sister, in a fit of insanity, has been the death of her own mother. I was at hand only time enough to snatch the knife out of her grasp. She is at present in a madhouse, from whence I fear she must be moved to an hospital. God has preserved to me my senses: I eat, and drink, and sleep, and have my judgment, I believe, very sound. My poor father was slightly wounded, and I am left to take care of him and my aunt. Mr Norris, of Bluecoat School, has been very kind to us, and we have no other friend; but, thank God, I am very calm and composed, and able to do the best that remains to do. Write as religious a letter as possible, but no mention of what is gone and done with. With me "the former things are passed away," and I have something more to do than to feel.

God Almighty have us all in His keeping!

Charles Lamb (1775–1834)

September 28

ST WENCESLAUS, Duke of Bohemia. His mother Drahomira was not a saint. In fact during her regency his grandmother, Ludmilla, who *was*, was murdered. When Wenceslaus came to power he tried to promote good order, Christianity, and to placate his German neighbours. He had a great reverence for priests, and with his own hands sowed the wheat and pressed the grapes used for the Mass. The bit about the page and the yule logs is legend. His murder in a church (in 929, say some; in 938, say others) by his brother Boleslav, instigated by Drahomira, is not.

1938: . . . then the PM played his trump ace, and read the message that had been handed to me—"That is not all. I have something further to say to the House" and he told how Hitler had invited him to Munich tomorrow morning, that Mussolini had accepted the same invitation, that M. Daladier in all probability would do so too—every heart throbbed and there was born in many, in me, at least, a gratitude, an admiration for the PM which will be eternal. . . .

I will always remember little Neville today, with his too long hair, greying at the sides, his smile, his amazing spirits and seeming lack of fatigue, as he stood there, alone, fighting the dogs of war single-handed and triumphant—he seemed the reincarnation of St George—so simple and so unspoilt—now in a few hours for the third time he takes a plane to a far country in the service of England. May God speed him, and reward him for his efforts. I don't know what England has done to deserve him.

"Chips" Channon (1897–1958)

196

September 29

"Benedicite Dominum, omnes Angeli ejus," sings the Introit for the Mass on the feast of St Michael (or used to): "bless the Lord all ye angels." Reaching far back into the Old Testament, the winged messengers of God, (Jophiel, who expelled Adam and Eve from Paradise, Chamuel who wrestled with Jacob, Zadkiel who stayed the hand of Abraham from slaying Isaac at that terrible command of God) passed into the New; Christian art is full of their majestic and mysterious wings, as they kneel at the Annunciation, or fill imagined heavens. It is they whose cry of *"Sanctus, sanctus, sanctus,"* as imagined by great composers, has inspired some of the noblest music ever to have come from— where? Traditionally the First Hierarchy is composed of Seraphim, Cherubim and Thrones engaged in constant adoration, the Second of Dominations, Virtues and Powers, engaged in the struggle with evil, and the Third of Principalities, Archangels and Angels, engaged in the care of creation. All are messengers and guardians, pure spirits. St Michael seems particularly associated with high places, which is where churches dedicated to him are often found. It is today's feast, of course, which gives its name to the whole Michaelmas Term.

1824: Took a walk in the fields, saw an old wood-stile taken away from a favourite spot which it had occupied all my life. The posts were overgrown with ivy and it seem'd so akin to nature and the spot where it stood as tho' it had taken on a lease for an undisturb'd existence. It hurt me to see it was gone.

John Clare (1793–1864)

September 30

St Jerome (about 331–419), chiefly famous as the translator of the Scriptures into Latin which we know as the Vulgate, was certainly a fiery character. Having studied rhetoric and law at Rome, he is said to have been amused by lawyers losing their tempers in argument, and perhaps got the habit there. He travelled to Trier, where he met his lifelong (though sometimes quarrelled-with) friend Rufinus, and saw some Scots (*Atticoti*), "a British nation who eat human flesh." In the east, during an illness, he had a vision in which God asked him what he was. He replied "a Christian," but received the reply "no, thou art a Ciceronian" (Cicero being his favourite author). His real conversion dates from this. There was an unfortunate row between him and his bishop, John of Jerusalem, which St Augustine (whom he warmly admired), begged him to moderate. No wonder he is represented with a lion. But his work on Scriptural interpretation (for which he learned Hebrew) makes his place as a major figure in the formulation of Christianity in its early days an unassailable one.

1675: More mirth at dinner this day than ever since we came on board. The wind blew very hard, and we had to dinner a rump of Zante beef, a little salted and well roasted. When it was brought into the cabin and set on the table (that is on the floor, for it could not stand on the table for the ship's tossing), our Captain sent for the Master, Mr Fogg, and Mr Davis, to dine with himself and myself, and the Lieutenant and the Purser. And we all sat close round about the beef, some securing themselves from the slurring by setting their feet against the table, which was fast tied down. The Lieutenant set his feet against the bed, and the Captain set his back against a chair which stood by the side of the ship. Several tumbles we had, we and our plates, and our knives slurred oft together. Our liquor was white rubola, admirable good. We had also a couple of fat pullets; and, whilst we were eating of them, a sea came, and forced into the cabin through the chinks of a port-hole, which by looking behind me I just discovered when the water was coming under me. I soon got up, and no whit wet; but all the rest were well washed, and got up as fast as they could, and laughed one at the other.

Henry Teonge, Chaplain on H.M.S. Assistance (1621–1690)

OCTOBER

October 1

ST REMIGIUS (Remi), (about 440–533) became archbishop of Rheims in his early twenties. When Clovis, king of the Franks, was about to do battle with the Allemanni, he promised to adopt the religion of his already Christian wife Clothild if he won, and he was duly baptized along with three thousand of his soldiers— It was said that St Remigius drove a huge fire that had broken out in Rheims before him, making the sign of the cross, till he drove it through a gate, which he ordered to be walled up "and forbade anyone ever opening it again. Many years later, the owner of the adjoining house, wanting an ash-pit, knocked a hole in the wall, that he might shoot his rubbish into it. Instantly out burst the demon of the conflagration and killed the man, his wife, children and servants."—But he *did* convert Clovis.

1844: As to Papa, why he knows nothing of Madame Dudevant*, and I don't feel inclined to explain her to him. Of course if I were to say . . . "she is a great genius, and no better than she should be, . . . and I had read her books and want to write to her,"—he would think I was mad and required his paternal restraint in all manner of ways. He has very strict ideas about women and about what they should read . . . if I were to *ask* him for that copy of the Eloise locked up in the drawer,—my dearest Miss Mitford,—he would as soon give me Prussic acid if I were thirsty!

Elizabeth Barrett (1806–1861)

October 2

ST LEODEGAR, better known to us as St Leger (about 616–679) was caught in the crossfire over the succession to the Frankish throne of Childeric and Theodoric (or, more accurately, *involved* in the crossfire, since he seems to have been a man of strong convictions). As bishop of Autun he supported Childeric;

* George Sand

his rival Ebroin, Mayor of the Palace, supported Theodoric
Eventually Ebroin besieged Autun, put out the eyes of St Leger,
cut his lips and tongue with a razor and later had him put to
death. St Leger bore all his sufferings, and the official ecclesiast·
ical tearing off of his episcopal robes, with great patience and
humility.

1857: [To M—(after speaking of extreme specimens of
the "strong-minded woman" type]. . . . One of the
pleasantest specimens of the type, because having so much
intellect as to be able to carry it off with a gentle manner,
called on me and we had a long talk on the subject. I
concluded it by saying that however people may differ as
to the theory and logic of the case, there was a *fact*,
independent of all theories, which seemed to me of
immense importance. That I am certain, from all I know of
human—and manly—nature, that if women became what
the "strong-minded" party would make them, there would
be one inevitable consequence—that no first-class man
would or could *fall in love* with them. He might admire them
as curious and interesting phenomena, but could not feel
towards them that inexpressible emotion we call *love*. The
unavoidable result would be that they must either die
spinsters or fall to the lot of inferior orders of men. She
seemed perplexed at this outlook; but, after thinking a little,
said she hoped it was not true, for she hoped both to be
married and to have children, because unless she passed
through both those experiences *she should not think her whole
nature developed*. Never dreaming—alas! poor clever girl—
that the maiden who had arrived at so much self-conscious-
ness as to be able to rationalize upon them as useful
"developments of her nature," had lost already without the
power of knowing it—one of the most exquisite attractions
to a high natured man, and one of the most delicious
differences of her sex.

Sidney Dobell (1824–1874)

October 3

Sᴛ Tᴇʀᴇsᴀ ᴏf Lɪsɪᴇᴜx (St Teresa of the Child Jesus), 1873–1897, led a life of heroic virtue, within the walls of an obscure provincial convent (she spoke of hers as "the little way"). She turned even the dismal, long-drawn-out agonies which tuberculosis in those days involved into spiritual gold; a fact which the *bondieuserie* surrounding her popular cult, making the hideous basilica built in her honour at Lisieux second only to Lourdes as a place of pilgrimage, has tended to obscure. She set out to prove that an "ordinary" person can be a saint; and she was made of the metal to succeed. She was canonised in 1925.

1711: A Believer may be excused by the most hardened Atheist for endeavouring to make him a Convert, because he does it with an Eye to both their Interests. The Atheist is inexcusable who tries to gain over a Believer, because he does not propose the doing himself or Believer any Good by such a Conversion.

The Spectator

October 4

Sᴛ Fʀᴀɴcɪs ᴏf Assɪsɪ (1181–1226); practically everyone's favourite saint. He was actually christened John, and "Franciscus" was a sort of nickname acquired because his merchant father taught him French after returning from a commercial trip. He had already shown by impulsive gestures, before he had his decisive vision at San Damiano, the blazing charity of that great heart which, as Chesterton wrote when he got to the Saint's deathbed in his marvellous little book about him, "had not broken till it held the world." He had overcome one of his last revulsions, and kissed a leper, before he heard the voice of God at the ruined church of San Damiano "Francis, do you not see my house is in ruins?" He took this literally (as we shall see in a moment, his entire life was a living metaphor of love), using some of his father's property for the purpose, being imprisoned by that father and jeered at by the people until it became clear to them that they had a very great soul indeed among them.

He just naturally attracted people, and in no time he had round him the first friars who (in Chesterton's words) "scattered what St Benedict had stored," pouring out charity, faith and hope to the poor and to anyone else good enough to receive them. The stories are well known; St Francis at Rome again seeking ratification for his Order, at first not received by the pope, then the pope (Innocent III) having his dream about the Lateran church collapsing, and being held up by two figures whom he was to recognize as St Francis and St Dominic (*see August 4*). Once a reminder of his old elegant life came to him and he felt, in his cell at the Portiuncula at Assisi, a longing to hear music. "The decorum of religion," said St Bonaventura "forbade his asking for it at the hand of man . . . but one night he heard the sound of a harp, of wonderful harmony, and most sweet melody. The sound came and went, as if the player were moving to and fro under the window." This for the man who wrote the first hymns of praise in the vernacular Italian, including that famous Canticle of praise for the whole of creation ("my brother the sun, my sister the moon"), starting something that was to culminate in Dante.

Once a brother saw him "heap up seven little figures of snow in the clear moonlight. 'Here is thy wife,' he said to himself; 'these four are thy sons and daughters, the other two are thy servant and handmaid; and for all these thou art bound to provide. Make haste, then, and provide clothing for them, lest they perish with cold. But if the care of so many trouble thee, be thou careful to serve the Lord alone.' What piteous human yearning," says Baring-Gould, "is manifested in this little scene . . . it is a remarkable peculiarity of the history of St Francis, that whereas every Saint in the calendar, from St Antony onwards, is sometimes troubled with visions of voluptuous delight, only Francis, in his pure dreams, is tempted by the modest joys of wife and children, the most legitimate and tenderest love."

When he was going blind, says Chesterton, "the remedy, admittedly an uncertain remedy, was to cauterize the eye, and that without any anaesthetic. In other words it was to burn his living eyeballs with a hot iron. Many of the tortures of martyrdom, which he envied in martyrology and sought vainly in Syria" (he had gone alone to try and convert the Sultan Melek-el-Khamed, who received him with touching courtesy and attention) "can have been no worse. When they took the brand from the furnace, he rose as with an urbane gesture and spoke as to an invisible presence: 'Brother Fire, God made you beautiful

203

and strong and useful; I pray you be courteous with me.' If there be any such thing as the art of life, it seems to me that such a moment was one of its masterpieces. Not to many poets has it been given to remember their own poetry at such a moment, still less to live one of their own poems. Even William Blake would have been disconcerted if, while he was re-reading the noble lines 'Tiger, tiger, burning bright,' a real large live Bengal tiger had put his head in at the window of the cottage at Felpham, evidently with every intention of biting his head off. . . . Shelley, when he wished to be a cloud or a leaf carried before the wind, might have been mildly surprised to find himself turning slowly head over heels in mid air a thousand feet above the sea. . . ."

At the age of forty-two he had the most ecstatic vision of his life, on Monte Alverno, an extraordinary combination of a winged seraph and the Cross, after which he bore the Stigmata, the wounds of the Passion of Christ, for the rest of his life. The world owes so much to him that it sometimes forgets one of his simplest gifts; it was St Francis who invented the idea of the Christmas Crib. No wonder he is called the Seraphic Doctor.

1918: My darling Mother. . . . You will guess what has happened when I say I am now Commanding the Company, and in the line had a boy lance-corporal as my Sergeant-Major.

With this corporal who stuck to me and shadowed me like your prayers I captured a German Machine Gun and scores of prisoners.

I'll tell you exactly how another time. I only shot one man with my revolver (at about 30 yards!); The rest I took with a smile. The same thing happened with other parties all along the line we entered.

I have been recommended for the Military Cross;* and have recommended every single N.C.O. who was with me!

My nerves are in perfect order.

I came out in order to help these boys—directly by leading them as well as an officer can; indirectly, by watching their sufferings that I may speak of them as well as a pleader can. I have done the first.

Wilfred Owen (1893–1918)

* The award was immediate. He was killed a month later,
seven days before the Armistice.

October 5

St Placid (born about 515) was in the charge of St Benedict as a boy when he was still at Subiaco, and was the subject of a legendary miracle. Having gone to fetch water he fell into the lake. St Benedict called out from his cell to another monk, St Maurus, who rushed out and pulled him up by the hair and then drew him to safety—only then realizing that he had walked over the water to do so. At one point St Placid was numbered among some martyrs in Sicily, but in the Roman missal today it merely says that he followed St Benedict to Monte Cassino and became one of his firmest supports.

1872: A goldencrested wren got into my room at night and circled round dazzled by the gaslight on the white ceiling; when caught even and put out it would come in again. Ruffling the crest, which is mounted over the crown and eyes like beetlebrows, I smoothed and fingered the little orange and yellow feathers which are hidden in it. Next morning I found many of these about the room and enclosed them in a letter to Cyril [his younger brother] on his wedding day.

Gerard Manley Hopkins (1844–1889)

October 6

St Bruno was born at Cologne about 1033. He taught theology at Rheims until he quarrelled with his archbishop, a scandalous person called Manasses de Gournai. When St Bruno with other clergy was successful in getting Manasses removed they asked St Bruno to be archbishop; but instead he went to a region where the bishop (of Grenoble) was a saint, St Hugh of Châteauneuf. With him, three other clergy and two laymen, in a wild and picturesque valley, he set up the first house, La Grande Chartreuse, of the Carthusian Order of which he is the founder. His rule was a combination of that of St Benedict with the solitude of the early desert hermits. His monks met only in choir, and spent the rest of their time in cottage-like cells, and in silence. Curious that in every cheerful, garrulous saloon bar there is a bottle of a certain famous liqueur.

✍ *1808:* Dear Lady Holland, I take the liberty to send you two brace of grouse, curious, because killed by a Scotch metaphysician; in other and better language they are mere ideas, out of a pure intellectual notion called a gun. Yrs ever very truely

Sydney Smith

I will do myself the pleasure of dining with you on Saturday next—tomorrow evening I am engaged. The modification of matter called Grouse which accompanies this note is not in the common apprehension of Edinburgh considered to be dependant upon a first cause, but to have existed from All Eternity. Allen will explain.

Sydney Smith (1771–1845)

October 7

S<small>T</small> O<small>SYTH</small> (d. 673) was a grand-daughter of the rather awful king Penda of Mercia. She was married to Sigher, king of the East Saxon, though not for long, if at all, if one story is true. Wishing for the religious life, she was nevertheless at the wedding banquet when "suddenly a magnificent stag bounded past the hall windows. Sigher was an ardent lover, but he was a more ardent sportsman. He blew his horn, mounted his horse, and followed by his men, went in pursuit of the stag. Osyth seized the opportunity, and fled the place with some of her maids." She founded a monastery at a place called Chich, on a creek of the river Colne, and here she was killed by Viking raiders.

✍ *1914:* To me woman is *the* wonderful fact of existence. If there be any next world and it be as I hope it is, a jolly gossiping place, with people standing around the mantel-piece and discussing their earthly experiences, I shall thump my fist on the table as my friends turn to me on entering and exclaim in a loud voice, "WOMAN."

W. N. P. Barbellion (1889–1917)

October 8

ST THAIS was the legendary (4th-century (?)) courtesan who, persuaded of the error of her ways by the famous desert monk Paphnutius, burnt her fine dresses in the street, retired to a convent and died there three years later in the odour of sanctity. In the opera of the same name by Massenet, Paphnutius, here named Athanael, is an ex-lover of Thais, and after her repentance he finds his motives were not as pure as he had thought, and thinks only of their love at the deathbed where she is thinking only of heaven. But that's *opera*.

1770: Ringmer nr. Lewes. A land-tortoise, which has been kept for thirty years in a little walled court belonging to the house where I now am visiting, retires underground about the middle of November, and comes forth again about the middle of April. When it first appears in the spring it discovers very little inclination towards food; but in the height of summer grows voracious: and then as the summer declines its appetite declines; so that for the last six weeks it hardly eats at all. Milky plants, such as lettuces, dandelions, sow-thistles, are its favourite dish. In a neighbouring village one was kept till by tradition it was supposed to be an hundred years old. An instance of vast longevity in such a poor reptile.

Gilbert White (1720–1793)

October 9

ST DIONYSIUS, or Denis, the patron saint of France, martyred about 258 on "the hill of the martyr" now known as Montmartre, was later amazingly confused with two other figures of the same name; Denis the Areopagite, hence the Epistle for the Mass of this day, from the Acts of the Apostles, where St Paul speaks of the resurrection of the dead, at which "some indeed mocked," but "certain men adhered to him, and believed, among whom was Dionysius the Areopagite"; and the "Pseudo-Dionysius," the Neoplatonist philosopher who influenced minds from St Augustine to St Thomas Aquinas.

1939: ... I can't sympathize with Hitler, by the way. His origins don't at all excuse his extreme brutality and treachery. The kink in his brain does more, of course. But he is so *horribly* cruel. It is the quality that is hardest to get over in any one, I suppose.

Rose Macaulay (1881–1958)

October 10

ST PAULINUS (d. 644), a Roman by birth, came up from Kent with the princess Ethelburga when she married the pagan king Edwin of Northumbria. At first Paulinus made no headway, but eventually Edwin was baptized on Easter Day 627. It was to Edwin that a pagan priest or noble, Coifi, developed the famous metaphor of—human *life* being like the sparrow's brief passage through the lighted hall—related by St Bede (*see May 27*).

1829: [To John Wilson Croker]. After all, however, the real question is—how will three shillings a day support a man? I speak as yet hesitatingly; but I have good reasons for thinking that one of my police constables, if a single man, can find out of his pay of a guinea a week: (1) lodgings, (2) medical attendance, (3) very comfortable subsistence at his mess, (4) clothing; and can, after finding these, save out of his pay ten shillings a week.

Sir Robert Peel (1788–1850)

October 11

ST ETHELBURGA (7th century) from a noble family, was the sister of St Erconwald, who became bishop of London. Erconwald founded a monastery at Cerotaesei (= Cerot's Island, = Chertsey) for men, and one for women at In-Berecingum (= Barking), of which Ethelburga became abbess. There was a legend that while Barking Abbey was being built a roof beam was found to be too short; "then Erconwald took one end and Ethelburga the other, and pulled it out to the proper length."

Baring-Gould also says that this was the first religious house for women in England.

✒ *1861:* Today I was consulted by a Mr Welby. I remarked that his name was uncommon, which led us into conversation. He told me that his father was a remarkable man in one particular; he had the art of making brick-layers' trowels; and he made them so well that every old bricklayer knows Welby's trowels. Indeed no manufacturer comes from the provinces to London without having visited Welby's factory. In a few years, however, the name of this man will be forgotten, while the benefits received through him will remain with mankind. What a benefactor was the man who made the first kettle, for instance; and yet we do now know who was this benefactor. So it is with respect to almost every invention; the result, the benefit becomes part of the wealth which anterior times bestow on posterior. The inventor, the benefactor, is forgotten.

John Epps (1805–1869)

October 12

Sᴛ Wɪʟꜰʀɪᴅ (634–709) was educated as a monk at Lindisfarne, and went to Rome in company with St Benet Biscop, that indefatigable traveller (*see Jan 12*). He built the first stone church at Ripon, a basilica said to be one of the finest buildings west of the Alps, but of which only the crypt of the present cathedral remains after a Danish raid two centuries later. The ability to squeeze through "St Wilfrid's Needle," the hole from the crypt to the passage outside, was held to be a test of chastity. St Wilfrid not only did much to consolidate Christianity in the north but was, on various of his travels, the apostle of the South Saxons and of the Friesians.

✒ *1932:* Dear Sir Edward [Elgar], . . . There are fleas of all grades; and so I have felt the awkward feeling of having smaller creatures than myself admiring me. I was so sorry to put you to that awkwardness: but it was inevitable. You have had a lifetime of achievement, and I was a flash in the pan. However I'm a very happy flash, and I am continually winning moments of great enjoyment. That

Menuhin Concerto is going to be a pleasure to me for years: and the news of your 3rd Symphony was like a week's sunlight. I do hope you will have enough enthusiasm left to finish it. There are crowds of us waiting to hear it again and again.

Probably it feels quaint to you to hear that the mere setting eyes upon you is a privilege: but by that standard I want to show you how good an afternoon it was for me, in your house.

T. E. Lawrence (1888–1935)

October 13

EDWARD THE CONFESSOR (about 1004–1066) was the last-but-one "English" king, and is said to have made a vow that if he succeeded to the English throne he would make a pilgrimage to Rome. He *did* succeed in 1042, on the death of King Hardacanute, his half-brother. He spent most of his time opposing Earl Godwin (father of Harold, the *last* English king) and favouring Normans in high places such as the see of Canterbury and, more unfortunately, Dorchester. There he appointed one, Ulf, who "almost caused Pope Leo to break his staff, because he was so ignorant he could hardly read the breviary." This same pope released Edward from the pilgrimage vow on condition that he gave the money it would have cost to the poor and built a great abbey at Westminster. This Edward did. He had a great love both of hunting and of the peaceful religious life and was the first king reputed able to cure the "king's evil" (scrofula) by his touch. He was canonized in 1161, and his tomb is of course in the successor to the great church he built.

1779: At Stowe. The buildings called Temples are most miserable, many of them both without and within. Sir John Vanbrugh's is an ugly clumsy lump, hardly fit for a gentleman's stable . . . the statues are full as coarse as the paintings, especially those of Apollo and the Muses whom a person not otherwise informed might take to be nine milkmaids.

John Wesley (1703–1791)

October 14

CALLISTUS, (d. 223) who began life as an odd kind of slave—a bank manager, no less—did something or other which resulted in hard labour in the Sardinian quarries, and on his emancipation he became a deacon and after being taken up by the pope St Zephyrinus, succeeded him. What is probable is that he was rather more tolerant of sinners than opponents who were to harden into Montanism, which said not only that there could be *no* forgiveness after mortal sin, but that Montanus himself was the paraclete (when the considerable thinker Tertullian joined this lot it was, said Ronald Knox rather snobbishly, as though Cardinal Newman had joined the Salvation Army). St Callistus is also credited with instituting Ember Days.

1944: [To Marie Belloc-Lowndes]. There is a wonderful picture of me on the cover [of his book, *The Shrimp and the Anemone*] looking like an elderly and dissipated bloodhound exhausted after a long chase. It was taken by my sister Norah's dog-photographer which explains the canine look.

L. P. Hartley (1895–1972)

October 15

ST TERESA OF AVILA (1515–1582) is the only woman to have been given the title Doctor of the Church (from Popes Gregory XV and Urban VII). As a girl she was high-spirited, to say the least; and a great novel-reader. "I spent many hours, both of the day and night, in this vain exercise," she wrote, "unknown to my father. But I was so addicted to the habit, that if I could not obtain a new book I was miserable." Her path to the religious life was by way of extraordinary and intense visions, some of her advisers urging her to forget them as being merely hysterical, others, including a Jesuit called Alvarez, encouraging her as the genuine mystic she in fact was. A great part of her life was spent travelling about Spain, taking over dilapidated mansions and turning them into strict-observance houses of the Discalced (Barefoot) Carmelites, often against violent opposition.

Her blazing sincerity won her friends both powerful (King Philip) and personally distinguished (St John of the Cross was one of the first of the many *men* to join her reform, in that classically male-dominated country). She seems to have spent almost as much time crossing flooded rivers, stifling in waggons, and founding her seventeen convents as in achieving the heights and depths of the contemplation for which she is famous; a classic fusion of Martha and Mary.

1774: . . . I caught a remarkable large Spider in my Wash Place this morning and put him in a small glass decanter and fed him with some bread and intend keeping him.

James Woodforde (1740–1803)

October 16

ST GALL (d. about 640) was one of twelve Irish monks who accompanied St Columbanus to Europe, where they settled for a time at Bregenz, converting the Woden-worshipping heathens. "The two missionaries, with daring zeal, burned the heathen temples, broke the boilers in which the sacred beer was brewed, and threw the gilded idols in the lake." Later, having parted with St Columbanus he became a hermit, and disturbed two water-sprites "who threw stones at him, and rebuked him for having intruded on their solitude. Gall ran up, and exorcised the nixies, and they fled up the cascade, filling the mountain with their musical laments." This was at St Gall, where later the famous monastery bearing his name grew; today a priceless repository of early Gregorian chant manuscripts.

1677: A scant wind. And this day I saw a woodcock and a wren on our ship; and yesterday many linnets, though so far at sea. Why should any man be afraid to go to sea when these birds dare cross the Bay of Biscay?

Between 12 and 1 of the clock, Summersett Evins, going up the mizzen chains to clear the pendant, fell down and was drowned.

Henry Teonge (1621–1690)

212

October 17

St Margaret-Mary Alacoque (1647–1690); a Counter-Reformation saint. At a time when there had been not only the Protestant breakaway from the Church but the emergence of stern elements still in it, such as the Jansenists, the idea of the Sacred Heart of Jesus as being full of love for all men was something likely to appeal to many. St John Eudes had already composed a Mass and Office of the Sacred Heart for his congregation of Eudists (who ran seminaries) in 1670. St Margaret-Mary, after an ailing childhood, entered the convent of the Visitation at Paray-le-Monial at the age of twenty-four; the tough mother superior, mistrusting her visions, sent her to work in the infirmary; but the visions persisted, culminating in four of the Sacred Heart and an injunction to spread the devotion (it is now a major feast, kept on the Friday following the Octave of Corpus Christi).

1875: Last Sunday was the principal day of the Festival called the Doorga Poojah, in honour of the Goddess Doorga, and in the evening we all walked out to the river to see the goddess bathed. The ceremony was rather grand. About twelve images of the goddess raised on platforms, and surrounded by tinsel ornaments, were ranged along the edge of the river, and behind them all the Rajah's elephants were drawn up in line. Both sides of the river were crowded with spectators, and as the time approached for the goddess to be let down into the water, fireworks and rockets were let off in the space between the elephants and the goddess.

H. M. Kisch (1850–1942)

October 18

The symbol of St Luke, Apostle and Evangelist, is a winged bull. St Luke was not a Jew, and is thought to have been born in Antioch. He was closely associated with St Paul, who describes him as "the beloved physician" (although this does not preclude his having been an educated and freed slave). In the Acts of the Apostles there is a sudden change to the first person *plural* at Troas which indicates that he joined St Paul there, similar clues pointing to his having been left at Philippi, preaching there, and rejoining Paul there later on his third journey. In the second Letter to Timothy, from Rome, where St Paul, nearing the end, says he has fought the good fight, he also says "only Luke is with me." St Jerome and St John Chrysostom describe his gospel as "the gospel of St Paul."

1703: I stood near a Lyon (w ᶜʰ came abot for a sight) w ᵗʰ my back to him & he rose vp (as I was told by some that called to me) to mischief me & I stept forward the same moment out of his reach & God knowes what the event might have been. (*See also November 18*)

William Coe of Mildenhall (1680–1729)

October 19

Sᵗ Frideswide (d. about 735) is the patron saint of Oxford, where she founded a monastery. Pursued to Abingdon by one Alfgar, who wanted to marry her, she hid in the forest and, as he drew close, she prayed for deliverance—and he was struck blind. "From this incident sprang a fantastic superstition, according to which the kings of England carefully avoided Oxford, for fear of losing their eyesight. Henry III was the first English king who disregarded this prejudice." Her monastery was on the site of what is now Christ Church (the cathedral of Oxford).

1821: .... I am glad you like what I said of Mrs Elizabeth Fry. She is very unpopular with the clergy: examples of living, active virtue disturb our repose, and give birth to distressing comparisons: we long to burn her alive.

Sydney Smith (1771–1845)

October 20

S T JOHN CANTIUS (1397 to about 1473) was born at Kenty in the diocese of Cracow, where he was ordained and became a professor in the university. He returned there after a not very successful spell as a parish priest of a village called Ilkutsi, where the people followed him with curses, to which his invariable reply was "above", meaning that Christ and the martyrs had undergone worse things. He was famous for his charity. On one of his four pilgrimages to Rome he was attacked by brigands, and told them they had taken all his money. When he remembered some gold coins sewn into his cloak he went back and offered them, not wishing to have told a lie; and, not surprisingly, they then gave everything back to him.

1841: [To Frederic Tennyson] . . . . in spite of your Vesuviuses and your sunshine, I love my poor dear brave barren ugly country. Talk of your Italians! why, they are extinguished by the Austrians because they don't blaze enough of themselves to burn the extinguisher. Only people who deserve despotism are forced to suffer it. We have at last good weather: and the harvest is just drawing to a close in this place. It is a bright brisk morning, and the loaded waggons are rolling cheerfully past my window. . . . Ah, Master Tennyson, we in England have our pleasures too. As to Alfred [Tennyson], we in England have heard nothing of him since May: except that some one saw him going to a packet which he believed was going to Rotterdam. . . . When shall you and I go to an Opera again, or hear one of Beethoven's Symphonies together? You are lost to England, I calculate: and I am given over to turnips and inanity. So runs the world away. Well, if I never see you again, I am very glad I *have* seen you: and got the idea of a noble fellow all ways into my head. . . .

Edward Fitzgerald (1809–1883)

October 21

S⊤ Hilarion (d. 371) spent his early youth as a hermit below Majuam (the port of Gaza) and was tormented by demons appearing in many forms. Sometimes, as he prayed "the whole pomp was swallowed up in the earth." As he grew older a great monastery grew round him, and he began to long for solitude again. After a journey to the tomb of St Antony he spent time in Libya, Sicily, Dalmatia, and finally Cyprus, where he died. The magnificent ruins of the castle above Kyrenia, looking across the strip of sea to Turkey, bear his name.

1783: . . . Garrick, Madam [Mrs Siddons], was no declaimer; there was not one of his own scene-shifters who could not have spoken *To be, or not to be*, better than he did; yet he was the only actor I ever saw whom I could call a master both in tragedy and comedy. A true conception of character, and natural expression of it, were his distinguishing excellencies. . . . Johnson, indeed, had thought more upon the subject of acting than might be generally supposed. Talking of it one day to Mr Kemble, he said, "Are you, Sir, one of those enthusiasts who believe yourself transformed into the very character you represent?" Upon Mr Kemble's answering that he had never felt so strong a persuasion himself; "To be sure, sir, (said Johnson) the thing is impossible. And if Garrick really believed himself to be that monster, Richard the Third, he deserved to be hanged every time he performed it."

James Boswell (1740–1795)

October 22

S⊤ Philip, bishop of Heraclea in Thrace (d. 304) suffered martyrdom in the persecution of Diocletian. Scourged under a governor called Bassus, he endured worse things under his successor, one Justin. Dragged by the feet to prison, he was then scourged again, so that he could not walk to the place where he was to be burnt (buried to the waist and with his hands nailed to the stake). Before they lit the fire he sent a cheerful message

216

to his son, telling him to work hard for his living and be courteous to everyone.

1766: Having no companion but such as the place [Bath] afforded, and which I did not accept, my excursions were very few; besides that the city is so guarded with mountains, that I had not patience to be jolted like a pea in a drum, in my chaise alone. I did go to Bristol, the dirtiest great shop I ever saw, with so foul a river, that, had I seen the least appearance of cleanliness, I should have concluded they washed all their linen in it, as they do at Paris.

Horace Walpole (1717–1797)

October 23

ST IGNATIUS OF CONSTANTINOPLE (d. 877) was very much at the centre of things when the Byzantine church was beginning to move away from the Latin. When he refused to give communion to Bardas, uncle of the emperor Michael III, on the grounds that Bardas was living in incest, he was imprisoned. Ignatius, later restored to his see after much complicated dealings by all parties with the pope, was a leader of the rigorist party in the Byzantine church.

1775: We went to see the looking glasses wrought. They came from Normandy in cast plates perhaps the third of an inch thick. At Paris they are ground upon a marble table by rubbing one plate on another with grit between them. The various sands, of which there are said to be five, I could not learn. The handle by which the upper glass is moved had the form of a wheel which may be moved in all directions. The plates are sent up with their surfaces ground but not polished and so continue until they are bespoken, lest time should spoil the surface, as we were told. Those that are to be polished are laid on a table covered with several thick cloths, hard strained so that the resistance may be equal, they are then rubbed with a hand rubber held down hard by a contrivance which I did not well understand. The powder which is used last seemed to me to be iron dissolved in aqua fortis. They called it, as Baretti

said, Mar de l'eau forte, which he thought was dregs. They
mentioned vitriol and saltpetre. The cannon ball* swam in
the saltpetre. To silver them, a leaf of beaten tin is laid, and
rubbed with quicksilver to which it unites. Then more
quicksilver is poured upon it by which its mutual attraction
rises very high. Then a paper is laid at the nearest end of
the plate, over which the glass is slided till it lies upon the
plate, having driven much of the quicksilver before it. It is
then, I think, pressed upon cloths, and then heightened to
drop the superfluous mercury, the slope is daily heightened
towards a perpendicular.

Samuel Johnson (1709–1784)

October 24

St Maglorius (d. 586), after education at the monastery of
Llantwit Major, under St Illtyd, Followed St Samson (*see July
28*) to Dol in Brittany, where he became bishop and ruled for
many years. In his old age, longing for solitude, he met one
Soiesco, who owned Jersey, and cured him of leprosy. In
gratitude the count gave him half the island. "As, however, all
the wild fowl and fish deserted the count's portion for that of the
saint, he made Maglorius change with him. All the fish and fowl
at once followed Maglorius. Then the count abandoned the
whole island to the monks."

1348: . . . . this cruel plague, as we have heard, has
already begun singularly to afflict the various coasts of
the realm of England. We are struck by the greatest fear lest,
which God forbid, the fell disease ravage any part of our
city and diocese. And although God, to prove our patience
and justly to punish our sins, often afflicts us, it is not in
man's power to judge the divine councels. Still, it is much
to be feared that man's sensuality which, propagated by the
tendency of the old sin of Adam, from youth inclines to all
evil, has now fallen into deeper malice and justly provoked
the Divine wrath by a multitude of sins to this chastisement.

William Edendon alias Edyndon or Edyngton,
Bishop of Winchester (d. 1366)

* *Cannon* ball?

218

October 25

Ss Crispin and Crispinian, reputedly brothers and shoemakers, were either martyred *at* Soissons (285, says Baring-Gould unequivocally), or these were the names of martyrs whose relics were brought from Rome *to* Soissons. They are certainly the patron saints of shoemakers; and their feast day will be remembered as long as Shakespeare is known:

> And Crispin Crispian shall ne'er go by
> From this day to the ending of the world,
> But we in it shall be remembered;
> We few, we happy few, we band of brothers . . .

1787: I should pity the man who expected, without other advantages of a very different nature, to be well received in a brilliant circle at London because he was a fellow of the Royal Society. But this would not be the case with a member of the Academy of Sciences at Paris; he is sure of a good reception everywhere. Perhaps this contrast depends in a good measure on the difference of the governments of the two countries. Politics are too much attended to in England to allow a due respect to be paid to anything else; and should the French establish a freer government, academicians will not be held in such estimation when rivalled in the public esteem by the orators who hold forth liberty and property in a free parliament.

Arthur Young (1741–1820)

October 26

St Evaristus (martyred in 109 under Trajan) was something much more possible in the centuries before the formal separation between Rome and Byzantium in 1054—a Greek Pope of Rome. It was he who first divided the city into parishes.

1757: [to his son]. . . . Go on so with diligence, and you will be, what I begin to despair of your ever being, *somebody*. I am persuaded, if you would own the truth, that

219

you feel yourself now much better satisfied with yourself, than you were when you did nothing.

Application to business, attended with approbation and success, flatters and animates the mind; which, in idleness and inaction, stagnates and putrefies. I would wish, that every rational man would, every night when he goes to bed, ask himself this question, *What have I done today?* ...

Lord Chesterfield (1694–1773)

October 27

ST FRUMENTIUS (d. about 380) is venerated as a pioneer of Christianity in Ethiopia. A native of Tyre, as a youth he accompanied a philosopher called Meropius "who had recently visited the Brahmins in India, determined to travel among the Hamyarites of Arabia Felix." There is also a tradition that he went to Axum, in Abyssinia, and spread the faith from there.

1910: The airship turns out to have been the largest yet launched and to have descended at Aldershot. It must have been travelling faster than I thought and at a greater height. On arrival at the garage at Aldershot it got torn and exploded, but the passengers, they say, were unhurt. It seems to have been the first regular passenger ship to cross the Channel.

Wilfrid Scawen Blunt (1840–1922)

October 28

SS SIMON and JUDE, Apostles. St Simon was called Zelotes, since he originally belonged to the "Zealots," a Jewish sect fiercely strict in their adherence to the Mosaic Law. It is not known for certain where he preached the Gospel, although Egypt and Persia are often mentioned. Nor is it certain where, how, or even if he was martyred, although again tradition couples him with St Jude. The latter, surnamed Lebbe ("the courageous") is the one described as "Judas, not Iscariot" by St John and as asking how God will manifest himself, and being told by Jesus, "if a

220

man love me, he will keep my words: and my Father will love him, and we will come unto him, and make our abode with him." St Jude was brother of St James the Less, nephew of St Joseph and Mary and therefore cousin of Jesus. His short Epistle is the last book in the New Testament before Revelation. He is traditionally the patron of impossible or seemingly hopeless causes.

1780: [To Thomas Bentley] Mr Stubs thinks he has quite finish'd our picture, but he is a little mistaken for I shall get him to make a few alterations still, but it must be by degrees, for I have plagued him a good deal in the last finishing-strokes & he has been very good in bearing with my impertinence. . . .

Josiah Wedgwood (1730–1795)

October 29

THERE ARE ninety-five saints called Colman in the Martyrology of Donegal (this, of course, does not mean that they were all martyrs). This one, COLMAN MAC DUACH or Kilmacduach (d. about 632) was eventually abbot-bishop of that place. "He had three pets—a cock, a mouse, and a bluebottle. The cock crowed at night when ever the turn came for him to rise and say his office; if he slept on, the mouse nibbled his ear, or fingers, or toes, till he got up; and the fly served as a book-marker. For when he read, the bluebottle hopped on, and formed a stop at the end of each sentence. And if St Colman was called away in the midst of his reading, the fly sat quiet at the end of the paragraph he had just completed till he returned and finished his reading." He was made bishop very much against his will. One Easter Day King Guair of Connaught, sitting down to roast stag, said this was something like an Easter meal; "I only wish the poor hermits in Burren wood had a bite at them." At this the venison flew out through the window. The king and his men followed its succulent smell over hill and dale, and found St Colman just sitting down to it. " 'O spits and skewers, what has brought you hither?' And the angels answered in chorus, 'your prayers and the charity of King Guair.' " The next day, "after an interchange of courtesies" the king having asked St Colman to be his

221

spiritual director, and sent masons to begin work on the church of Kilmacduach.

1870: Today I found in a book a red silk handkerchief worked with the words "Forget me not," and I am sorry to say that I have entirely forgotten who gave it to me. One of my many lovers no doubt. But which?

Francis Kilvert (1840–1879)

October 30

ST MARCELLUS THE CENTURION (d. about 298) was yet another victim of Diocletian. After service in Spain he became a Christian; and one account says that he had twelve children who were also martyred, the governor shortening their tortures so that the constancy of one should not encourage another. He is specially venerated at Leon in Spain.

1892: Rabbits are creatures of warm volatile temperament but shallow and absurdly transparent. It is this naturalness, one touch of nature, that I find so delightful in Mr Benjamin Bunny, though I frankly admit his vulgarity. At one moment amiably sentimental to the verge of silliness, at the next, the upsetting of a jug or tea-cup which he immediately takes upon himself, will convert him into a demon, throwing himself on his back, scratching and spluttering. If I can lay hold of him without being bitten, within half a minute he is licking my hands, as though nothing has happened.

He is an abject coward, but believes in bluster, could stare our old dog out of countenance, chase a cat that has turned tail.

Benjamin once fell into an Aquarium head first, and sat in the water which he could not get out of, pretending to eat a piece of string. Nothing like putting a face upon circumstances.

Beatrix Potter (1866–1943)

October 31

S⊤ WOLFGANG (about 925–994), a nice comfortable Benedictine saint, was for a time at the famous monastery of Einsiedeln, and also on a short and apparently not very successful mission in Pannonia (Hungary). He became bishop of Ratisbon (Regensburg), and also abbot of the Benedictine monastery there. He found it in some disorder, and put in a good reforming abbot whom he had known at Trier, in his pre-Einsiedeln days. There were also some convents badly in need of reform, which he managed with firmness and a charity which was evidently greater than that of the prince-bishop under whom that composer served, eight centuries later, who made the name of Wolfgang brilliant for ever.

1777: [To his father]. . . . I went with Herr Danner today to M. Cannabich, who was exceedingly courteous. I played to him on his pianoforte, which is a very good one, and we went together to the rehearsal. I thought I should not be able to keep myself from laughing when I was introduced to the people there [Mannheim]. Some who knew me by repute were very polite and fearfully respectful; others, however, who had never heard of me, stared at me wide-eyed, and certainly in a rather sneering manner. They probably think that because I am little and young, nothing great or mature can come out of me; but they will soon see. . . . I kiss Papa's hands and my sisterly beloved I embrace shortly and sweetly, as is proper.

JOHANNES*** CHRYSOSTOMUS
SIGISMUNDUS** WOLFGANG* GOTTLIEB MOZART
* Today is my name-day! ** That is my confirmation name!
*** January 27th is my birthday!
Wolfgang Amadeus Mozart (1756–1791)

NOVEMBER

November 1

A LL SAINTS DAY. In 610 the old Roman Pantheon, the temple of all the gods, became the basilica of St Mary and the Martyrs; but by this time the notion of "saint," although it had never been synonymous with that of martyr, had become more general, and now includes all those, known and unknown, who have entered heaven. The Council of Trent codified the belief that it was good and useful, though not *necessary*, to pray to the saints but to accept that any benefit, spiritual or temporal, came from God through Christ. This feast was fixed on November 1 in 835 by Gregory IV.

1857: At Dovercourt saw Mrs—, a wonderful old lady, managing a farm and a large household at seventy-five years of age, her intellect still powerful. The daughter mentioned that when her mother was young, a fortune-teller told her to keep off water, lest she should be drowned. So now, in coming to Dovercourt, she travelled all the way in her carriage, a distance of twenty-four miles, when she could have come at a quick rate by water over a distance of five miles.

John Epps (1805–1869)

November 2

S T MARCIAN (d. 388) was an anchorite in the Syrian desert, and after a long period of solitary prayer and fasting found he was rather plagued with a reputation as a miracle worker. Once three bishops came to see him. He received them with respect but in total silence. One of them asked for some words of edification. "God speaks to us from all Creation," Marcian said, "and He speaks to us from the Scriptures. What more can you want from a poor learner like Marcian?"

Today is also the feast of All Souls, on which intercession is made (as throughout the month of November) for the souls in Purgatory—the Church Suffering united with the Church Triumphant of the saints and the Church Militant of the living.

226

1811: [To John Constable] My dear Sir,. . . . I dare not suffer myself to think on your last letter. I am very impatient as you may imagine to hear from Papa on a subject so fraught with interest to us both—but was unwilling to delay writing to you as you would be ignorant of the cause of such seeming inattention . . . you know my sentiments, I shall be guided by my Father in every respect.

Should he acquiesce in my wishes I shall be happier than I can express, if not, I shall have the consolation of reflecting that I am doing my duty, a charm that will stifle every regret and in the end give the greatest satisfaction to my mind. I cannot write any more 'till the wished but fearfully dreaded letter arrives, with the most ardent wishes for your health.

believe me, dear Sir, your obliged friend
Maria E. Bicknell
(*see also November 4*)
Maria Bicknell (1788–1828)

November 3

ST HUBERT (d. 727), son of Bertrand, Duke of Aquitaine, was the bishop of Tongern-Maastricht and missionary of the Ardennes. The story is that he led the life of a young noble and was fond of hunting. While so engaged on a Good Friday he saw a great stag with a crucifix between its horns, and heard a voice warning him to turn to God or fall into hell. St Hubert is the patron saint of hunters, and the saint appealed to after the bite of a mad dog.

1770: This day I visited his Neapolitan majesty's museum, at Portici, where I had enquiries to make concerning ancient instruments. . . . the most extraordinary of all these instruments is a species of trumpets, found in Pompeia not a year ago, it is a good deal broken, but not so much so as to render it difficult to conceive the entire form. There are still the remains of seven small bone or ivory pipes, all of the same length and diameter which surround the great tube, and seem to terminate in one mouthpiece. Several of the small brazen pipes are broken, by which the ivory ones are laid bare; but it is natural to suppose that they were all blown at once, and that the small pipes were

227

unisons to each other, and octaves to the great one . . . . this
singular species of trumpet was found in the *Corps de Garde*,
and seems to be the true military *Clangor Tubarum*.
Charles Burney (1726–1814)

November 4

S<small>T</small> C<small>HARLES</small> B<small>ORROMEO</small> (1538–1584), son of the Count of Arona
took a doctorate in law and was made a cardinal by his
uncle, Pius IV, before he was ordained. But he had a natural
integrity in that corrupt world, and when he became archbishop
of Milan he set about reforming a diocese where things, after his
absentee predecessors, had got very lax indeed. One order, the
Frati Umiliati, who had 90 monasteries, a mere 170 members,
and a lot of money, put up an unsuccessful assassination attempt
on him. He started seminaries, gave heroic leadership during
the plague of 1575–6, and by his whole life gave serious
expression to the reforms of the Council of Trent in which he
had taken part. There is an enormous statue of him overlooking
Lake Maggiore.

1811: Dear Miss Bicknell, Can I ever sufficiently thank
you for the happiness your letter this morning has given
me. My health if so much better that I think I may consider
myself nearly recovered.
I trust that I cannot have deceived myself as to a too
favourable reception in Spring Garden. Your father told me
he should write to you, and that I should hear from him
when he had your answer—let me hope that there will not
be so much (as you imagine) depending on one letter alone
from your Father, thought it certainly must be of the
greatest consequence.
Beleive me, dear Miss Bicknell,
always most affectionately yours
John Constable
John Constable (1776–1837)

November 5

SS ZACHARY AND ELIZABETH, the parents of St John the Baptist. Since St Elizabeth was beyond child-bearing age, Zachary asked for a sign, the angel Gabriel appeared and Zachary was struck dumb. During her confinement she was visited by Our Lady, who was her cousin (the Visitation, second of the Joyful Mysteries of the Rosary). When her child was born, Zachary, still without his speech, confirmed by writing on a tablet "his name is John," and his speech was restored.

1876: ... You spoke once more of even trying Walpole's Letters. ... I can scarce imagine better Christmas fare: but I can't, I say, guess how you [Miss Anna Biddell] would relish it. N.B. It is not gross or coarse: but you would not like the man, so satirical, selfish, and frivolous, you would think. But I think I could show you that he had a very loving Heart for a few, and a very firm, just understanding under all his Wit and Fun. Even Carlyle has admitted that he was about the clearest-sighted Man of his time.

Edward Fitzgerald (1809–1883)

November 6

ST ILLTYD (6th century) was one of the great Welsh saints (5th-6th century). Of noble birth in Glamorganshire (he was related to King Arthur), he founded "and governed for many years the most famous monastery and school then in Britain, called from him Llan-Iltut or Llan-twit." (Butler.) Among his pupils were St David (*see March 1*), St Samson (*see July 28*) and St Maglorius (*see October 24*).

1721: [To Luise von Degenfeld] .... I write until half-past ten, then I send for my honey-water and wash myself as clean as I can, rub my painful knees and thighs with *eau vulneraire*, which my doctors recommend, ring, sit down at my dressing table and everybody, men and women, enters while my hair is being done. When I am coiffed all the men, except for my doctors, surgeons and apothecaries, leave the room and I put on my shoes, stockings and *caleçons* [*caleçons*, or drawers, were only worn by the most old-fashioned and straight-laced women of the old régime] and wash my hands. While this is taking place the ladies have arrived to attend on me and pass me the things I need for washing my hands and hand me my chemise. Then the doctor-crew leaves the room and my tailor comes in with my dress. I put this on as soon as I have put on my chemise. When I am laced up all the men come back in, for my manteau is so constructed that I am fully dressed as soon as the laces are tied. All my underskirts are tied to the bodice with tabs, and my *manteau* is sewn on to it. I find this very convenient.

> *Elizabeth Charlotte (Liselotte) Princess Palatine*
> *and Duchess of Orléans (1652–1722)*

November 7

ST WILLIBRORD (d. 739), educated at the monastery of Ripon, was a great apostle of Holland and Belgium. Having been made bishop by Pope Sergius, at the request of King Pepin, he founded the see of Utrecht, and was followed by many missionaries both Saxon and Irish, e.g. St Boniface (*see June 5*) and he baptized Pepin's redoubtable successor, Charles Martel. "He once gave twelve men to drink from one pocket flask of wine. They all professed that they had had quite enough of his wine. We should be more certain that this was a miracle," says Baring-Gould, "if we knew what the quality of the wine was."

1478: [from Eton] To hys worchepful brodyr John Paston be thys delyvered in hast.

Ryght reverent and worchepful brodyr, I recommaunde me onto yow, desyrynge to here of yowe welfare and prosperite, letynge yow wete that I have resevyd of Alwedyr a lettyr, and a nobyll in gowlde therin. Ferthermore, my creansyr,[1] Mayster Thomas, hertely recommaundyd hym to yow, and he praythe yow to sende hym sum mony for my comouns; for he seythe ye be xx^ti s.[2] in hys dette, for a monthe was to pay for whe(n) he had mony laste.

1. Tutor
2. Twenty shillings

Also I beseche yow to sende me a hose clothe, on for the halydays of sum colore, and anothyr for the workyng days—how corse so ever it be it makyth no matyr; and a stomechere, and ii schyrtys, and a peyer of sclyppers. And if it lyke yow that I may come wyth Alwedyr be watyr and sporte me wyth yow at London a day or ii thys terme, than ye may let all thys be tyl the tyme that I come. And than I wol telle you when I schall be redy to come from Eton, by the grace of God, whom have yow in hys kepyng.

Wretyn the Saturday next aftyr All Halowyn Day, wyth the hand of your brodyr.

William Paston III (1459–?)

November 8

S⊤ GODFRID, Godrey or Geoffrey (1065–1115) was bishop of Amiens, and seems to have combined integrity with crustiness in a very satisfying manner. Before his elevation he reformed a corrupt monastery at Nogent-sous-Coucy. After it he fought energetically against infringements of clerical celibacy. One wife, or concubine, sent him some poisoned wine, but he tried it on his dog, being not unnaturally suspicious at a gift from such a source—and the dog died. He seems to have gone to Rome simply to get redress over a row about who had the right to consecrate altar linen. Later, outspoken about papal submission to the emperor in the matter of church appointments, he withdrew to the Grande Chartreuse, but was ordered to return to his diocese. He was buried at Soissons.

1779: .... Doctʳ Darwin was here on Friday & order'd our little girl to be electrified two or three times a day on the side affected, & to be continued for some weeks. We are willing to flatter ourselves that she has received some benefit from electricity already, as she begins to move her arm & leg a little, and this will encourage us to proceed in the same course. The Doctʳ gives us great hopes of our poor little girls limbs being restored, even without the assistance of the electric shocks, but apprehends they will hasten the cure. . . [*See also November 9*]

Josiah Wedgwood (1730–1795)

November 9

S^T THEODORE, sometimes known as Theodore the Recruit, was a newly-joined soldier in the Roman legion at Amasea in Pontus (the north-eastern region of Asia Minor) and when the persection of Diocletian broke out. The story is that after deliberately setting fire to a temple of Cybele he was cruelly tortured with iron hooks, "his ribs being laid bare," then burnt alive. Attwater says this is "untrustworthy . . . but there is good evidence that there was a martyred Theodore in Pontus."

1756: Having procured an apparatus on purpose, I ordered several persons to be electrified who were ill of various disorders, some of whom found an immediate, some a gradual cure. From this time I appointed, first some hours in every week, and afterwards an hour in every day, wherein any that desired it might try the virtue of this surprising medicine. Two or three years after, our patients were so numerous that we were obliged to divide them. So part were electrified in Southwark, part at the Foundery, others near St Paul's, and the rest near the Seven Dials. The same method we have taken ever since; and to this day, while hundreds, perhaps thousands, have received unspeakable good.

John Wesley (1703–1791)

November 10

S^T JUSTUS OF CANTERBURY (d. about 627) was sent to England by Pope St Gregory 'to help St Augustine, in 601. By 616 a heathen reaction had set in. King Ethelbert, the protector, died, and his son Eadbald refused Christianity. Justus, Mellitus, and Laurence of Canterbury "agreed to desert England, and return to the peaceful enjoyment of their religion and leisure in their own sunny Italy, away from the cold autumn mists, cheerless winters, and rude manners of England." The first two actually left; but Laurence, recovering from a rheumatic attack caught by sleeping on the damp floor of his cathedral, had another attack, of conscience. He won over Eadbald, then recalled Mellitus and

Justus from France (not Italy). The former, and then the latter, succeeded him at Canterbury.

1871: I think—The Northern Lights. Fine clouds that day and hail for a day or two before.

Gerard Manley Hopkins (1844–1889)

November 11

S T MARTIN OF TOURS (about 315–400) was born in Pannonia (Hungary) and became a soldier in the Roman army, and it was during this time that the famous episode of his giving half his cloak to a beggar took place. Later, in the fighting under Julian against the Franks and the Allemanni, he refused to fight and, when accused of cowardice, offered to stand between the opposing armies. To the credit of the Romans he was allowed to leave the service, and became a hermit on the island of Gallinaria, off the Ligurian coast. Even after he was made unwilling bishop of Tours he lived as a monk, in what was the first monastery in Gaul. He pleaded successfully for the captives of Avitian, Count of Ambianum (Amiens), unsuccessfully against the torture and execution of one Priscillian for a mystical–pantheist heresy— "the first infliction of death for heresy which had stained with blood the annals of the church," says Baring-Gould.

1878: School. Flood falling. So far the greatest flood of this century. Before breakfast I went down to the bridge to see how the Jenkins family were. Soon after I passed last night the river came down with a sudden rush and wave and filled the road full of water and they had to escape to the trap, carrying their two children on their backs, wading through water knee deep, the house also being surrounded by water and the water running in at front and back.

Francis Kilvert (1840–1879)

233

November 12

ST MARTIN (d. about 655) was pope while a controversy was raging about Monothelitism—the doctrine that Christ had only one will, not the two separate ones, the divine and the human, which were eventually to be confirmed as a constituent of His uniqueness. The Byzantine Emperor Constans published a document, known as the Type, which really tried to stop the factions from quarrelling (and he did remove a statement of the one-will doctrine from the great church at Constantinople). But Martin called a great council at the Lateran in 649 at which Monothelitism was condemned, and the Type with it. Eventually he was taken by the emperor's troops, ill-treated in prison, tried, and put back in prison where he died. He is the last bishop of Rome to be venerated as a martyr "so far," says Attwater ominously.

1828: Dear Schober, I am ill. I have eaten nothing for eleven days and drunk nothing, and I totter feebly and shakily from my chair to bed and back again. . . .

Be so kind, then, as to assist me in this desperate situation by means of literature. Of Cooper's I have read "The Last of the Mohicans," "The Spy," "The Pilot" and "The Pioneers." If by any chance you have anything else of his, I implore you to deposit it with Frau von Bogner at the coffeehouse for me.

Your friend—
Franz Schubert (1797–1828)

November 13

ST FRANCES CABRINI (1850–1917) died at what seems at first sight an unlikely place for a saint, until one realizes that God is not a historical snob; for it was Chicago. She was in fact the first American citizen to be canonized (in 1946). Born in Lombardy, she founded the Order of the Missionary Sisters of the Sacred Heart in 1880. Her original ambition had been to work in China, but in 1889 she went to America, to look after the Italian immigrants then flooding the country. She opened schools and institutions all across America, conquering one difficulty after another, including the English language, which she found "hard to learn." She is the patroness of all emigrants.

1930: Interesting, but disconcerting, train of thought started by prolonged discussion with Vicky as to the existence or otherwise of a locality which she refers to throughout as H.E.L. Am determined to be a modern parent, and assure her that there is not, never has been, and never could be, such a place. Vicky maintains that there *is*, and refers me to the Bible. I become more modern than ever, and tell her that theories of eternal punishment were invented to frighten people. Vicky replies indignantly that they don't frighten her in the least, she *likes* to think about H. E. L. Feel that deadlock had been reached, and can only leave her to her singular method of enjoying herself.

(Query: Are modern children going to revolt against being modern, and if so, what form will reaction of modern parents take?)

E. M. *Delafield,* Diary of a Provincial Lady

November 14

Sᴛ Lᴀᴡʀᴇɴᴄᴇ O'Tᴏᴏʟᴇ (d. 1180) grew up as a boy hostage to a rather unpleasant Irish king called Dermot MacMurrough, who had a penchant for putting people's eyes out. When later the saint was elevated (against his will) from the solitudes of Glendalough, where he was abbot, to be archbishop of Dublin, King Dermot's continuing cruelties led to his being expelled from Ireland. He sought the aid of Henry II. (who had a bull from Adrian IV, admittedly an English, indeed the *only* English pope, Nicholas Breakspear, authorising him to "enter Ireland, subject the people to obedience of laws, eradicate the seeds of vice, and also to make every house pay the annual tribute of one penny to the blessed Peter"), but in the end got only the aid of Strongbow, his Norman and Welsh as well as Saxon followers, the entire band now being known to the Irish as "the English", as some of them were of course; and it was while St Lawrence was trying to negotiate with them that they conducted a characteristic massacre. He later took part in the Romanizing church council of Cashel in 1172, and finally died at Rouen on

235

a journey back from Rome on a mission which had incurred Henry II's displeasure.

1666: ... there was a pretty experiment, of the blood of one dogg let out (till he died) into the body of another on one side, while all his own run out on the other side. The first died upon the place, and the other very well, and likely to do well. ... may if it takes be of mighty use to man's health, for amending of bad blood by borrowing from a better body.

Samuel Pepys (1633–1703)

November 15

S⊤ GERTRUDE (1264–1334, say some; 1256–1334, say others; 1256–1302 say yet others) was a Benedictine abbess at Helfta (Helpede) in Saxony. Dissuaded from technical scholastic theology she had many ecstatic visions and has always been revered as a mystic. She was an early proponent of the devotion to the Sacred Heart.

1885: Mr Millais came here 15th in the evening to get papa to photograph next morning. He seemed in good health and high spirits. "I just want you to photograph that little boy of Effie's. I've got him you know, he's (cocking up his chin at the ceiling), he's like this, with a bowl and soap suds and all that, it's called *A Child's World*, he's looking up, and there's a beautiful soap bubble; I can't paint you know, not a bit, (with his head on one side and his eyes twinkling) not a bit! I want just to compare it, I get this little thing (the photo of the picture) and I hold it in my hand and compare it with the life, and I can see where the drawing's wrong.'

Beatrix Potter (1866–1943)

November 16

S T MARGARET (d. 1093) was the granddaughter of Edmund Ironside, the sister of Edgar Atheling (who would have succeeded to the English throne if the Normans had not invaded). In 1070 she married Malcolm III of Scotland. She was famous for her austere and devoted life and her charity to the poor. She also founded many churches, including that of the Trinity at Dumfermline. She had six sons and two daughters, and three sons were successively kings of Scotland (the youngest being another saint, David). She died within days of hearing of her husband's death at Alnwick. With St Andrew she is the patron saint of Scotland, where her feast is kept today. (*See also June 10*).

1892: First comes the redoubtable Mr Lunn... I disgree with him flatly in his denunciation of the vowel *oo* for practice.... But if Mr Lunn will teach his pupils to round the back of the throat (the pharynx) as they sing— and this is a trick of the old school which he does not seem to know—he will find that they can "compress the air," as he puts it, just as effectually on *oo* as on Italian *a*. ...

George Bernard Shaw (1856–1950)

November 17

S T GREGORY OF TOURS (538–594) is remembered as a historian "from the beginning of the world till the sixth century," and was one of those civilized men who were well skilled at dealing delicately with the rude chieftains and kings in the days when Gaul was slowly becoming France. He even managed to shelter the prince Meroveus from the wrath of his father, the king Chilperic, at his marrying his (Meroveus's) *aunt*.

Today is also the feast of St Hilda, first abbess of Whitby where the famous Synod of 664 brought Britain firmly into the Roman and out of the Irish orbit (although she herself had been an adherent of the Celtic usage). (*See also St Wilfrid, October 12.*)

1716: [To the Countess of Mar] I have already been visited by some of the most considerable ladies [of

Prague], whose relations I know at Vienna. They are dressed after the fashions there, as people at Exeter imitate those of London: that is, their imitation is more excessive than the original; 'tis not easy to describe what extraordinary figures they make. The person is so much lost between head-dress and petticoat, they have as much occasion to write upon their backs, "This is a Woman," for the information of travellers, as ever sign-post painter had to write, "This is a Bear."

Lady Mary Wortley Montagu (1689–1762)

November 18

ST KEVERNE. "There are no written records, but it is well established that he was one of several Gaelic missionaries who brought the Christian faith to Cornwall from Ireland or Wales during the period from 500–800 A.D.," says a note in the church of his eponymous village. "Two legends are associated with his name.

(1) Disrespect having been shown to him by local inhabitants he caused the mineral lodes to become barren, hence the saying 'no metal will run within the sound of St Keverne's bell.'

(2) A friend of St Keverne was St Just. The latter, however, coveted his friend's chalice. After a visit St Just took the coveted article away with him. On discovery of the theft St Keverne set off in pursuit, picking up three stones on the way. He overtook his ungrateful friend and threw the stones whereupon St Just dropped the chalice and fled."

1715: As I came from the ferry ab^t 9 at night comeing over the stile into my Croft, my foot slipped off the stepp when I was stradling over the stile & I jolted down on my members being Cross the stile & brussed myself & might have spoyled me, I felt at times uneasy for some months after, blessed be God it proved noe worse.

(*see also December 7*) *William Coe of Mildenhall (1680–1729)*

238

November 19

Sᴛ Eʟɪᴢᴀʙᴇᴛʜ ᴏꜰ Hᴜɴɢᴀʀʏ (1207–1231) actually spent the whole of her life in Germany, having been brought from the Hungary of which her father was king in a silver cradle as the child bride of the child Ludwig, landgrave of Thuringia. She grew up in the Wartburg castle among a hostile family, but from the first showed signs of a deeply compassionate, tender and religious nature. But she loved Ludwig deeply and was deeply loved in return, and when he died in Italy during preparations for a Crusade, she rushed through the castle shrieking "dead, dead, dead!" At Marburg, she founded a hospital at which she personally washed lepers and wore the dress of the Franciscan Third Order.

1914: I am sitting hunched up by the fire in my lodgings after a meal of tough meat and cold apple-tart. I am full of self-commiseration. It is very cold and I cannot get warm—try as I will. . . . London in November from the inside of a dingy lodging-house can be very terrible indeed. This celestial isolation will drive me out of my mind. I marvel how God can stick it lonely, damp, and cold in the clouds. That is how I live too—but then I am not God. . . .

W. N. P. Barbellion (1889–1917)

November 20

Sᴛ Eᴅᴍᴜɴᴅ, King and Martyr, is *the* great East Anglian hero (d. 870). The story preceding his martyrdom is that he had befriended a shipwrecked Danish prince called Lodbrog (Hairy-breeches), that one Bjorn, jealous of Lodbrog's influence, killed him and, his crime being discovered by Edmund, was put into the boat that had brought Lodbrog. In it Bjorn drifted back to Denmark where he told the Danes that Edmund had killed Lodbrog; hence the avenging raid. The whole story is delightfully told in Suffolk dialect in Julian Tennyson's *Suffolk Scene*. Of Edmund's discovery of Lodbrog's death. "My, young Edmund he got in a turr'ble state, he jump up and down an he say 'Whew's the fule done this ere?' he say. 'Come on together, spik up! Which o' yew min bin an done such damrotten tricks? Show me that faller an I'l trosh the arse orf o' him.' Well one way an nuther he fount out it was Barn done it and Lor, he got so angry he coulden hardly spik. 'Whoi, yew bloody fule yew,' he say, 'yew mis'rable bloody ould warment . . . thass what I'll dew, dret if I 'on't, I'll put yew in is little ould boot, an if yew get drownded that on't matters, an if yew wash up tuther side I hoop them Deens'll give yew a damgret hidin . . . of all the bloody fules', he say, 'to goo an dew a snakin, brutal thing like that.' " And of Edmund's martyrdom, " 'But ere's one thing,' they say, 'will yew give up Chrisheranity afore yew're kilt, y'know kind o' change yer relijun like, cause thass the wrong un yew got there, boy.' But young Edmund he was a werry kerajus chap, he whully stuck by what he thot was roight, dew they moight ha let im orf. 'I ain't a going to give up nuthen for yew,' he say, 'yew're a rotten lot o' barstids the whull bloody bag of ye.' " No wonder his shrine became the greatest Benedictine abbey in England.

1873: Edward Humphries married a young woman when he was 83 had a son within the year. "Leastways his wife had," said Mrs Hall.

Francis Kilvert (1840–1879)

November 21

ST COLUMBANUS (about 540–615) was one of the most famous Irish missionaries to *Europe* (and is not to be confused with St Columba, *see June 9*). An impetuous and courageous man, he was advised by an old hermitess to go to some country where the girls were less pretty than in Ireland. He found favour with the Frankish king Gontram, and established the great monasteries of Luxeuil and Fontaines. Later he incurred the enmity of the redoubtable Queen Brunehild and the grandson Thierry for whom she had provided concubines and he was expelled, but returned from semi-shipwreck on another missionary journey, with St Gall (*see October 16*). He arrived in Milan in 612 and three years later died in Italy while founding the great abbey of Bobbio.

1739: I never beheld anything more aimiable [than Genoa]. . . . The rest of the day was spent, much to our

240

heart's content, in cursing French music and architecture, and in singing the praises of Italy.

Thomas Gray (1716–1771)

November 22

A GREAT DAY for musicians, although legend and fact are inextricably mixed in the story of St Cecilia. She is said to have been married to Valerian who became a Christian and respected her vow of virginity, and was martyred—as was she, by beheading, in 229, after an attempt to suffocate her in some baths had failed. In 1502 a musical society at Louvain was founded which wanted to put itself under the patronage of Job, and it was the magistrates who said no, it must be St Cecilia. It seems a better choice. "At the sound of musical instruments," says the 1st response at Matins for her feast, "the virgin Cecilia sang to God in her heart."

1666: This day the King begins to put on his vest. . . . being a long cassocke close to the body, of black cloth, and pinked with white silk under it and a coat over it, and the legs ruffled with black ribbands like a pigeon's leg. . . . a very fine and handsome garment. . . . the King of France hath, in defiance to the King of England, caused all his footmen to be put into vests.

Samuel Pepys (1633–1703)

November 23

A LTHOUGH St Alexander Nevsky defeated the Swedes, the Teutonic Knights and the Lithuanians, he said "God is not on the side of force, but of truth and justice." He trod a delicate balance between his people and the Mongols and Tartars, and was a deeply religious man who wore a monk's habit on his deathbed. He was canonized by the Orthodox Church in 1547.

1828: I was at Hampstead a few days before [Mrs Constable] breathed her last. She was then on a sofa in

241

their cheerful parlour, and although Constable appeared in his usual spirits in her presence, yet before I left the house, he took me into another room, wrung my hand, and burst into tears, without speaking. She died on the 23rd of November.

C. R. Leslie (1794–1859)

November 24

S⊤ JOHN OF THE CROSS (1542–1592); the great Spanish mystic and poet whose name is forever associated with that of St Teresa of Avila (*see October 15*). It was by her he was dissuaded from leaving the Carmelite Order for the stricter Carthusians, and to join her in founding the Reformed (Discalced) Carmelites. He was thrown into prison and brutally treated by one Tostado, a Visitor appointed by the Order. He mistrusted visions, indeed one of his works was called by a title now so famous that hardly anyone knows he first used the words: *The Dark Night of the Soul*. "All the grace and comeliness of creation, compared with the Grace of God, is supreme disgrace and supreme disfavour," he wrote, "and that soul, therefore, which is captivated by the grace and comeliness of created things is in the eyes of God in disfavour and disgrace." He prayed that no day would be without suffering, that he would die in disgrace and contempt— and this indeed happened, during another semi-imprisonment. Yet his poems use marvellously sensuous imagery. "The 'Living Flame of Love' ", says Baring-Gould, "is descriptive of the human passion of a mistress for her lover, whom she has admitted to her chamber, which may be compared with one of Herrick's warmest compositions. It has, however, quite another signification in the mouth of a mystic to whom earthly passion is unknown." (So, of course, has the Song of Solomon, on which St John also drew.)

1850: There cannot be any moral turpitude in being born of Adam, because no one had a choice in the matter.

John Epps (1805–1869)

November 25

ST CATHERINE OF ALEXANDRIA was said to have resisted the
advances of Maxentius, the emperor who was defeated by
Constantine. She was also said to have won a kind of massed
argument with pagan philosophers, and to have been beheaded
after the wheel on which she was to be tortured (the "Catherine
wheel") broke down. Attwater calls this "preposterous" and
says there is no trace of her name in early martyr records.

1940: Letter from a soldier at the front to his wife:
"No, dear Mabel, I am not spending any money on
mademoiselles or beer. I am sending it all to you. So let me
fight this bloody war in peace."

James Agate Ego IV

November 26

ST SYLVESTER (1177–1267) gave up the study of law to become
a priest and eventually a canon at Osimo. Struck one day by
the hideous appearance of the corpse of man whom he had
known in his handsome prime, he said, "I am today what he
was, and one day I shall be as he is," gave up everything for a
life of solitary meditation, and eventually founded the Sylves-
trines, a strict offshoot of the Benedictine Order.

1744: .... The town has been trying all this winter to
beat Pantomimes off the stage, very boisterously; for it
is the way here to make even an affair of taste and sense a
matter of arms. Fleetwood, the master of Drury-Lane, has
omitted nothing to support them, as they supported his
house. About ten days ago, he let into the pit a great number
of Bear-garden *bruisers* (that is the term), to knock down
everybody that hissed. The pit rallied their forces, and
drove them out: I was sitting very quietly in the side-boxes,
contemplating all this. On a sudden the curtain flew up,
and discovered the whole stage filled with blackguards,
armed with bludgeons and clubs, to menace the audience.
This raised the greatest uproar; and among the rest, who

flew into a passion but your friend the philosopher? In short, one of the actors, advancing to the front of the stage to make an apology for the manager, he had scarce begun to say, "Mr Fleetwood—" when your friend, with a most audible voice and dignity of anger, called out, "He is an impudent rascal!" The whole pit huzzaed, and repeated the words. Only think of my being a popular orator! But what was still better, while my shadow of a person was dilating to the consistence of a hero, one of the chief ringleaders of the riot, coming under the box where I sat, and pulling off his hat, said, "Mr Walpole, what would you please have us to do next?" It is impossible to describe to you the confusion into which this apostrophe threw me. . . .

Horace Walpole (1717–1797)

November 27

S T VIRGILIUS (d. 780) was an Irish missionary who came to the France of Pepin and later to Salzburg, of which he became bishop. He upheld, against St Boniface, the apostle of Germany (*see June 5*) baptisms by priests ignorant enough of Latin to say, for instance, *in nomine Patria et Filia* (which means, if it means anything, "in the name by the Fatherland and the Daughter". St Boniface then accused him of believing in an underground world of Germanic elves "whose little hammers, clinking as they worked the ore, were heard by the miners in their shafts." The quarrel seems to have been allowed to drop in the end. St Virgilius organized the infant church in Carinthia.

1095: Jerusalem is the centre of the earth; its land fruitful above others, like another paradise of delights. The Redeemer of the human race honoured it by coming thither, adorned it by His sojourn, hallowed it by His passion, redeemed it by His death, glorified it by His burial. This royal city, placed at the centre of the world, is now held captive by her enemies and is made by men ignorant of God to minister to heathen worship.

She seeks and desires to implore your aid. . . . Therefore undertake this journey for the remission of your sins, assured of the imperishable glory of the kingdom of heaven.

Pope Urban II (1042–1099)

November 28

ST KATHERINE LABOURÉ (1806–1876), known to be an unemotional and hard-working nun in the very practical Order of the Sisters of Charity of St Vincent de Paul (*see July 19*), nevertheless combined Mary with Martha by having visions of Our Lady of which the form was preserved in the cult of the "miraculous medal."

1784: [Dr Johnson] told me he was going to try what sleeping out of town might do for him.

"I remember," said he, "that my wife, when she was near her end, poor woman, was also advised to sleep out of town; and when she was carried to the lodgings that had been prepared for her, she complained that the staircase was in very bad condition—for the plaster was beaten off the walls in many places: 'Oh,' said the man of the house, 'that's nothing but by the knocks against it of the coffins of the poor souls that have died in the lodgings!' "

Fanny Burney (1752–1840)

November 29

ST SATURNINUS (3rd century) is particularly associated with Toulouse, to which he was sent by Pope Fabian in 245. Taken into the chief pagan temple by priests angered at the success of his mission, he refused to offer sacrifice and was tied to the tail of a bull by his feet and dragged through the streets till he was dead.

1789: In the morning, deliver letters to Signor Vassari and the Messieurs Zappas, gentlemen in commerce, from whom I might receive information relative to the exports, etc., of the Milanese. At noon to the society of agriculture (called the Patriotic Society). . . . An artist in the town had made a button and half a pair of scissors, one half English and the other half of his own manufacture, for which he claimed and had a reward. Similar are the employments of societies everywhere! In England, busied

245

about rhubarb, silk and drill-ploughs;—at Paris with fleas and butterflies;—and at Milan with buttons and scissors! I hope I shall find the *Georgofili* at Florence employed on a top-knot. I looked about to see a practical farmer enter the room, but looked in vain. A goodly company of i Marchesi, i Conti, i Cavalieri, i Abati, but not one close-clipped wig, or a dirty pair of breeches, to give authority to their proceedings.

Arthur Young (1741–1820)

November 30

ST ANDREW was among the first apostles to be called by Our Lord. According to St John, it was on the day that St John the Baptist seeing Jesus, spoke the words "the Lamb of God," *Agnus Dei*, that St Andrew went to his brother St Peter and said "we have found the Messiah" and brought him to Jesus. It was St Andrew who noticed the boy with the five loaves and two fishes when the five thousand were in the wilderness. He is said to have conducted his missions in what is now Turkey, Macedonia and even Scythia (Russia) and to have been crucified, on an X-shaped cross, at Patras in Greece. From this comes the flag of Scotland, of which country he is of course the patron saint. Scotland's oldest university, like the town at once dignified and romantic in which it is situated, bears his name. (Relics of St Andrew were brought to the town by St Regulus, or Rule.)

1884: The joyous mood left when the jubilant sounds of the *Freischutz* overture had died away immediately received a damper: it was the turn of Brahms's F major Symphony. Regarded as a Symphony by Dr Johannes Brahms, it is partly a competent, meritorious work; as that of a second Beethoven it is wholly and entirely a failure, because all that is expected of a Beethoven No 2 is completely lacking in a Dr Johannes Brahms:- originality. . . .

Hugo Wolf (1860–1903)

DECEMBER

December 1

S<small>T</small> E<small>LIGIUS</small> (588–660), born at Limoges, was a goldsmith and metalworker, who first came to the notice of King Clothair II when, entrusted with metal for a throne, he found there was enough for *two* thrones, which he made for the king instead of keeping the surplus. Later a trusted adviser of King Dagobert, who wore sackcloth under his rich clothes, he became bishop of Noyon, and founded several religious houses. One of his sermons against lingering pagan superstitions gives an interesting picture of them. Women must not wear amber bearing invocations to Minerva, fountains or trees must not be held sacred, sneezing must not be regarded as ominous, bits of paper with quotations from Scripture are not to be worn round the neck, people must not celebrate the "festivals of moths and mice" or the solsticial feast of St John with "capers, carols and diabolical songs." He is the patron saint of metalworkers.

1816: . . . I read yesterday the evidence of the Elgin Marble Committee. Lord Elgin has done a very useful thing in taking them away from the Turks. Do not throw pearls to swine; and take them away from swine when they are so thrown. They would have been destroyed there, or the French would have had them. He is underpaid for them. . . .

Sydney Smith (1771–1845)

December 2

T<small>HE</small> basilica of St Mary Major in Rome is built over the tomb of S<small>T</small> V<small>IVIANA</small>, of Bibiana (363?), and there was a church in her honour there in the fifth century. She was said to have been scourged to death in the time of the emperor Julian; but "all historical knowledge of her is lost" according to Attwater.

1815: . . . I am sorry my Mother has been suffering, & am afraid this exquisite weather is too good to agree with her.—*I* enjoy it all over me, from top to toe, from right to left, Longitudinally, Perpendicularly, Diagonally;—& I cannot but selfishly hope we are to have it last till Christmas;—nice, unwholesome, unseasonable, relaxing, close, muggy weather. . . .

Jane Austen (1775–1817)

December 3

S⊤ Francis Xavier (1506–1552) was the extraordinary "Apostle of the Indies." He met St Ignatius Loyola (*see July 31*) when they were both at the University of Paris; sceptical at first, he performed St Ignatius's *Spiritual Exercises* in 1535 and was associated with him in the founding of the Jesuit Order. His voyages and travels were incredible. Sailing from Lisbon in 1541 he arrived in Goa the next year, and after an arduous and successful mission moved on to Cape Comorin, endlessly preaching, helping the sick, baptising. 1545 found him in Malacca, then back to Cochin and south India. In 1549 he was in Japan, and in forty days had mastered that totally alien language enough to translate the Creed into it, and subsequently much of the Scriptures. 1551 India again, 1552 Malacca again, where he behaved with characteristic courage and charity in an epidemic. He died while making the final arrangements for getting into China from Macao. Sometimes he would cry out in his ecstasies, "it is enough Lord, it is enough!" In Japan alone there were 400,000 Christians forty years after his death.

1957: Fr Harris preached so well on Sunday about Christmas, and not making it an orgy of present-giving to each other but sending the money saved to refugees and others in need. I think he got some of his ideas from a Xmas article I wrote in *The Spectator* which had pleased him. Is it part of my mission, do you think, to give the clergy good ideas?

Rose Macaulay (1881–1958)

December 4

S⊤ Peter Chysologus ("golden-tongued"), about 400–450, was bishop of Ravenna, and is chiefly remembered for his replies to Eutyches, a main propounder of the Monophysite heresy which denied the human nature of Christ, saying it was entirely swallowed up in the divine. "If they obtained for him the title of 'Golden Speaker' ", says Baring-Gould rather coldly, "the average powers of preaching at the time must have been very leaden."

1762: The Peak, a countrey beyond comparison uglier than any other I have seen in England, black, tedious, barren, and not mountainous enough to please one with its horrors.

Thomas Gray (1716–1771)

December 5

S⊤ Birinus (d. 650) was sent by Pope Honorius to England "to sow the faith in the inner parts beyond the dominions of the English, where no other teacher had been before him;" but finding the West Saxons still pagan, he became their apostle, baptising their king Cynegils. He established his see at Dorchester.

1910: ... I walked through the doorway of the Parthenon, and on into the inner part of it, without really remembering where I was. A heaviness in the air made my eyes swim, and wrapped up my senses: I only knew that I, a stranger, was walking on the floor of the place I had most desired to see, the greatest temple of Athene, the palace of art, and that I was counting her columns, and finding them what I already knew. The building was familiar, not cold as in the drawings, but complex, irregular, alive with curve and subtlety, and perfectly preserved ... about Athens ... there is an intoxication, a power of possession in its ruins, and the memories which inhabit them, which entirely prevents anyone

250

attempting to describe or to estimate them. There will never be a great book on Athens, unless it is one by an enemy: no one who knew it could resist its spell, and who can attack it now of artists, when Tolstoy is dead? He, and he alone, could have uprooted Greek culture in the world. . . .

T. E. Lawrence (1888–1935)

December 6

S<small>T</small> N<small>ICHOLAS</small> (fourth century) only got the name "Santa Claus" via Dutch and German American immigrants. But, as all who have heard the charming cantata about him by Benjamin Britten know, this fourth-century bishop of Myra restored to life three children who had been butchered and pickled—a legend said to have grown from pictures of a real act, when he got three men pardoned who were in a tower prison, so that he was shown beside a tower with three little *men* rising from it. The three golden balls (he is patron of pawnbrokers) represent three bags of gold thrown through a window to save three girls from prostitution. At the Council of Nicaea he spoke doughtily against Arius, and indeed is reputed to have socked him on the jaw. And everybody knows what he does on Christmas Eve.

1851: The Grange, Alresford, Hants. There is to be a fine Christmas tree for Lady A.'s school children and *seven* dolls form part of the gifts. They were bought *naked*, except for a wrappage of silkpaper and a piece of cotton wool on each of their noses to prevent damage to that interesting feature and Lady A., tho' not much given to a credulous faith in her fellow creatures, *actually* hoped that her Lady's Maid and the Housekeeper, and *their* numerous subordinates would *take an interest* in these dolls and dress or assist *her* dress them. But not a bit. . . . The very footman won't *carry the dolls* backwards and forwards! When told to bring one or to desire Josephine (the Lady's Maid) to bring one they simply disappear and no doll comes!—I remarked on this with some impatience yesterday, and Lady A. answered, "Perfectly true, Mrs Carlyle—they *won't bring the doll!*—I know it as well as you do—but what would you have me do?". . . . Such is the slavery the grandest people live under *to what they call* their *"inferiors"*. . . .

Jane Welsh Carlyle (1801–1866)

251

December 7

ST AMBROSE (about 335–397) is one of the four great Doctors of the Latin Church. The governor of Liguria, he was made bishop of Milan by popular acclaim on the death of the bishop Auxentius, an Arian, before he had been baptised. He was the first personification of the church as a power able to stand up to the imperial power. His firmness during the last real organized pagan military threat from Arbogastes of Gaul and his puppet-emperor Eugenius helped the final overthrow of the old gods. He was a prolific writer and apologist during a time when definitions of the faith were needed as it spread. It was he who helped to convert St Augustine, and he was the first in the western church to write and use hymns, many of which survive.

1703: I went into my Cart-horse stable & nigh my Darby Colt to put his shackles upon his fetlock & when I was stooping he bitt att my head & if my hat had not been on he might have done me a great mischief, or if he had got hold of my arm or shoulder, but I thank God who continually preserves us I got noe hurt.

William Coe of Mildenhall (1680–1729)

December 8

ST BUDOC (6th century), whose name is commemorated in place-names in Devon and Cornwall, is right in the Celtic tradition, that is, he certainly existed, and became bishop of Dol in Brittany, but acquired a legendary life that began with his very birth—in a barrel at sea, into which his mother Azenor had been cast. At Dol he succeeded St Maglorius (*see October 24*).

1844: Snow over the ground. We have our wonders of inundation in Suffolk also, I can tell you. For three weeks ago such floods came, that an old woman was carried off as she was retiring from a beer house about 9 p.m. and drowned. She was probably half seas over before she left the beer house.

Edward Fitzgerald (1809–1883)

December 9

THE SEVEN MARTYRS OF SAMOSATA, in Syria (297) were SS HIPPARCHUS, PHILOTHEUS, JAMES, PARAGRUS, HABIBUS, ROMANUS and LOLLIANUS. The first two were elderly officials, the other five were young men converted by them at a time when the emperor Maximian had ordered sacrifices to the gods to celebrate a victory over the Persians. Hipparchus said he could no more change than that hair could grow on his bald head. They nailed a goatskin to it. After scourging and starvation they were variously crucified, stabbed, or finished off with spikes through the head.

1859: Saw Mrs S., who said the new curate had paid them his first visit. They had a talk about the poor people amusing themselves in their gardens on Sundays. Mrs S. maintained that *that* is better than going to the beer-shop. "Oh, no," said the curate: "there is no commandment against drinking; there is against *Sunday labour.*" Mrs S. maintained that the question was not one of labour; in their own gardens they were really resting; and she urged, moreover, that there are many implied commandments against excess, whether in drinking or in other things.

Mrs S. said the argument put her in mind of a council held in Russia some century ago, as to whether smoking or brandy should be prohibited. The decision was to forbid smoking, not brandy, because the Scripture saith it is not that which goeth into the man defileth the man, but that which cometh out from him.

John Epps (1805–1869)

253

December 10

Sᴛ Mᴇʟᴄʜɪᴀᴅᴇꜱ (or Miltiades) (d. 314) became pope just before the emperor Constantine's decree allowing Christians freedom and the right to build churches. He presided over a council at the Lateran, dealing, it seems with tact and moderation, with unsubstantiated charges against Cecilian, bishop of Carthage.

1943: Lying in the bath this evening, with the hot tap gently running and the water making throaty noises down the waste-pipe—a thing one is strictly enjoined not to allow in war-time—I thought how maddening it is that the worst sins are the most enjoyable. . . . the lusts of the flesh, instead of alienating me from God, seem to draw me closer to him in a perverse way. He on the other hand may not be drawn to me. Yet I feel he ought to know how to shake me off if he wants to. Can it be that he is too polite, as I am when Clifford Smith button-holes me at a party, and I am longing to escape?

James Lees-Milne (1908–   )

December 11

Sᴛ Dᴀᴍᴀꜱᴜꜱ (d. 384), a Spaniard either by birth or descent, was skilled in Latin and Greek, and left behind verse epitaphs for the martrys' tombs (and did much to preserve the catacombs). His accession to the papal throne was accompanied by violence and bloodshed between his party and that of the other candidate, Ursinus. It was he who put the Doxology at the ends of Psalms.

1775: In the Morning left Orleans and went of to Paris a foot by the Chapell des Aides; about a league from the toun begines the forest which is about two Leagues to pass. There is no doubt of roberys being comitted here; there is six remains of bodys upon wheels where they have been brock, this was the first time that I had ever seen this horrid spectacle; this was not all for upon a large oak there was twelve others some of which seemed not to have been long there.

Thomas Blaikie (1750–1838)

December 12

S T FINIAN, bishop of Clonard (d. about 550) was one of the greatest of the "second wave" of saints after Patrick in Ireland. He is said to have crossed to Wales, meeting among others St David (*see March 1*) and founding many churches. Back in Ireland he was traditionally the founder of the organized monastic-teaching movement, numbering among his pupils such as the great St Columba (*see June 9*) and St Brendan the Voyager (*see May 16*).

1822: A Staffordshire Application for Relief.

Jeantlemen at this time I ham In grate distress my youngest son is dad and I have another daughter vury bad and I my sealfe am hill.

Sir the cofin will be 12s. and the ground with the fees will be 5s. 6d. and the shroud 3s. 6d. Sir threaugh stoping my trifle of pay I have 14s. in det for seame and if not paid by christmas I must be trioublead.

Jeantlemen I hope you will not stop my trifle of pay at this time your humble sarvant

Thos Bannister
W. E. Tate, The Parish Chest

December 13

S T LUCY (d. about 304) was martyred in the time of Diocletian at Syracuse; that much is certain, although there have been several variations on the story of her rejection of a pagan suitor. Her mass, curiously, used to be *Dilexisti* "For a Virgin *not* a Martyr," but it is full of the idea of *light* from the lamps of the wise virgins (possibly also from the verbal association of her name) and she was invoked in case of eye disease. She is named in the Canon of the Mass.

1759: When I first went to Cambridge, I was to learn mathematics of the famous blind professor Sanderson. I had not frequented him a fortnight, before he said to me, "Young man, it is cheating you to take your money: believe me, you never can learn these things; you have no capacity for them." I can smile now, but I cried then with mortification. The next step, in order to comfort myself, was not to believe him: I could not conceive that I had not talents for anything in the world. I took, at my own expense, a private instructor, who came to me once a-day for a year. Nay, I took infinite pains, but had so little capacity, and so little attention (as I have always had to anything that did not immediately strike my inclinations), that after mastering any proposition, when the man came the next day, it was as new to me as if I had never heard of it; in short, even to common figures, I am the dullest dunce alive.

Horace Walpole (1717–1797)

December 14

ST SPIRIDION (d. about 350) was a sheep farmer who became bishop of Tremithus on the beautiful, legend-haunted island of Cyprus. He remained a sheep farmer, and was probably the uncouth-looking fellow who pushed his way to the front where a really tremendous intellectual was scoring all round the wicket, and said "there is one God, maker of heaven and earth, and of all things visible and invisible, who made all things by the power of his word, and by the holiness of his Spirit. This Word, by which name we call the Son of God, took compassion on men for their wandering astray, and for their savage condition, and chose to be born of a woman. . . . these things we believe without curious enquiry."

1610: The University [of Oxford] is much reformed about drinking, long hair and other vices, especially our house [University College], out of which I have lately gone to avoid expulsion for drunkenness.

Sir G. Radcliffe

December 15

NO APOLOGY for returning to Helen Waddell's *The Wandering Scholars*. ST VENANTIUS FORTUNATUS (d. about 600) is one of its earliest heroes. Educated at Ravenna "when he left it, it was to step into a world where the barbarians were masters: in North Italy the Lombards: the Goths in Spain: the Burgundians in Auvergne: the Franks in France and the Low Countries: and on every frontier the menace of the Huns. . . . the Church taught the good monsters language, and their profit on't was they knew how to swear and also write verses." He became bishop of Poitiers, he wrote a famous Epithalamium for the wedding of Sigebert and Brunhild, he produced eleven volumes of collected verse, he "wandered through the terrifying courts of the giants, a little like Gulliver. . . . a life so gentle and blameless that they made him a saint." But he also wrote, for the arrival of relics of the True Cross at Poitiers "the greatest processional of the Middle Ages," the *Vexilla Regis*, "the banners of the King go forth. . . ."

1941: . . . I get news of France mostly through the Free French, for no day goes by without someone escaping to England. Also, Susan sees a certain number of them in London. The conditions in Paris are indescribably terrible. . . . I much regret the abuse of old Pétain. He ought to be left to history. All the Free French I meet, who of course are followers of de Gaulle, regret what is published about Pétain. I much fear there will be violent revolution in France after the War.

Marie Belloc-Lowndes (1868–1947)

December 16

YET ANOTHER ST EUSEBIUS (d. 370) who became bishop of Vercelli, in Piedmont, in 340, was a stout upholder of Trinitarian Catholicism against Arianism; in his later years he worked together with St Hilary (*see January 13*). This was after he, like many orthodox bishops, had been banished by the Arian

257

emperor, Constantius II. He is credited with a Latin translation
of the Gospels which antedates that of St Jerome.

1796: Buttal's sale I went to. Gainsborough's picture
of a Boy in a Blue Vandyke dress sold for 35 guineas.
Several of His drawings were sold in pairs, some went so
high as 8 guineas and half the pair.

Joseph Farington (1747–1821)

December 17

St Sturm, or Sturmi (d. 779) was a younger assistant of St
Boniface (*see June 5*) in the evangelisation of Germany; no
easy task especially in his later years when surrounded by sullen
Saxons lately vanquished by Charlemagne. He founded the great
abbey of Fulda, and returned to it after a removal caused by
some rather unsaintly opposition by St Lullus, bishop of Mainz.
On his first arrival at Fulda, says Baring-Gould, "he saw a swarm
of naked Slavonians bathing in the river. The sight of their
naked bodies 'and their smell' filled him with terror . . . the
good-natured barbarians let the hermit go his way, and they
went theirs. It is curious to remark even in the eighth century
the antipathy of the German for the Slav, manifesting itself in a
belief that the latter is naturally endowed with an ill savour,
which even water will not remove. But the barbarous Slavs on
this occasion set a good example of bathing, which it would
have been well if certain ascetic saints had followed. The odour
of sanctity would not have been removed from them by an
ablution."

1825: [Visiting Blake] Nothing could exceed the
squalid air both of the apartment and his dress; but in
spite of dirt—I might say filth—an air of natural gentility is
diffused over him; and his wife, notwithstanding the same
offensive character of her dress and appearance has a good
expression of countenance, so that I shall have a pleasure in
calling on and conversing with these worthy people . . . nor
would he admit that any education should be attempted
except that of cultivation of the imagination and fine arts.
"What are called the vices in the natural world, are the
highest sublimities in the spiritual world." When I asked

258

whether if he had been a father he would not have grieved if his child had become vicious or a great criminal, he answered: "I must not regard when I am endeavouring to think rightly my own any more than other people's weaknesses." And when I again remarked that this doctrine puts an end to all exertion or even wish to change anything, he had no reply. . . .

Of the faculty of vision he spoke as one he had had from early infancy. He thinks all men partake of it, but it is lost by not being cultivated. . . .

Henry Crabb Robinson (1775–1867)

December 18

S⊤ Wynbald (about 700–786) was one of the English monks who, like St Boniface himself, brought Christianity to Germany. The brother of St Willibald (*see July 7*) he was the first abbot at Heidenheim in Bavaria.

Today is, or was, also the feast of the Expectation of the Confinement of Our Lady, instituted in 654 because the Annunciation usually fell in Lent and could not be properly observed.

1765: Riding through the Borough all my mare's feet flew up and she fell with my leg under her. . . . After resting a few minutes, I took a coach; but when I was cold, found myself much worse, being bruised on my right arm, my breast, my knee, leg and ankle, which swelled exceedingly. However, I went on to Shoreham, where, by applying treacle twice a day, all the soreness was removed and I recovered some strength. . . .

John Wesley (1703–1791)

December 19

S⊤ Nemesion (d. 250) was acquitted on a charge of theft, but immediately afterwards found guilty of being a Christian, for which he received, during the persecution of Decius, scourging and torture double that given to thieves, before being burnt.

1857: The country people are much amused at [Ten-nyson's] bad hat and unusual ways, and believe devoutly that he writes his poetry while mowing his lawn. However, they hold him in great respect, from a perception of the honour in which he is held by their "betters." Our housewife here is a friend of his servant, and she entertained us with an account of how said servant had lately been awed. Opening to a ring at the door, when the Tennysons were out, she saw a "tall handsome gentleman" standing there, who on learning they were not at home turned to go. "What message shall I give?" quoth the maid. "Merely say Prince Albert called."

Sidney Dobell (1824–1874)

December 20

ST PAUL THE HERMIT (d. 956) lived on Mt Latrus in Greece, at first, for some weeks, feeding "on green acorns, which caused him to vomit, even to blood." In no time other people came to live near him, in a "laura" or group of cells. He fled higher up the mountain, only visiting them occasionally. Then he went to the island of Samos, but was followed there and had to restore the lauras destroyed by the Saracens. He returned to Mt Latrus where he remained. Popes, bishops and princes sent messages to him, and "the emperor Constantine Porphyroge-netta wrote frequently to him, asked his advice in affairs of importance, and had always reason to repent if he did not follow it."

1891: I remarked to one of the young persons serving, that carelessness seemed to be a disease with some purchasers. The observation was scarcely out of my mouth, when my thick coat-sleeve caught against a large pile of expensive [Christmas] cards in boxes one on top of the other, and threw them down. The manager came forward looking very much annoyed, and picking up several cards from the ground, said to one of the assistants, with a palpable side-glance at me: "Put these amongst the six-penny goods; they can't be sold for a shilling now." The result was, I felt it my duty to buy some of these damaged cards.

I had to buy more and pay more than intended. Unfortunately I did not examine them all, and when I got home I discovered a vulgar card with a picture of a fat nurse with two babies, one black and the other white, and the words: "We wish Pa a Merry Christmas."

George and Weedon Grossmith, The Diary of a Nobody

December 21

IT SEEMS very appropriate somehow that the feast of ST THOMAS, the Apostle who doubted the Resurrection until he had seen the marks of the nails (and uttered the most concentrated of all prayers, "My Lord and my God!") should be not near Easter but near Christmas.

The word *Thomas*, like *Didymus*, means "twin", though there is much argument about whom he was twin of (St James, say some). It was he who, saying to Jesus, "Lord, we know not whither thou goest" received the reply, "I am the way, the truth and the life." There is a strong tradition that St Thomas took the Gospel to India.

1895: . . . the amusement of the last month has been the question whether Sir Lewis Morris is married or not, that hypocritical Welshman having suddenly electrified his most intimate friends by sending out cards Sir Lewis Morris and my Lady. How he has possibly kept it quiet so long, living at an address in Maida Vale with his christian name spelled wrong in the Blue Book, I cannot imagine. He has always passed as a bachelor. Luckily, too frightfully ugly to break hearts, but a certain elderly lady, now justly enraged, is said to have taken gratuitous trouble to introduce him to likely parties. . . .

Beatrix Potter (1866–1943)

261

December 22

S<small>T</small> I<small>SCHYRION</small> was a steward or servant of a magistrate in Alexandria who died in 250. After persistent refusal to sacrifice to the gods, he was impaled.

1782: [To his father] . . . [Constanze's guardian] forbade me to have anything more to do with Constanze, unless I would give him a written contract—or to desert the girl. What man who loves sincerely and honestly can forsake his beloved? Would not the mother, would not my loved one place the worst interpretation upon such conduct? That was my predicament. So I drew up a document to the effect that I bound myself to marry Mlle Constanze Weber within the space of three years and that if it should prove impossible for me to do so owing to my changing my mind, she should be entitled to claim from me three hundred *gulden* a year. Nothing in the world could have been easier for me to write. For I knew that I should never have to pay these three hundred *gulden*, because I should never forsake her, and that even should I be so unfortunate as to change my mind, I should only be too glad to get rid of her for three hundred *gulden*, while Constanze, if I knew her, would be too proud to let herself be sold. But what did that angelic girl do when the guardian was gone? She asked her mother for the document and said to me: "Dear Mozart! I need no written assurance from you. I believe what you say," and tore up the paper. This action made my dear Constanze yet more precious to me. . . .

Wolfgang Amadeus Mozart (1756–1791)

December 23

S<small>T</small> T<small>HORLAC</small> is the most popular in what can surely not be a very long list, that of Icelandic saints. Born in 1133, he was ordained priest and then studied in Lincoln and Paris. He became bishop of Skalholt, and had to lay about him a good deal with excommunication in a fight against lay appointments of clergy, the marriage of clergy, and, in one celebrated case, the marriage of a priest's daughter to another priest very remotely related to her.

1917: [To his mother] . . . I can think of nothing at the moment but Robert Graves' letter, which came by the same post as the parcel.
He says "Don't make any mistake, Owen, you are a—fine poet already, & are going to be more so. I won't have the impertinence to criticize. . . ."

Yours ever, Robert Graves.
Wilfred Owen (1893–1918)

December 24

THE STORY OF St Irmina (d. 707) would make a very good opera, in perhaps the Bellini idiom. A daughter of the Frankish king Dagobert II, she was on her way to Trèves (Trier) to marry one Count Hermann, whom she loved passionately, when a youth, Edgar, in her retinue, fell equally passionately in love with her. He went on ahead, told Hermann there was a foreign merchant with jewels nearby from whom a surprise wedding gift could be bought, offered to take Hermann to him, led him to a rock overlooking the Moselle and seized him so that they both plunged to their deaths. Irmina thereupon took the veil in the convent at Trèves which Dagobert founded for her.

1942: [Midi] said, "Your mother told me in confidence that whenever she wants to get out of the Red Cross functions she puts her thermometer on the hot-water bottle, and shows it to your father, who positively forbids her to leave her bed. Your mother, to make her feigned illness more convincing expostulates with your father just a little, but not too much, knowing that he will not give his consent."

James Lees-Milne, (1908–)

263

December 25

H—stands for *bomb*. It stands for *happy*, too;
A—toms, and letters, are a neutral crew
P—repared to sing, at our creative urge,
P—aean or threnody, love-duet or dirge.
Y—et now, while angels bid the world rejoice,

C—onsider what we are that have this choice;
H—oped for in Heaven? Spirits in a void?
R—easoning animals, soon to be destroyed?
I—n vain we merely reason, since we are
S—till amateur creators on our little star.
T—his was the magic of the three wise kings;
M—agic was left behind with childish things;
A—dmitting deeper truths not known, but felt,
S—ilent they looked on Love and, silent, *knelt*.

1675: [In the eastern Mediterranean] Christmas Day we keep thus. At 4 in the morning our trumpeters all do flat their trumpets, and begin at our Captain's cabin, and thence to all the officers' and gentlemen's cabins; playing a levite at each cabin-door, and bidding Good morrow. Wishing a merry Christmas. After they go to their station, viz. on the poop, and sound three levites in honour of the morning. At 10 we go to prayers and sermon: text, *Zacc., ix,* 9. Our Captain had all his officers and gentlemen to dinner with him, where we had excellent good fare; a rib of beef, plum puddings, mince-pies etc., and plenty of good wines of several sorts; drank health to the King, to our wives and friends; and ended the day with much civil mirth.

Henry Teonge (1621?–1690)

December 26

S⊤ S⊤EPHEN (d. 33), the first person to die for the Christian faith, is commemorated on the first day after the birth of Christ. Preaching in Jerusalem, he reminded the Jews of how they had turned away from Moses. "Which of the prophets have not your fathers persecuted? and they have slain them which showed before of the coming of the Just One; of whom ye have now been the betrayers and murde̤ ̤rs." The passage in the Acts of the Apostles goes on, ". . . when they heard these things, they were cut to the heart," and they stoned him, having "laid down their clothes at a young man's feet, whose name was Saul."

1794: . . . Thank God! had a pretty good Night last Night, and I hope am something better, but rather languid and low. Could eat but very little for dinner today. Appetite bad. To Weston Ringers, gave 0.2.6. To Christmas Boxes &c. gave 0.4.0. Dinner today, Calfs Fry & a Rabbit rosted. I drank plentifully of Port Wine after dinner, instead of one Glass, drank 7. or 8. Glasses, and it seemed to do me much good, being better for it.

James Woodforde (1740–1803)

December 27

S⊤ JOHN ⊤HE EVANGELIST, St John the Divine, St John the Beloved Disciple, St John whose Gospel begins with that huge unanswerable statement from eternity, *"In the beginning was the Word . . ."* and whose vast vision in *Revelation*, the last book of the New Testament, well justifies his symbol of the soaring eagle. The brother of James, with whom he was nicknamed by Jesus "Son of Thunder" (Boanerges), he was always close to the heart of the mystery. He was among the chosen few who saw the Transfiguration, he was with Peter and James in the Garden of Gethsemane, it was to him that Jesus, dying, commended his Mother. At some later period of his life he was in Ephesus, and was also exiled to the island of Patmos. The manner of his death is not certain.

🖋 *1873:* [To Gaynor Simpson] As to dancing, my dear, I *never* dance, unless I am allowed to do it *in my own peculiar way.* There is no use trying to describe it: it has to be seen to be believed. The last house I tried it in, the floor broke through. But then it was a poor sort of floor—the beams were only six inches thick, hardly worth calling beams at all: stone arches are much more sensible, when any dancing of *my peculiar kind* is to be done.

C. L. Dodgson (Lewis Carroll), 1832–1898.

December 28

THE FEAST of the Holy Innocents—the victims of Herod's reaction to the prophecy of the Magi that the Child born at Bethlehem was a king—was initiated in the 5th century. Its subsequent history is a reminder of how long Christianity has had time to become entwined with western folk-ways, for by the Middle Ages, combined with memories of the Saturnalia, when slaves took the place of masters and there was no restraint, this was the time of the Feast of Fools. In Constantinople "priests and clerks danced in the choir, and sang obscene songs. The deacons and subdeacons ate cakes and sausages at the altar, played cards and dice on it, and made offensive odours issue from the censer." As late as 1444 in "the Liberty of December" they elected "an archbishop of fools . . . danced in the choir and sang indecent songs, and burned their old shoes in the censers." A long way from the Gospel of the Mass for this day: *"vox in Rama audita est, ploratus, et ululatus multus: Rachel plorans filios suos, et noluit consolari, quia non sunt."* A voice in Rama was heard, lamentation and great mourning: Rachel bewailing her children, and would not be comforted, because they are not. And there are, of course, the words of one of the most beautiful (and early) of all carols, the Coventry Carol, "Herod the king, in his raging. . . ."

🖋 *1870:* As we passed Langley Burrell Church we heard the strains of the quadrille band on the ice at Draycott. The afternoon grew murky and when we began to skate the

266

air was thick with falling snow. But it soon stopped and gangs of labourers were at work immediately sweeping away the new fallen snow and skate cuttings of ice. The Lancers was beautifully skated. When it grew dark the ice was lighted with Chinese lanterns, and the intense glare of blue, green, and crimson lights and magnesium riband made the whole place as light as day. Then people skated with torches.

Francis Kilvert (1840–1879)

December 29

ST THOMAS À BECKET (1119–1170) was of course the victim of one of the endless church-v.-state quarrels on so high and famous a level that it was only three years after his "Murder in the Cathedral" by the four knights getting rid of Henry II's "troublesome priest" that he was canonised. His shrine at Canterbury became one of the most famous in Europe (it was to it that Chaucer's *Canterbury Pilgrims* were making their way 150 years later). It was not all good against all evil. The Constitutions of Clarendon, of 1164, where it all really began, did remove some injustices (such as the immunity for all crimes, however bad, committed by clergy) from lay trial. St Thomas later went back on his original adherence to them, and during his subsequent exile in France, when many legates and intermediaries between him and Henry and the Pope and the French king came and went for six years, he brandished furious excommunications against such as Gilbert, bishop of London. But at the same time he was developing the inner life of austerity so dramatically revealed when the hair shirt was found on his body after the murder; and there was no doubt about his love and concern for the poor. He was a martyr with all the unyielding toughness of his Norman ancestry (his father was from Rouen and his mother from Caen).

1779: Our dear little girl has got her sight again very perfectly we hope, & her limbs are recovering their wonted use every day. She is quite well & as wild as a little buck, or rather a doe if you please.

I thank you for a catalogue, but have not found time to read a page. My wife says I must read no more books "till

I build another house" & advises me to first read some of those I have already—What nonsense she talks sometimes!

Josiah Wedgwood (1730–1795)

December 30

ST AMYSIUS (d. about 410) had the misfortune to be bishop of Thessalonica during the time when the emperor Theodosius had 7000 people massacred in the stadium where they had rioted. St Amysius later presided over a council which condemned one Bonosus, who had stated that Mary had other children and was not virgin, and had also disputed the divinity of Jesus.

1787: This morning my dear father carried me to Dr Herschel. This great and very extraordinary man received us with almost open arms. He is very fond of my father, who is one of the Council of the Royal Society this year, as well as himself, and he has invited me when we have met at the Lodge or at Mr de Luc's.

At this time of day there was nothing to see but his instruments: those, however, are curiosities sufficient. His immense new telescope, the largest ever constructed, will still, I fear, require a year or two more for finishing, but I hope it will then reward his labour and ingenuity by the new views of the heavenly bodies, and their motions, which he flatters himself will be procured by it. ... By the invitation of Mr Herschel, I now took a walk which will sound to you rather strange; it was through his telescope and it held me upright, and without the least inconvenience; so would it have done had I been dressed in feathers and a bell hoop—such is its circumference.

Fanny Burney (1752–1840)

December 31

S^T S<small>ILVESTER</small> succeeded St Melchiades (*see December 10*) immediately after the victory of Constantine over Maxentius which gave the church its first Christian emperor. His pontificate (314–335) saw the perhaps inevitable institutional development. The "Donations of Constantine" giving Rome complete temporal and spiritual primacy were 8th-century forgeries (and of course even if they hadn't been, they would only have been imperial decrees). But the great central doctrines were now being defined "by the exclusion of opposites." Perhaps the most famous of all the great councils, that of Nicaea, which condemned Arianism and from which the Nicene Creed is traced, took place in 325, when St Silvester was too old to attend personally, though he sent two legates. He was one of the first non-martyrs to be venerated as a saint.

1877: ... the old woman was full of stories of the countryside. ... "There are strange things about the Black Mountain," she said, "but I have travelled the hills at all hours, night and day, and never saw anything bad. One time I had been working late at the Parc on the southern side of the Mountain down in the dingle and I was coming home pretty late in the dark. It was about February or March. As I came over the Bwlch y fingel I was singing to keep my courage up, and I was singing a hymn out of an old book for I thought I wouldn't sing anything but what was good then. It was a fine starlight night and just as I got down into the plain I heard beautiful singing overhead, like the singing of birds. They seemed to be some great birds travelling. I could not see them but they sang and whistled most beautiful. They seemed to be going away down the mountain towards Caedwgan. And I said to myself, 'God bless me from here, there will be a funeral from that house,' and sure enough within a month a dead person was carried out from Caedwgan." I sat up till after midnight to watch the Old Year out and the New Year in. The bells rang at intervals all the evening, tolled just before the turn of the night and then rang a joy peal. . .

Francis Kilvert (1840–1879)

269

INDEX
OF SAINTS, MARTYRS AND FESTIVALS

INDEX

OF AUTHORS AND PERIODICALS QUOTED